FRASIER

THE CULTURAL HISTORY OF TELEVISION

Series Editors: Bob Batchelor, M. Keith Booker, Kathleen M. Turner

Mad Men*: A Cultural History*, by M. Keith Booker and Bob Batchelor
Frasier*: A Cultural History*, by Joseph J. Darowski and Kate Darowski

FRASIER

A Cultural History

Joseph J. Darowski
Kate Darowski

ROWMAN & LITTLEFIELD
Lanham • Boulder • New York • London

Published by Rowman & Littlefield
An imprint of The Rowman & Littlefield Publishing Group, Inc.
4501 Forbes Boulevard, Suite 200, Lanham, Maryland 20706
www.rowman.com

86-90 Paul Street, London EC2A 4NE, United Kingdom

British Library Cataloguing in Publication Information Available

Library of Congress Cataloging-in-Publication Data

Names: Darowski, Joseph J. author. | Darowski, Kate, 1988– author. Title: Frasier : a
    cultural history / Joseph J. Darowski and Kate Darowski.
Description: Lanham : Rowman & Littlefield, 2017. | Series: The cultural history of
    television Includes bibliographical references and index.
Identifiers: LCCN 2017001797 (print) | LCCN 2017017625 (ebook) | ISBN
    9781442277977 (electronic) | ISBN 9781442277960 (hardback : alk. paper) | ISBN
    9781538188156 (pbk : alk. paper)
Subjects: LCSH: Frasier (Television program)
Classification: Classification: LCC PN1992.77.F72 (ebook) | LCC PN1992.77.F72 D38
    2017 (print) DDC 791.45/72—dc23
LC record available at https://lccn.loc.gov/2017001797

To Les and Glen Charles for creating a great character,
to Kelsey Grammer for playing him,
and to David Angell, Peter Casey, and David Lee
for giving him a family

CONTENTS

ACKNOWLEDGMENTS

There are several people who personally helped us by reading chapters of the book and giving us some feedback, including John Darowski, Joe and Kay Darowski, and Gary Hoppenstand. We'd also like to thank Tom Hubbell, KACL780.net webmaster, and John Taylor, administrator of the Frasier Forums, who were kind enough to respond to our email inquiries. We'd also like to acknowledge Ken Levine's blog, . . . *by Ken Levine* (kenlevine.blogspot.com), which provided invaluable insights into some of the behind-the-scenes work that happens on sitcoms.

INTRODUCTION

Welcome to Camp Crane.

The premise is strong and likely to generate a lot of comedy. Frasier Crane is a pompous psychiatrist who moves back to his hometown of Seattle as the host of a radio advice show. His father, Martin, is a gruff cop who was shot in the hip in the line of duty. He can't live on his own anymore because of his injury, so Frasier takes him into his home, even though their relationship has never been great. Throw in an uptight brother, an eccentric home health care worker, and a sassy producer for the radio show and you have all the ingredients for a good sitcom.

So what made *Frasier* great?

There are any number of accolades that *Frasier* earned during its run that stand as evidence that it is one of the most successful TV shows of all time.

- Thirty-seven total Emmy wins, the most ever for a sitcom
- 108 Emmy nominations across all categories
- Five consecutive wins for Outstanding Comedy Series, a record later tied by *Modern Family* (a show that shares many behind-the-scenes talent with *Frasier*)
- Twenty-four Golden Globe wins
- Six nominations for the Humanitas Award (recognizing writing that promotes human dignity, meaning, and freedom) and two wins
- The 1994 Peabody Award (recognizing excellence in quality in broadcast radio and television)

- David Hyde Pierce was nominated for a Best Supporting Actor Emmy all eleven seasons, winning four times.
- Kelsey Grammer is the only actor to have been nominated for an Emmy for playing the same character on three separate series (*Cheers*, *Wings*, and *Frasier*).

Or you could talk about the fan base for the series. During most of its run, despite NBC shifting its time slot around multiple times, *Frasier* was consistently one of the twenty most viewed shows on television.

Significantly, many of the fans of the series carry their love for the show on to the present day. There are multiple active fan sites available online where fans still discuss the show. One *Frasier* fan site, KACL780.net, hosts transcripts, made by fans, of every episode of the series. Tom Hubbell, KACL780.net webmaster, says that he did not make

Kelsey Grammer and Moose. © *NBC; NBC/Photofest*

any of the transcripts—other fans did and his site just hosts them—but even more than a decade after *Frasier* went off the air he is still "contacted frequently by fans who write to correct phrases, translations, and even subtext."[1] The site hosts transcripts that fans have translated into other languages, including Japanese. Another fan site, frasieronline.co.uk, has episode guides, fan-generated ratings for each episode, trivia and background information about the show, and a fan forum for discussion about the series.

There are also multiple podcasts that plan to discuss the series episode by episode. These include *The Frasier-Philes Podcast* and *Talk Salad and Scrambled Eggs*, the latter of which is cohosted by the filmmaker Kevin Smith.

During the show's run several books were published for fans, including an official companion book, an unauthorized guide to the series, multiple books reprinting scripts, a trivia book, a cookbook titled *Café Nervosa: The Connoisseur's Cookbook*, and even an autobiography "written" by Moose, the dog who played Eddie on the show. One of the stranger artifacts is a CD titled *Tossed Salad and Scrambled Eggs*, which features a few selections of Kelsey Grammer singing on the show interspersed with tracks by jazz artists such as Ella Fitzgerald, Nat King Cole, and Louis Armstrong. Of course, there were also assorted Café Nervosa mugs and *Frasier* T-shirts, but the merchandizing never reached the successful level NBC experienced with *Cheers*.

Besides the longtime fans who watched the show during its initial run, new fans also discover the show through its DVD sets, reruns, and availability through streaming services such as Netflix and Amazon Prime. Also, entertainment websites routinely preach the show's quality, with articles appearing periodically recommending that people who never gave the show a chance go back and enjoy the show.

Obviously, with this fan engagement, enduring interest, and repeated recommendations, the show must be funny and stand up even more than a decade after it went off the air. That is perhaps what stands out most about the series. This show is incredibly funny. And the writers, actors, and directors managed to find humor in very different and unique ways. As Joe Keenan, a writer of many of the best episodes of the series, notes:

I have to say, my favorite thing about *Frasier*, and the thing I'm proudest of, and that everyone was with the show, is that it had such a wide tonal palette. You could do shows as sexy and silly and romping as this one, and the same characters swing into heartbreak the week before and the week after without feeling that it was two different shows and that we couldn't make up our mind on the tone. The tone was very, very broad, from very silly to very emotional.[2]

Whether it was a pun about Rachmaninoff, an unbelievably absurd monologue by Daphne, a carefully orchestrated farce that needed every minute of an episode to culminate, or a pratfall by Niles in the background, any type of comedy was fair game for this show.

All these things clearly establish *Frasier* as a great sitcom. But what made *Frasier* so great to us? Why did we do this to ourselves? Why did we write a book about *Frasier*? Although siblings, we each had very different first exposures to *Frasier*. When Joseph was a high school student in the 1990s, his sister, Virginia, would sometimes let him use the computer in her room to do homework. One night she had *Frasier* on and it was the episode where Niles throws a costume party and through a series of misunderstandings everyone ends up with just the right amount of information to reach the wrong conclusion. From then on he made sure to always try to do his homework when *Frasier* was on. On the other hand, Kate, being younger, never watched during its initial run on air. The summer before her first year of college, Joseph brought home the DVD set of the first season, found his younger sister, and said something like, "We're watching this. It is the best writing we'll ever see." That was the summer of 2006. Ten years later we've completed a book on the show and love it more than we ever have before. We're amazed by the talent behind the show, the actors performing on the show, and the overall strength of the series from start to finish. Sure, there are a few dips in quality, and every season has at least one episode that doesn't work, but on the whole, *Frasier* is an amazing creative achievement. With the close study of the series we've come to notice and appreciate more intricate details in the writing and performances than comes with just one casual viewing. Truly, we love *Frasier* and we hope this book demonstrates why, besides the constant laughter it provides, this show is worth emotionally investing yourself in eleven years of fictional characters' lives.

Part I

Making a Classic

The cast of *Frasier*. Top row: David Hyde Pierce and Jane Leeves; bottom row: John Mahoney, Kelsey Grammer, Moose, Peri Gilpin. © *NBC; Photographer: Chris Haston; NBC/Photofest*

I

FRASIER BEFORE *FRASIER*

Where everybody knows your name . . .

Before *Frasier* there was *Cheers*. *Cheers* is legendary, but it almost didn't have a chance to become a legend because its ratings were so demonstrably horrible. The primary way networks track the audience size of a show is through Nielsen ratings, and after its premiere ratings for *Cheers* were among the lowest for any program on television. This was an unlikely start for a show that ended its run with eight consecutive years as one of the top ten highest-rated shows on television[1] and a well-earned status as a classic.

When *Cheers* went off the air it had won twenty-seven Emmy Awards and was nominated for the Outstanding Comedy Series Emmy every year of its original run. Acclaimed author Kurt Vonnegut even praised the series, stating, "I would say that television has produced one comic masterpiece, which is *Cheers*. . . . I wish I'd written that instead of everything I HAD written. Every time anybody opens his or her mouth on that show, it's significant."[2] With no sense of shame (or scale), NBC promoted the finale as "the television event of a lifetime."[3] The finale of *Cheers* is an iconic moment of television history, with NBC estimating that ninety-three million viewers, almost 40 percent of the country,[4] watched it.

Not only was the finale a triumph in the ratings, it was a strong creative close to a long-running series. The show about a sports bar and its regulars had one of the most perfect final lines for a series in television history—"Sorry, we're closed"—and satisfyingly wrapped up an eleven-year journey.[5] The final shot beautifully bookends the pilot in its closing scene, while also honoring one of the cast members who passed away during the show's run. Both the pilot and the finale were written by Glen and Les Charles and directed by James Burrows, the three men who created the series. The first shot of the series, aired in September 1982, is Sam Malone, the owner of Cheers, entering down the hallway from the back room and straightening a picture on the wall as he prepares for the bar to open.[6] The final shot of the show, aired in May 1993, is Sam Malone straightening a picture on the wall before exiting down the hallway to the back room of the bar.[7] The picture Sam straightens in the finale hung in the dressing room of Nicholas Colasanto, the actor who portrayed Coach for three seasons before he passed away.[8]

BUILDING AN AUDIENCE

Tracking the trajectory of *Cheers* from an almost unwatched failure to a popular classic is a lesson in patience. In the early 1980s, NBC was a struggling third-place network (of only three), and executives were looking to rebrand. The network's lack of significance had already been an issue the previous decade, when "NBC was in certain respects a nonentity in 1970s television's industrial and cultural history."[9] Several of the executives were well aware that their network needed a major overhaul in terms of content and identity. NBC had been defined by the ethos of Paul Klein, who argued the network would find success by airing the least objectionable programming (LOP) and thus find the widest possible audience.[10] As Klein explained in a 1971 *TV Guide* article, "Why You Watch What You Watch When You Watch,"

> The fact is you view TV regardless of its content. Because of the nature of the limited spectrum (only a few channels in each city) and the economic need of the networks to attract an audience large enough to attain advertising dollars which will cover the cost of production of the TV program, pay the station carrying the program, and also make a profit, you are viewing programs which by necessity must appeal to the rich and poor, smart and stupid, tall and short, wild and tame, together. Therefore, you are in the vast majority of cases viewing something that is not to your taste.[11]

This philosophy inevitably led to shows that would offend the fewest but also excite the fewest. Klein seems to have recognized this theory worked best when there were only limited options, because as technologies evolved he left work at NBC and began developing the first pay-per-view channels, including founding the Playboy Channel, which certainly falls outside the confines of LOP.[12] And, it should be noted, the theory was not working very well in the closed system of the 1970s, with NBC ranking last among three networks. Coming out of the LOP era, NBC was trying to distinguish itself by having programming that stood out from the competition and that viewers would seek out, rather than programs a viewer just wouldn't turn off if they happened to be on.

Brandon Tartikoff, the president of NBC's entertainment division at the time, heard "the head writers and director of *Taxi* had formed their own production company" and urged his boss, Fred Silverman, to make a deal with them right away.[13] Charles/Burrows/Charles was the new company named for two writers, the brothers Glen and Les Charles, and the director James Burrows, a man who would go on to become a legend in the television industry—"the Willie Mays of directing"[14] —after directing more than one thousand episodes of television. The Charles brothers and Burrows met while working on *Taxi* and bonded immediately, with Glen Charles joking, "We were a Jew and two Mormons, so we kind of banded together," and Burrows recalling, "We wanted to call our company that: 'A Jew and two Mormons.' But unfortunately, it was taken."[15]

The trust in the company was so great that Silverman offered "to finance their first series—with a guarantee that NBC would buy at least thirteen episodes, regardless of the show's initial ratings."[16] Unfortunately for Silverman, NBC would shake up its executives and he would be let go before *Cheers* ever reached the air. But, fortunately for the creators of *Cheers* and fans of great television, *Cheers* had other champions at NBC, notably Warren Littlefield.

Warren Littlefield would one day become president of NBC, but when *Cheers* premiered he worked in comedy development for the company. Littlefield was familiar with the talent of Charles/Burrows/Charles and notes that "the desire to work with [them] was really to change NBC's identity, to say, 'We want to be in the sophisticated-adult-comedy business.'"[17] This aligned with the vision of Grant Tinker, the new president of NBC. His new focus was on quality, trusting that an audience would eventually find a well-written, well-acted, and well-produced show even if it took some time.

The reviews were positive[18], but in the ratings, *Cheers* "flopped like a flounder."[19] Literally, there were weeks where the show could not have possibly done worse. A few episodes into its run "*Cheers* had finished dead last—68th out of 68 prime-time shows" in Nielsen ratings.[20]

A few factors saved the series. NBC executives reportedly loved the series; the show also helped NBC's reputation and critical credibility when awards season came around. The chasm between audience indifference and critical praise was never more apparent than when a show almost nobody was watching was nominated for eleven Emmy Awards its first year and won five, including Outstanding Comedy Series. But, perhaps most importantly, NBC had nothing better to put on its place.[21] Tinker asked Littlefield and Tartikoff if they had a good show with which to replace *Cheers*, they said no, and *Cheers* stayed on the schedule.[22]

In an era when on-demand viewing of any sort was unimaginable, reruns proved a vital tool for networks. The summer months were a boon for *Cheers*. Viewers who had missed the series while watching first-run episodes of the competition on ABC and CBS discovered the sitcom on NBC. Ratings for *Cheers* improved during the second season, but it was a middle-of-the-pack show in terms of ratings. In its third season it moved up to the twelfth most watched show on television. After that, it was a Top 10 show in Nielsen ratings for the rest of its run, being ranked fifth, third, third, fourth, third, first, fourth, and eighth in its last eight seasons.[23] As surprising as the fact that *Cheers* went from almost unwatched to a perennial Top 10 show is that it did so with major changes to the cast. A core cast member passed away, another left after five years, new characters were periodically shuffled in, but the show's excellence remained.

CHANGING IT UP

Perhaps more than any sitcom, *Cheers* survived and thrived through major cast shake-ups. At least in part this is the result of the steady excellence of the writing and directing. "Frequent cast shifts, which destroyed other sitcoms throughout the years, could not make a dent in the quality of *Cheers*."[24] In the pilot we are introduced to the initial core characters, all with their defining traits and personalities well in place. Sam Malone

(Ted Danson) is the dim-witted owner of Cheers, a former professional baseball player, and a narcissistic lothario. Diane Chambers (Shelley Long) is a pompous intellectual, a permanent grad student and aspiring artiste, who ends up as a cocktail waitress at the end of the pilot. Carla Tortelli (Rhea Perlman) is a smart-aleck waitress with a propensity for unplanned pregnancies. Coach (Nicholas Colasanto) is the intellectually challenged bartender who offers sage wisdom even when he doesn't know what is going on. Norm Peterson (George Wendt) is the most regular of the bar regulars, and eventually settled into a groove as a mostly unemployed accountant who is completely content to watch life from his bar stool. When auditioning for the role that became Norm Peterson, an actor named John Ratzenberger realized that "his reading did not enthrall the producers" and asked if they had considered having a blowhard in the bar.[25] Ratzenberger used a character from his improv act to pitch an intellectual windbag to the producers and "practically created the role" of Cliff Clavin.[26] Originally, Ratzenberger was given a seven-episode contract as a recurring character,[27] but he appeared in every episode of the first season and was officially made a regular cast member for the second season.[28]

These characters filled roles that were familiar to viewing audiences, but had been tweaked enough to make it unique. *Cheers* was a variation, or a blending, of two staples of television. As Gary Hoppenstand contends, the show was a "reworking and updating of the popular family sitcoms of the 1950s, with the formula twist that features the characters of the cast as a dysfunctional 'symbolic' family: the 'father' with the wandering eye (Sam), the overbearing 'mother' (Diane), the daffy uncle (Coach), the underachieving 'children' (Norm and Cliff), and the promiscuous 'sister' (Karla)."[29] The series would not be a classic if it just put a fresh spin on an old formula; there has to be good comedy and hopefully something of substance to the show. *Cheers* managed both. Again, Hoppenstand points out:

> The show fundamentally satirizes social class in a very effective way, establishing humorous contrasts (which makes for great comedy) between the jock (and the common laborer) with the intellectual, the highbrow with the lowbrow, having both groups portrayed as unable (or unwilling) to fully understand each other's worldview or social culture (which, again, makes for great comedy). It is the humorous "clash of cultures" and their subsequent attempts at social integration

which is fundamentally American in nature, and thus appealing to an
American television audience.[30]

Eventually audiences discovered the pseudofamily that inhabited a bar
and became quite fond of them. But would they enjoy the creation of new
characters that inevitably changed the dynamic of the series?

The first change to this core group came with a recurring character
added to the cast in Season 3. As Frasier Crane, an intellectual psychiatrist who is a new love interest for Diane, Kelsey Grammer was originally only signed to a limited contract. He was guaranteed seven episodes,
with an option for the producers to pick up more episodes if the character
worked,[31] and ended up appearing in fifteen episodes that season. Still
only a recurring character in Season 4, in which he appeared in fifteen of
the twenty-six episodes, Grammer was not made an official part of the
main cast until the fifth season.

The next cast change was unplanned. Tragically, Nicholas Colasanto,
who played Coach, died of a heart attack while the third season was
filming. Many episodes of *Cheers* feature precredit cold opens—short,
self-contained scenes that set up a joke but have little to no bearing on the
plotlines. Knowing that Colasanto's health was struggling and he needed
time off from the show, producers filmed enough cold open scenes featuring Coach that his appearances are scattered throughout the third season
all the way to the finale even though Colasanto died before many of the
season's latter episodes were written and filmed. Besides his heart troubles, he was also beginning to have difficulty remembering his lines, and
he began writing his dialogue down in places on the set that wouldn't be
seen on camera, so that he could prompt himself during filming. Ted
Danson recalls that one of the lines he couldn't remember was "It's as if
he's still with us now," and that the cast saw those words written by
Colasanto the first time they entered the set after hearing he had passed
away.[32] That meant a lot to the cast, and Danson notes that "one year,
they repainted the sets and they painted over the line. People almost quit.
Seriously. They were so emotionally infuriated that that had been taken
away from them."[33]

Cheers, which largely avoided heavy messages and sentimentality, did
not have a funeral episode for the beloved character. Instead, in the
fourth-season premiere Sam Malone acknowledges that Coach recently
passed away and that they need a new bartender. The new bartender is

The Season 3 cast of *Cheers*. Front row: Woody Harrelson and Rhea Perlman; middle row: George Wendt, Shelley Long, Ted Danson, John Ratzenberger; top: Kelsey Grammer. © *NBC; NBC/Photofest*

Woody Boyd, played by Woody Harrelson. The character was already created and named Woody before Harrelson read for the role, the shared name between character and actor being a complete coincidence. While Coach's simplemindedness is explained by how many fastballs he took to the head during his baseball career, for Boyd, producers went with the tired trope of the rural bumpkin entering the big city. In this case, Boyd hails from Hanover, Indiana, a small farm town of simpletons. Boyd is a great character who provided many laughs, but the regional stereotypes at play in his naiveté and stupidity are unfortunate.

At the end of the fifth season, Shelley Long decided to leave the series. Over the years, multiple explanations have been provided for Long's departure. They generally fall into three categories: (1) Long wanted to leave television for a career in film; (2) there was tension on the set and Long, being perceived as either a perfectionist or a diva during rehearsals, was "a source of constant friction with the cast and crew";[34] or

(3) Long felt that the Sam-and-Diane relationship had run through every permutation and didn't see a way a sixth year would not be repetitive.

In her farewell episode, Sam and Diane have scheduled a wedding. However, Diane receives word that a book she had submitted to publishers has received interest, but needs major revisions. Diane and Sam agree to call off the wedding while Diane leaves to focus on her writing, but she promises to return in six months. Sam tells Diane, "Have a good life," to which she responds, "That's something you say when something's over. Sam, I'm going away for six months, that's all." After some final repartee, Diane exits Cheers and a lonely Sam repeats, "Have a good life" to the now empty room,[35] and Diane isn't seen again until the series finale six years later.

For a show that had been built around the will-they-won't-they dynamic of Sam and Diane to lose one-half of that equation could have been crippling to its creative dynamic. But the serious, business-oriented Rebecca Howe (Kirstie Alley) introduced a new vein of comedy for the series. Of course, as Rebecca spent years circling the absurd comedic gravity center of the bar, her no-nonsense businesswoman would devolve into a farcically broad and inept mess by the final season.

The final character to be added as a main cast member is Lilith Sternin-Crane. After his breakup with Diane, Frasier eventually began dating a fellow psychiatrist, played by the inimitable Bebe Neuwirth. First appearing in the fourth season, and not beginning a serious relationship with Frasier until the fifth season, it is revealed in the sixth season that Lilith and Frasier are married (the wedding occurred offscreen). Lilith is upped from a recurring character to a regular cast member for the tenth and eleventh seasons. All the actors and actresses who played regular characters on *Cheers* were nominated for either Best Actor/Best Actress or Best Supporting Actor/Supporting Actress Emmy Awards. Ted Danson, Shelley Long, Rhea Perlman, Woody Harrelson, Kirstie Alley, and Bebe Neuwirth all won Emmy Awards.

THE EMINENT DR. CRANE

Of all the characters introduced on the show, the one with the largest impact in popular culture is undeniably Frasier Crane. There are any number of things that are odd about this. He was introduced as a wedge to

Sam and Diane but kept hanging around the bar after she dumped him. He watched Sam and Diane get back together and stage a wedding in the bar. Then he stayed around long after she moved on. At the end of *Cheers*, a poll was taken asking viewers what character they would want to see spun off into a new series, and only 2 percent chose Frasier Crane.[36] And yet something about Frasier Crane allowed the character to swing from a peripheral character on *Cheers* to the centerpiece of a new show. So, how did Frasier Crane come to be, and what was his trajectory on *Cheers*?

At the end of Season 2, Sam and Diane had fought with each other so emotionally and painfully the writers knew they could not simply reset for Season 3. To demonstrate the repercussions of their actions, it was decided that Sam, a recovering alcoholic, would turn back to the bottle for the first, and only, time on the show. Diane would spend time at a sanitarium in Connecticut to regain emotional stability. But, to add stakes for viewers, in addition to the emotional hurt both characters were experiencing, producers looked for a character that could keep Sam and Diane apart for Season 3. They envisioned the opposite of Sam Malone. So rather than a jock, they created an intellectual. Rather than a lover of sports, a lover of museums. Rather than a self-assured, egotistic lothario, a pompous but needy romantic.

Kelsey Grammer would certainly not have been at the top of the producers' list of actors to cast in the role. Grammer had some experience, but nothing that said he was ready for a recurring role on a prime-time sitcom. Following high school, Grammer attended Juilliard (with other actors such as Mandy Patinkin, Robin Williams, and Christopher Reeve),[37] but Grammer was "expelled for lack of discipline" after his second year.[38] Eventually the acting bug returned to him, and he worked for two years doing plays in San Diego[39] before returning to New York, where he got a small role on a daytime soap opera[40] and then did more regional theater all over the country.[41]

While the Charles brothers and James Burrows were looking for an actor for the role of Frasier Nye (the character was renamed Frasier Crane after Grammer insisted he did not look like a Nye), Kelsey Grammer was an understudy in a New York production of *Hurly Burly*. Initially, the role was offered to John Lithgow, who turned it down without any consideration: "It was like swatting a fly away. At that time, I just wasn't going to do a series."[42] Mandy Patinkin recommended Grammer to a

Paramount casting director,[43] and Grammer did a video audition in New York, then was flown out to Los Angeles for an audition with Glen and Les Charles and James Burrows, then flown out to Los Angeles again to audition for Paramount executives.[44]

He learned he was hired when a bottle of Dom Pérignon was delivered to his hotel room with a card reading "Welcome to *Cheers*."[45] Grammer viewed Frasier Crane as "an intellectual at some points but also an Everyman—flawed and very insecure."[46] The contrast of pomposity and neediness at the core of Frasier was a comedic font for writers that resulted in a character who thrived on television for twenty years.

When Frasier is first introduced on *Cheers*, Diane brings him to the bar to help counsel Sam, who has begun drinking again. The fact that in Grammer's first performance he is aiding an intervention for someone struggling with substance abuse would take on a bitter irony later when Grammer's wild lifestyle caused problems on both *Cheers* and *Frasier*. The twist at the end of the episode is that Frasier is not just an acquaintance of Diane's, but they're actually dating.

Though Frasier and Diane become engaged, Diane is shown still pining for Sam and using Frasier as a means of getting over her past relationship. Eventually, Diane leaves Frasier at the altar, and he goes into a downward spiral (not the only one we'll see on *Cheers* and *Frasier*) but slowly recovers. In Season 5, Frasier begins to date Lilith Sternin. Season 6 sees the progression of Frasier and Lilith's relationship toward marriage. Early on in Season 6, Frasier and Lilith get engaged, we see the bachelor and bachelorette party for Frasier and Lilith, and then four episodes later Frasier acknowledges that it is his one-month anniversary. Thus, with Frasier's attempted marriage to Diane being an elopement in Europe and his wedding to Lilith taking place off camera, there is no need to later explain the absence of Martin and Niles from the festivities.

In Season 8, Frasier and Lilith become parents when their son Frederick is born. In the final season it is revealed that Lilith has had an affair. Lilith announces her intention to separate from Frasier, leaving him full custody of Frederick while she lives in an underground eco-pod with Dr. Louis Pascal, the man with whom she had an affair. Frasier does not take this news well and climbs onto a third-story ledge and threatens to jump unless Lilith returns to him. Needless to say, he does not jump, and Lilith does leave him. Later in the season she attempts to reconcile with Frasier. The series ends on an ambiguous note in the Frasier-Lilith relationship.

As the exact nature of the Frasier spin-off was not decided, the lack of a firm commitment to either reconciliation or a divorce allowed producers flexibility and viewers the chance to assume a happy ending if the spin-off had not occurred.

Years later, in a conversation with Daphne Moon, Frasier would look back on this era of his romantic life and describe it like this:

> I met a lovely barmaid—sophisticated, if a bit loquacious. We fell madly in love, we got engaged. Of course, she left me standing at the altar. But the point is, I didn't give up. I took my poor, battered heart and offered it to Lilith. Who put it in her little Cuisinart and hit the purée button! [47]

After such misadventures it is understandable why Frasier Crane would look to start a new chapter in his life. Viewers could follow that new life on a series whose critical acclaim would eclipse the classic where Frasier Crane first appeared.

2

FRASIER ON HIS OWN

We should do something special, be bold!

TO SPIN OFF OR NOT TO SPIN OFF

"It's not great, but here and there it has moments."[1] That line comes from the *New York Times* review of the first spin-off from *Cheers*. Of course, the reviews for *Frasier* were more positive ("The cast are putting on a splendid act"),[2] but *The Tortellis* is the first, almost forgotten "disastrous"[3] chapter in NBC's goal to create a *Cheers*-inspired franchise of shows. Naturally NBC wanted more shows associated with *Cheers*; it had become a bona fide cash cow.[4] Near the end of *Cheers'* run, John Pike, a Paramount television executive who was involved in both *Cheers* and *Frasier*, "put together a piece of paper called 'The Value of *Cheers*.' We calculated that net dollars to NBC for one year of *Cheers* was $75 million. The *Cheers* asset over the years was about three-quarters of a billion dollars of profit for the network."[5]

Knowing that *Cheers* was ending, executives began looking for a way to ensure continued success. NBC had considered a new show about Cliff and Norm,[6] but it is hard to imagine those two characters in a universe that didn't center on the bar. Television history's mix of failure and success when it came to spin-offs signaled that quality mattered more than anything else when it came to finding an audience. The hope would be that fans of the original series would at least give a spin-off a try, with something of a built-in audience. Of course, solid creative talent would be a key.

The producers of *Wings*, David Angell, Peter Casey, and David Lee, had formed a production company, Grub Street Productions, after they met while writing on *Cheers*. Knowing that *Cheers* was coming to a close, and having had good experiences working together on both *Cheers* and *Wings*, Grammer and Angell, Casey, and Lee began planning to work together after the *Cheers* finale. However, perhaps wary of the very mixed success of new shows based on beloved characters in new settings, they tried to create a brand-new sitcom rather than attempt the continuing adventures of Frasier Crane. After all, though popular spin-offs can be identified, Martin Gitlin correctly points out, "there have been far more bombs when attempts have been made to give characters from one show a sitcom of their own."[7]

In an effort to break out and really create their own show, they first pitched a series that would be completely unrelated to *Cheers*, even if it borrowed an actor. Casey, Angell, and Lee wanted to work with Kelsey Grammer, but they "weren't going to do *The Frasier Crane Show*. Kelsey didn't want to play the character again, and Casey/Angell/Lee didn't want to be the spin-off guys."[8] The show they pitched would have Grammer playing a "bedridden mogul who had been crippled in a motorcycle accident. A man so driven and wealthy that being in bed didn't stop him from virtually running the country."[9] Lee explains, "Kelsey was going to play a Malcolm Forbes type of guy. Big motorcycle. Really rich guy. He becomes paralyzed, and the relationship would be between him and his physical therapist."[10] This pitch was not what Paramount or NBC were looking for. Pike called it "the worst idea I'd ever heard in my life"[11] and after reviewing the pitch told Grammer, "Kels, I think a comedy should be funny."[12]

Instead, it was firmly suggested that they look at continuing the story of Frasier Crane. Why, of all the characters from *Cheers*, was the network pushing Frasier Crane for his own series? It likely has something to do with the richness of his character, as identified by television critic Ken Tucker:

> At first, he was the usual sort of TV intellectual: a pompous blowhard ridiculed by the *Cheers* barflies with whom we were supposed to identify. Soon enough, however—partly because of Grammer's skill as an actor and, I'll bet, partly because the *Cheers* writers were bored with

their established characters and wanted to try something new—Frasier became a sympathetic, well-rounded character, capable of horsing around with Norm and Cliffie while still radiating an intelligent demeanor. [13]

Grammer insisted that if the show was about an established character everything else about the series would have to be new and unique. This meant the new show would not be about Frasier and Lilith raising Frederick. [14]

To bridge the two series, a monologue was delivered in the first minute of the *Frasier* pilot that explained why Frasier Crane, who was last seen leaving Cheers in Boston, is now sitting in a radio booth in Seattle:

Six months ago I was living in Boston. My wife had left me, which was very painful. Then she came back to me, which was excruciating.

Kelsey Grammer. © *NBC/Photofest*

On top of that, my practice had grown stagnant and my social life
consisted of hanging around a bar night after night. I was clinging to a
life that wasn't working anymore and I knew I had to do something . . .
anything. So I ended the marriage once and for all, packed up my
things, and moved back here to my hometown of Seattle.[15]

On the commentary track for the episode, Peter Casey and David Lee
explain that the first joke that landed was based on Frasier's relationship
with Lilith on *Cheers*. "So we went, 'Okay, we're on our way, we scored
with a joke based on somebody else's character, now let's score some of
our own.'"[16] *Cheers* had eight main characters in its final year, and Angell, Casey, and Lee ended up writing for nine cast members on *Wings*, so
they knew how tricky it could be to service a lot of characters in a twenty-
two-minute episode. Deliberately keeping the cast small, in the pilot,
"The Good Son," viewers are introduced to the four new characters
around whom Frasier's life revolved for eleven years.

FINDING A CAST

The talent of the *Frasier* cast is undeniable. And, perhaps the greater
miracle, it was largely put together because everyone agreed that these
actors would all be perfect for their roles. Jeff Richman, a writer and
producer for the show, argued that the "lightning in a bottle" magic of the
cast required the writing to step up to the talent of the actors.[17]

The Producer

Roz Doyle, the snarky producer of Frasier's call-in radio show, was not a
fully fleshed-out character when the casting process began. Peter Casey
recalls that "she was supposed to be someone who Frasier was smarter
than, more educated than, but was completely inferior to in the setting of
the radio station. That was her stomping ground and she was the alpha
dog there."[18] Because of that, producers wanted an actress who could
"really stand toe to toe with Frasier."[19] After seeing dozens of actresses
from a wide spectrum of ages and ethnic backgrounds, it came down to
either Lisa Kudrow or Peri Gilpin.[20] Both Kudrow and Gilpin had appeared on *Cheers* in guest roles, so the producers and network knew

them.[21] When Grub Street Productions had created *Wings* in 1990, Angell, Casey, and Lee had considered Gilpin for a role in that series but didn't think she was ready to be a regular prime-time character.[22]

John Pike, the Paramount executive, pushed for Kudrow or perhaps against Gilpin. "Pike wasn't a fan of Peri [Gilpin]'s. When it came time to decide, John said, 'Not Peri.'"[23] Kudrow was cast and participated in table reads and rehearsals for *Frasier*'s pilot. Peter Casey remembers that Kudrow played Roz as more quirky than bold, which could still get laughs but was not what they planned for the character. "Lisa didn't exactly fit the mold of what we were looking for in terms of a strong-willed character, but she was really funny. Her quirkiness made lines that weren't intended as jokes hilarious."[24] During the rehearsal time for a pilot it is necessary to tweak the script to allow actors' strengths to come through. As Angell, Casey, and Lee rewrote Roz for Kudrow, the dynamic they wanted disappeared. "Although she remained funny in her quirky way, we found that each day we were re-writing the character less strong because Lisa just didn't play forceful. More importantly, what Jimmy [Burrows] noticed was that Kelsey was pulling back in scenes with her because if he went all out like he usually did, he completely overpowered her."[25] Four days after she was cast, Kudrow was told that she was being let go. Kudrow says, "Getting fired was devastating, because that was the best pilot."[26] Burrows, who directed Kudrow as one of the main characters in the *Friends* pilot[27] one year later, notes, "For awhile she didn't like me. Then *Friends* came along. We're good friends now."[28]

Gilpin was called and offered the role. Peter Casey explains, "From that point on through the rest of rehearsals things went smoothly. We rewrote Roz back to her original character and Peri made it work wonderfully."[29] As Grammer recognized, Roz Doyle was not an easy character to make work right away, but with the combination of "the writers' exploration and Peri's skills" she came to life.[30] In the end, though, the show needed Roz Doyle as a foil to both Frasier and Niles, and Gilpin delivered the harder edge the character required to hold her own.

The Brother

The first plans for *Frasier* did not include Niles Crane or any sibling at all. Producers did not consider adding a sibling for Frasier until Sheila Guthrie, an associate of casting director Jeff Greenberg, suggested David

Hyde Pierce purely because of his close resemblance to Grammer. Peter Casey recalls, "She showed us a picture of David Hyde Pierce. [She asked,] 'Doesn't he look like Kelsey ten years ago?'"[31] Based on this physical similarity with Grammer, producers met with Pierce before they'd written a script with the character. Pierce remembers, "All they could tell me was that Frasier was a Freudian and Niles was a Jungian. Frasier had gone to Harvard and Niles had gone to Yale."[32] The meeting evidently went well because Pierce was "settled on for the role of Niles without a second thought,"[33] at least by the creators. Casting can be a tedious process, requiring lots of auditions and network approval. When making the official pitch to the network, the producers would reference an actor as a template to help the executives get a picture in their mind. "So when we pitched Niles, we said think of David Hyde Pierce. That's when something else amazing happened. At the mention of DHP's name, Warren [Littlefield] said, 'We love him. If you can get him, he's pre-approved.'"[34] So, beginning with one suggestion because Pierce looked like a younger Grammer, a character had been created and the casting approved without an audition.

So similar are Grammer and Pierce in appearance that Pierce claims, "I even get a jolt talking to Kelsey sometimes. It's like looking at myself."[35] Grammer also admits, "David's picture could be mistaken for another me."[36] Their close resemblance to one another was even more notable when they were younger. Pierce recalls meeting Grammer, years before *Frasier* was even an idea:

> The first time I met Kelsey, he and I were doing plays together at the Long Wharf Theater in New Haven. I was doing *Holiday* and he was doing *The Common Pursuit*. We had our meals in the same place and I went in to have dinner and he was sitting at the table and I looked at him and thought I was already eating. Because we looked that much alike. And if you see pictures of him in his twenties in New York, he looks like me in my twenties. It's amazing. We still have a certain resemblance, but when we were both younger, we really looked alike.[37]

Their resemblance definitely lessened as the actors aged, but David Hyde Pierce's appearance at the beginning of *Frasier* is remarkably close to Kelsey Grammer's when he began on *Cheers*. This was acknowledged when Ted Danson was a guest star as Sam Malone in the second season of *Frasier*:

Frasier: Oh, Sam, this is my brother, Dr. Niles Crane.

Niles: Pleasure to meet you.

Sam: Yeah, you too. Wow . . . man, this is freaky. He looks just like you did when I met you. What happened, huh?

Frasier: Wasn't exactly a health club you were running there, Sam.[38]

The series also humorously noted that though they have similar facial features, Kelsey Grammer is physically larger than David Hyde Pierce. When the brothers find their mother's journal and believe they are reading her description of her sons (though she was really writing about her lab rats named Frasier and Niles), a laugh is earned when they read, "Frasier never seems to get enough at mealtime. He's nearly twice the size of Niles and often, when he thinks I'm not looking, steals his brother's food." Naturally, Frasier looks a bit put out by this statement.[39]

While a physical resemblance made Niles Crane possible, it must be noted that Pierce's incredible talent made the role unforgettable. As critic Scott D. Pierce notes, Niles "looks exactly like you'd expect Frasier's brother to look" but also, thanks to the writers and Pierce, "acts as you'd expect Frasier's brother to act."[40] Casey and Lee praised the actor, saying "David Hyde Pierce is a once in a lifetime find."[41] Ken Levine, who has written for shows from *M*A*S*H* to *Cheers* to *Everybody Loves Raymond*, was asked who was the funniest actor he got to write for and he answered, "David Hyde Pierce. The man is a comic God."[42] Perhaps the greatest compliment came from James Burrows. After working on the pilot for *Frasier*, Burrows "told the boys they had to go back to Niles" more often.[43] Pierce was recognized with eleven Emmy nominations for Best Supporting Actor and won four times.

The Father

When Angell, Casey, and Lee first began brainstorming ideas for the Frasier spin-off, they latched onto a concept for an episode of *Cheers* that had never been used. Frasier doing a guest spot on a call-in radio show was a leftover story idea from *Cheers* that they'd never been able to make work. Knowing that they wanted to move Frasier away from Boston, they decided to also give him a new career rather than having him in private practice as a psychiatrist, which might have felt too much like *The Bob Newhart Show*.[44] With that in mind, they started plotting a workplace comedy at a radio station.[45] In this version of *Frasier* "the entire show was going to be set at the radio station, with a full range of characters that included a station manager, head of advertising sales, and a bombastic Rush Limbaugh–type commentator."[46] But now producers began to worry that while trying to avoid having the show be too close to *Cheers* they were veering too close to another classic sitcom, *WKRP in Cincinnati*.[47]

David Lee drew on his own experience for inspiration in how to differentiate the show from any that had come before. He thought a lot of people were going through a stage of life he was experiencing and that hadn't been explored very much on television. "David's father had suffered a stroke, and David is an only child, so he was helping his mother take care of his father," which was a phase of life that they thought would be "an incredibly fertile field" for storytelling.[48] Thus, what had been a workplace sitcom became something of a hybrid of the classic workplace and home sitcoms, as they removed most of the radio station staff and added a father to the mix.[49] With the pilot titled "The Good Son," it is clear that the parent-child dynamic was going to be a key to the series.

In looking for who could play a cantankerous father, producers thought of an actor they had worked with on the last season of *Cheers*. John Mahoney had played a jingle writer who was hired to write a song for a radio ad for *Cheers*.[50] "Casey, Lee, and Angell saw him on that episode and thought he would be perfect for Frasier's dad."[51] They were not the only ones who thought Mahoney would be perfect; the network said if they could get him, Mahoney was preapproved and didn't have to audition.[52]

Being offered a role in a major network sitcom without an audition was a fairly stunning turn of events for Mahoney from where he'd been earlier in his life. In his thirties he had settled into a career in Chicago editing medical journals when, at age thirty-seven, he quit that job to pursue acting. Mahoney recalls:

> It was a huge challenge, but it's a fairy story, because . . . to go from a
> well-paid job in middle age, into a profession that at any given time 90

percent of its union members are out of work, is a rather silly, cavalier move to make. But I was never as happy in my life, and it must have been the right thing to do, because everything fell into place. I've never been without a job, and I haven't lost one ounce of that exhilaration and happiness.[53]

Mahoney so inhabited the role of Martin Crane that it is impossible to imagine anyone else playing the character. We should all be thankful that he was bored with a career as an editor.

To help create the tension and conflict that drives story, Martin Crane is very different from his pompous sons. He is blue collar in terms of taste, career, and attire. Again, the creators drew from their own experience for inspiration. "There's a lot of Martin in Casey's and Lee's real dads. Casey's father was a San Francisco cop, and Lee's dad grew up on a dirt farm in Texas."[54] Lee specifically notes that "a lot of the relationship between Frasier and Martin came from my parents looking at this kid who wanted to be in show business from the time he was nine years old as 'Where did we get this kid?'"[55] Peter Casey says that this became their go-to response when they were frequently asked how Frasier and Niles ended up so different from Martin: "We told them the truth. . . . David Lee is every bit as different from his father as the Cranes."[56] The pilot hinges largely on Martin's hip injury from his time as a cop, forcing him to move into Frasier's apartment, thus disrupting the plans and lifestyle Frasier had prepared. Casey says, "To create Frasier's father we wanted to have someone very different than Frasier. Those differences create conflict; conflict creates humor, so we came up with Martin, a down-to-earth, no-nonsense ex-policeman."[57] From the pilot on, that contentious father-son dynamic is the cornerstone of the series.[58]

The Home Health Care Worker

When Angell, Casey, and Lee had been preparing to pitch NBC a show with Kelsey Grammer as a bedridden mogul, the caretaker with whom he would interact was planned to be a street-smart Latina. They specifically had Rosie Perez in mind.[59] So when plans changed and they began working on the show that became *Frasier*, they carried over the idea of a live-in health care worker, but now the character would be helping out Frasier's father. They debated between having the character be Hispanic or

English for some time.[60] Jane Leeves had gained particular notice from NBC executives when she guest-starred in a *Seinfeld* episode as "the virgin."[61] Warren Littlefield told the producers that if they went with Jane Leeves she was preapproved and would not have to go through traditional casting either.[62] This would mean that four-fifths of their cast—Frasier, Niles, Martin, and Daphne—would not have to go through casting calls.

When writing the script, Angell, Casey, and Lee still waffled back and forth between a Hispanic character or an English one until they actually wrote the scene where Frasier and Martin interview Daphne. At that point, they decided to make her English.[63] With network preapproval, the casting seemed to be a slam dunk. However, Kelsey Grammer did not like the idea. He thought a British woman living in the house with an American man sounded too much like the 1970s television show *Nanny and the Professor*.[64] He was quite wary and asked the producers to consider a different route.

The producers asked Grammer to come in and read some lines with Jane Leeves. Grammer describes that experience: "She came in and read. We thanked her. She left. I turned to the producers. 'Okay,' I said, 'you got me. She's great. She was brilliant.'"[65] Now with the blessings of the network and the titular star of the show, the role of Daphne was cast.

While not nearly as abrasive as Martin, adding a "daffy physical therapist" to Frasier's daily life was intended to also add the type of conflict that easily led to comedy.[66] Of course, for fans of the show it is Daphne's relationship (or lack thereof) with Niles that is most important to the series. But, as Niles and Daphne do not even meet until the third episode, the idea that Niles's unrequited and secret crush on Daphne would become *the* source of comedy and story for much of *Frasier* does not seem to have been part of the initial concept of the show. The course correction happens rather quickly, however, and the Niles-Daphne relationship becomes as important, if not more so, than the Martin-Frasier dynamic.

MAKE IT DIFFERENT

Clearly, NBC and the producers of *Frasier* hoped that the massive audience that had come to know the character of Frasier Crane on *Cheers* would follow him to his new titular sitcom. But, from the very beginning, efforts were made to differentiate *Frasier* from *Cheers*. The new show must not be a watered-down version of what viewers had loved on *Cheers*.

Frasier determinedly declared its uniqueness from its predecessor in terms of style and tone. And it worked. In retrospect, "*Frasier* managed the rare feat of standing on its own as a successful sequel to a hit show."[67] As Martin Gitlin put it, *Frasier* is the only spin-off that "stands out for brilliance that rivals that of a critically acclaimed program" that launched it.[68] *Frasier*'s status as one of the most successful spin-offs in television history is at least in part due to the way the series established its own identity that allowed it earn a following, reputation, and critical acclaim apart from *Cheers*.

On the surface, there are several points from basic plot and setting that already set up a contrast between *Frasier* and *Cheers*. One of the most significant changes between the two series is that *Cheers* was a workplace sitcom (where admittedly the employees and patrons came to rely on one another like family), while *Frasier* was a family sitcom. Certainly, Frasier's work at the KACL radio station (whose call sign represents the show's creators Angell, Casey, and Lee) provides regular plot points and Roz from KACL is a core cast member. However, Frasier's apartment is the main setting of the series and his relationships with Martin and Niles are at its core.

The creators also set an entire continent between the location of *Cheers* and *Frasier*. This was done to (1) have a different atmosphere than Boston and (2) make it hard for the network to insist on guest stars from *Cheers*.[69] The creators knew Lilith would appear at least once a season. As the mother of Frasier's child and the *Cheers* character who had the most cause to interact with Frasier, this made sense. But the producers did not want Norm or Cliff just popping by periodically. After a year for *Frasier* to establish its own identity they were comfortable with additional cast members from *Cheers* guest-starring once a season or so.

Frasier's ex-wife Lilith makes the most appearances, twelve episodes during *Frasier*'s eleven-season run. Frasier's son Frederick, who was played by several different actors on *Cheers* and on *Frasier*, appeared six times on *Cheers* and nine times on *Frasier*. But the characters that were less related to Frasier made much less frequent appearances on the *Cheers* spin-off. Sam appears in Season 2, Diane in Season 3, and Woody in Season 6. Diane also appeared for a few seconds as the punch line to a nightmare Frasier is having in the second season and in a Season 9 epi-

sode in which Frasier has an imaginary conversation with his most significant ex-girlfriends/wives.

Of course, though these *Cheers* crossovers were fairly infrequent, the
NBC promotional department made the most of them. When Sam Malone
was going to appear, NBC ran numerous ads promoting it as "Home
Malone Tuesday" and declared that there was a full hour of *Frasier*
scheduled for that night. This implied, but never stated, that Sam Malone
would be in a special hour-long episode of *Frasier*. Of course, what aired
was the new Sam Malone episode followed by a repeat episode from
earlier that season. As Scott D. Pierce notes, "While the commercial spots
are careful not to say anything that's not true, what they do say is mis-
leading."[70]

The largest reunion, which saw Frasier and his family visiting Boston,
occurred in Season 9. Once in Boston, they run into Cliff Clavin, who
invites Frasier to his retirement party. The party is not held at Cheers but
in a hotel lounge, which definitely sticks out as odd. Within the story both
the unexpected location and Sam's absence are explained away when
Cliff says Sam has rented out the bar for a Red Sox party. The absences
were most likely because, productionwise, it would have been too expensive to re-create the old set, and because Ted Danson was starring in the
CBS sitcom *Becker*. It was reported through secondhand sources (but not
Kirstie Alley herself) that Rebecca Howe never made an appearance on
Frasier because, as a Scientologist, she would not appear on a show with
a psychiatrist as the main character.[71]

At Cliff's party, viewers are treated to a mini-*Cheers* reunion, with
Cliff, Norm, Carla, and Paul all making guest appearances. Really, there
is very little plot to this episode and it likely only entertained those who
were nostalgic for *Cheers*. This episode was part of a nostalgia-fueled
celebration that dominated NBC in April 2002. Celebrating its seventy-
fifth anniversary as a broadcasting entity—it began as a radio network
known as the Radio Broadcasting Network of America—the network had
multiple specials honoring itself. Casts from previous hit shows appeared
in episodes of current series. Members of the cast of *St. Elsewhere* appeared on *Scrubs*, while the cast from *Quincy* dropped in on *Crossing
Jordan*, and, the most natural of these exercises, characters from *Cheers*
appeared on *Frasier*.

Contemporary articles from 2002 speculate that this wave of nostalgia
(that went beyond just NBC throwing itself a party; most networks were

having reunion shows or specials), was because "in the wake of 9/11, American viewers are looking for familiar TV that takes them back to a happier time."[72] Others, such as Carol Burnett, who had a very successful reunion show that year, argued it was simply a search for simplicity and less cynicism.[73] Kelsey Grammer, who cohosted two NBC specials and had his *Cheers* castmates appear on his show, saw a less complex reason for the nostalgia: network executives were out of ideas: "Basically, it's because they don't know where they're going. They've got to look back. . . . They're stalled right now a little bit."[74] Whatever the reason behind the reunion, this was the last of the *Cheers* cast to appear on *Frasier*, other than the most frequent guest, Bebe Neuwirth as Lilith.

In the 264 episodes of *Frasier*, familiar adult characters from *Cheers* (mostly Lilith) appear in only sixteen episodes, a scant 6 percent of the series. Producers clearly did not want *Frasier* to simply feel like a sequel to *Cheers*. In addition, *Frasier* developed its own storytelling style, one that was markedly different from its predecessor.

First, there is the general tone of the two series. *Cheers* was a decidedly working-class setting; *Frasier* has a much more elitist aesthetic. As critic Lynn Elber puts it, "When the blue-collar barroom comedy Cheers ended its run in 1993, it managed the neat trick of turning beer into champagne."[75] Frasier stuck out in *Cheers*, a quirky upper-class character in the blue-collar world of a Boston sports bar. In *Frasier*, the audience is now in Frasier's world, and his blue-collar father sticks out in his apartment. Kelsey Grammer says that on *Cheers* he could engage in what he called "hit-and-run" comedy, getting in and out to add some humor to a scene.[76] On *Frasier*, he became the canvas of the show, whereas on *Cheers* he was a bright spot of color.[77] If Frasier Crane is the canvas for the series, it is undoubtedly a high-priced designer canvas.

For example, on *Cheers*, the first episode featured a debate about the sweatiest movie ever made, with popular movie titles like *Rocky II*, *Ben-Hur*, *Alien*, and *Cool Hand Luke* being tossed out. In the pilot of *Frasier*, designer names like Corbusier and Eames get casually mentioned. The two shows are operating in different milieus, but that doesn't make one better than the other. As Caryn Mandabach, the president of the Carsey-Werner television production company, said of *Cheers*, "You could basically retitle that show *Everybody's Dumb*, because in truth all of those characters were stupid, but the show was very wittily written."[78] Conversely, noted critic Ken Tucker says of *Frasier*, "But, I must add adamantly, I always hated the notion that *Frasier* was an intelligent show because it was filled with references to the opera and fine wines; it was an intelligent show because its best plots were immaculate farces and its jokes little treasures of verbal dexterity."[79] The writing of both series made them classics, not the tone or setting.

But, in order to blaze their own trail, the producers of *Frasier* employed differences in presentation and editing that make the show quite different from *Cheers*. In many instances, it was as though they looked at what *Cheers* had done and chose to present the exact opposite to viewers. While shows inevitably evolve and shift course across multiple seasons, the pilots of the respective series represent the efforts of the showrunners to set a tone and style for a series. Clearly the tone that is being established from the very beginning with *Frasier* is "not-*Cheers*."

"Give Me a Ring Sometime," the series pilot of *Cheers*, opens with a precredits gag about an underage drinker trying to order a beer. Then the opening credits, which last a full minute, roll with the now-classic theme song "Where Everybody Knows Your Name" playing. A design studio named Castle/Bryant/Johnson located "archival illustrations and photographs of bar life, culled from books, private collections, and historical societies" and then hand-tinted each image.[80] Over the vintage images, cast and crew names appear in a bold, wide orange-and-yellow font. Then, the plot is introduced, in which Diane enters the bar and waits all day for her prospective lover to return before she is offered a job as a waitress. Then, the final credits roll over a still shot of the bar as an instrumental version of the theme song plays.

This is the pattern that most episodes of *Cheers* would follow. For much of the series, there would often be only a single A-storyline, one that would be introduced with someone entering the bar. As Bob Broder notes, "The beauty of having set the show in a bar meant when the door opened, the story started, and any story could walk in that door. It wasn't like doing a family comedy where you had to figure out how you were going to service your six characters."[81] The *Cheers* cast who did not have significant roles in the plot would sit at the bar cracking jokes about what was happening like an alcoholic Greek chorus.

Contrast this with the first episode of *Frasier*, "The Good Son." First, there is no cold open. The title card announcing the series title appears during a six-second jingle while a simplistic animation outlines the Seattle skyline. Castle/Bryant/Johnson also designed that six-second opening credit sequence. Then, an intertitle card with the words "The Job" in plain white text over a black background appears, before the audience enters a scene in medias res. While credits play over the action, Frasier delivers a monologue that acknowledges his roots in Boston but also definitively separates him from his past in Boston. The editing style of this new show has already, in a matter of minutes, established itself as unique from *Cheers*. Throughout the episode, new scenes are introduced with intertitle cards. Action moves from the radio station, to the coffee shop Café Nervosa, to Frasier's apartment, then moves between those three locales one more time before wrapping up. The episodes end with a silent comedic scene acted out as credits are displayed on the bottom of the screen and Kelsey Grammer sings a song titled "Tossed Salad and Scrambled Eggs."

In the twenty-three-minute pilot (NBC stole fifteen seconds from each of the other shows airing in its prime-time block that night to allow *Frasier* one extra minute for the pilot),[82] a unique relationship between Frasier and each of the other characters is established in scenes that rotate between the three most common settings. An antagonistic work relationship is set up with Roz at the radio station. Frasier and Niles demonstrate similar taste and style, but with an underlying sibling rivalry at the Café Nervosa. Frasier's broken relationship with his father is established at Frasier's apartment, the same setting where Daphne is interviewed and given a job as Martin's physical therapist (over Frasier's protestations that she's a "loon"). This is quite different from *Cheers*, where all the action took place in the bar and the characters' relationships largely were coworkers or employee-patron.

Peter Casey has acknowledged that many decisions were made "to make *Frasier* different from *Cheers*."[83] Choices in terms of style and editing that may seem minor end up building a whole that stands apart from *Cheers*. For example, on *Frasier* there is deliberately no music between shots or musical cues to start a scene. Also, there are no establishing shots outside before cutting into the scene taking place inside a building. *Cheers* had often used an establishing exterior shot of the bar before showing the interior scenes, and on the few occasions where other locations, such as Carla's house, were used, there was a generic shot of an individual house before beginning a scene inside. For *Frasier*, the producers "always thought that it might be fun to trust America's intellect to imagine that if indeed they are inside a coffee house that the outside of it looks like a coffee house. Same thing with an apartment building. If you're inside Frasier's apartment you're going to pretty much know that it's a building on the outside."[84]

Several of these differences grew and evolved into distinctive parts of *Frasier*'s identity. For example, the intertitle cards began in the pilot as a means of cutting out unnatural expositional dialogue.[85] Rather than have Frasier say, "How's my brother Niles doing?" when viewers first meet Niles, they have a title card up that says "The Brother." Frasier and Niles can then simply have a normal conversation without revisiting aspects of their relationship of which they're both well aware but the audience needs to learn. However, once that was a tool in the writers' and editors' bag of tricks, the intertitle cards were employed in many different ways throughout the show's eleven years.

At times, intertitle cards warn the audience to pay extra close attention. "This Gets Tricky, So Pay Close Attention" appears at the beginning of an episode with alternate timelines playing out. They may seem like a complete non sequitur until several minutes later, such as when "How Many Sharks Died . . . ?" precedes a scene in which Martin proudly models a sharkskin suit. Or, perhaps the funniest example, an intertitle card gives multiple punch lines to a joke that hasn't been told yet. "It Was Either 'The Wheat Field' or 'The Sandstorm'" appears before a scene that ends with Martin asking for help assembling a ten-thousand-piece jigsaw puzzle called "The Wheat Field." Likely the debate in the writer's room about which was funnier led to a title card giving both options.

The intertitle card became such an iconic part of *Frasier*'s identity that it was satirized in an episode of *The Simpsons*. Kelsey Grammer voices Sideshow Bob, a minor character in that series, and in the eighth-season episode "Brother from Another Series," David Hyde Pierce voices Cecil, Sideshow Bob's brother. Numerous allusions to *Frasier* occur in the episode, but the most in-your-face one is the intertitle card that appears after the first commercial break reading "*Frasier* is a hit show on the NBC television network."[86]

Similarly, the very odd closing song that played over the closing credits has become a key part of the show's identity. "Tossed Salad and Scrambled Eggs" had music written by Bruce Miller, with lyrics by Darryl Phinnessee (though Miller suggested a couple of lines), and was sung by Kelsey Grammer.[87] Grammer called the song "sonic liquid gold drizzled on top of a pile of laughs every week."[88] "Tossed Salad and Scrambled Eggs" has what appears to be nonsensical lyrics that, at the very least, are inscrutable. As a 2012 *Entertainment Weekly* article by Lanford Beard put it, the song "has likely haunted, perplexed, and/or eroded [*Frasier* fans] from the inside out for the better part of 20 years."[89] Fortunately, Miller has shed some insight into their meaning.

Miller had specific instructions not to include anything that was an explicit character name or mention of a radio show or psychiatry.[90] Through opaque symbolism, they did make many references to what happened on the show. As explained by Miller, "Hey baby, I hear the blues a-callin'" refers to depressed callers on Frasier's radio show.[91] "Tossed salad and scrambled eggs" are mixed up, again, like his callers.[92] "And maybe I seem a bit confused / Yeah maybe, but I've got you pegged" represents the idea that Frasier can't quite get his life in order, but he is a good psychiatrist and can analyze others.[93] "But I don't know what to do with those tossed salad and scrambled eggs" is an acknowledgment that psychiatry is a tough business, and "They're callin' again" is a nod to Frasier's daily call-in show.[94]

The song was played over a silent scene to close out each episode. Those comedic scenes were generally not written into the script; they would brainstorm them with the writer, cast, and crew on the last day of filming. Joe Keegan says, "All those silent tags tended to be very last minute. More often than not, we would come up with them on the day of the shoot, just a few hours before, because there was no dialogue and they were only meant to be something visual to accompany the credits."[95] The only episodes without the silent codas are season finales, which would reveal what celebrities had called in to the radio show the previous year. Additionally, there are a few episodes that originally aired as special one-hour shows but were chopped into two parts for syndication, DVD sets, and streaming services. In these cases, the first half of hour-long episodes has credits added that play over stock images of Frasier's apartment.

Aside from the new cast, setting, and style of the show, it should be noted that the character of Frasier Crane changed in several ways between *Cheers* and *Frasier*. Most obviously, the Frasier on *Cheers* who frequents a sports-themed bar was often shown enjoying beer and even sometimes becoming engrossed in sporting events. This wasn't a defining aspect of his character on the show, and in fact he sometimes pushed for the clientele of the bar to change the channel away from sports, but it stands in stark contrast to the Frasier Crane on *Frasier*.

There are also some rather significant differences in the biographies of the two characters, some which are explained away in *Frasier*. For example, on *Cheers* Frasier discussed his dead father (a research scientist, according to Frasier), but when Sam visits Seattle and meets Martin he remembers that Frasier said he was dead. In response, Frasier offhandedly defends himself: "We were fighting."[96] On *Cheers* it was also established that Frasier was an only child, which quite obviously was not the case on his spin-off series.

And, in one of the stranger instances, in Frasier's fifth appearance on *Cheers*, we meet Hester, Frasier's mother. Sometime between this meeting and the pilot of *Frasier* Hester dies, though it is not shown on *Cheers*. During the eighth season of *Cheers* as Frasier is trying to help Carla through the grief process after she loses her husband, Frasier does have a breakdown that acknowledges Hester's passing: "Studies of human behavior tell us that we need to grieve. And until we do allow ourselves that emotional release we can never get back on the course of life. You see, some people hold in their grief for literally years and years, and all they accomplish is to prolong the grief and the agony, casting a pall over their remaining days on this Earth. [Begins sobbing] Oh . . . Oh Mommy! Mommy! Why you?"[97]

The Hester we meet on *Cheers* is a far cry from the one described on *Frasier*. On *Frasier* we are told that she was a psychiatrist and all the Crane men idolize her, though she was not a perfect woman (in "Beloved Infidel" Frasier learns she had an affair but Martin forgave her). The Hester on *Cheers* threatens the life of Frasier's girlfriend, Diane, and even admits to going gun shopping in order to shoot her. She is portrayed as riding the borderline between sanity and lunacy—Diane describes her as an "evil, psychotic, dark-hearted murderess"[98]—nothing like the loving descriptions provided on *Frasier*.

SIMILARITIES

There are, naturally, still many similarities between the two shows. They were shot on the same soundstage, Stage 25 at Paramount Studios.[99] Both are classic multicamera sitcoms, rather than the single-camera style that came into more prominence in the twenty-first century with shows like *Scrubs*, *Arrested Development*, *The Office*, or *Modern Family*. Also, and this can be a distraction for some modern audiences, both shows have an at-times intrusive laugh track. Not canned laughter, but the actual laughter from the studio audience accompanies each episode. This can be invaluable for comedic timing: you never miss the next joke because you're laughing at the last one when the actors can time delivery with a live audience giving feedback about how well a joke landed. But, if a viewer is more accustomed to the laugh-track-free style that has become more common, revisiting a classic-style sitcom can be frustrating.

Besides these production styles, both series had iconic, never seen characters—Norm's wife Vera and Niles's wife Maris. Furthermore, Roz Doyle and Sam Malone are cut from the same cloth when it comes to their proclivity for finding temporary romantic partners, a point made clear when they meet each other in "The Show Where Sam Shows Up" and Frasier dryly notes, "Oh, boy. Just look at the two of you face to face. I imagine wild animals all over the Northwest are lifting their heads, alerted to the scent."[100] We also learn that Roz has a little black book of her previous dates, much like Sam's famed little black book.

And, like *Cheers* with its Sam-and-Diane storyline, *Frasier* had several long-running plots. Most famously, the Niles-Daphne relationship that began with a smitten Niles in the third episode and ended when their son was born in the finale. David Lee says, "We consciously fought against what was happening at the time. The world of the sound bite was being translated to TV scenes, and they were becoming shorter and shorter."[101] Trusting the audience with longer scenes also led to longer plots.

This long-form storytelling is meant to reward committed viewers who stick with a show consistently and even engage in repeat viewings. Of course, in any long-running show, hiccups in the storytelling may arise that actually make the most committed viewers cry foul. For example, in "The Perfect Guy," KACL's restaurant critic Gil Chesterton reveals that he is not gay and has been happily married for years. Frasier responds in mock surprise, "That's the first time I've ever seen anyone *in* himself."[102] Except, of course, it's not. On *Cheers*, Frasier and Lilith encourage Norm to pretend to be gay in order to be in higher demand as an interior decorator. In the end, when the charade has gone too far, Norm "ins" himself as a straight man (and faces prejudice in the workplace because of his heterosexuality). Even more personally, in Season 2 Frasier had to correct his own boss who thought he was on a date with Frasier after assuming Frasier was gay (Frasier thought his boss was on a date with Daphne). Just three episodes earlier Frasier saw his own brother "in" himself, when Niles had to explain to a homosexual ski instructor who assumed Niles was gay and Daphne was a lesbian, "I am not gay, Guy!"[103]

There are other instances where repeat viewings of the twenty years of continuity built up between *Frasier* and *Cheers* reveals contradictions. In one episode, Niles and Frasier debate how many sexual partners it is reasonable for a man to claim to have had in his life, settling on seven. This completely ignores Frasier's long-running friendship with Sam Malone, a character whose defining characteristic was a never-ending parade of romantic escapades. Of course, their discussion also ignores their mutual friendship with Roz, whose romantic life is essentially the same as Sam Malone's.

COMING INTO ITS OWN

There is no debate that *Frasier* stepped out of the shadows of *Cheers* and became its own show. With a unique tone and style the creators of *Frasier* can rest assured that it is a classic in its own right, which is no small feat when the original show was so beloved. It does stand as evidence that quality writing, directing, and acting can exceed any amount of unrealistic expectations a show may be burdened with before it even begins airing. Having a quality team in front of and behind the camera can ensure that a show carries on despite tragedy. And *Frasier* had its fair share of issues to work through, from Kelsey Grammer's well-documented substance abuse issues to tensions between the creators and the network over time slot changes. But no single moment was as impactful for the cast and crew as the tragedy of September 11, 2001.

September 11 obviously shook the entire nation, but it had a heartbreakingly personal element for the cast, crew, and creators of *Frasier*. David Angell, the A of KACL, and his wife, Lynn, were returning home from attending a family wedding that day.[104] Both were aboard American Airlines Flight 11, the first airplane to hit the World Trade Center.

The premiere of Season 9 was the first episode of *Frasier* to air after 9/11. Airing on September 25, 2001, the hour-long episode, which had clearly been produced prior to 9/11, had only one acknowledgment of 9/11. A title card at the end of the episode read "In loving memory of our friends Lynn and David Angell." In a more subtle homage, while Niles Crane was played by a David, it has been surmised that when Niles and Daphne have a son named David in the series finale, it is a poignant, final way of remembering the late David Angell.

3

THREE CRANES AND A DOG

We're an odd little family, aren't we?

Characters drive story. Characters drive comedy. Characters bring the audience back. As television writer David Isaacs has said, "I learned early in my writing career that character rules. It's the two-word mantra I repeat to myself, and to anyone who asks me how to become a Successful TV Writer."[1] More than a setting or a great hook or a show's mythology, it is good characters that will ensure quality for a series. The creators of *Frasier* all came out of the *Cheers* writers' room and they learned an important lesson from Les Charles: if you have great characters "you can do very good shows without a lot of plot."[2]

One of the goals on *Frasier* was to ensure that story came from the characters, not the characters reacting to a plotline.[3] As Peter Casey recalls, "We kept the story very simple, which gave us the room to do a lot of character humor. We painted very vivid characters, we had a lot of laughs, but also dramatic moments."[4] Undeniably there are episodes that are memorable because of a plot point. The one where they buy a restaurant. The one where they pretend to be Jewish on Christmas Eve. The one with the dead seal. But there are also episodes that are almost devoid of plot. The one where Frasier and Niles get coffee. The one where they talk about throwing a party. The one where Niles asks Frasier a question.

It may seem a little odd to say that these characters are experiencing the mundane when Frasier and Niles are two of the more elitist characters to appear on television. But their ostentatiousness is balanced by the much more down-to-earth trio of Roz, Daphne, and Martin. A key to having such pompous characters be popular with the widest audience possible is to frequently make the airs they put on the butt of jokes. The punch lines often are delivered from the middle class to the upper class, not in an arrogant, top-down direction. As Ken Tucker notes, "One of the small miracles of *Frasier* is the way the show's high-strung, highbrow characters have managed to become mass-appeal favorites. Granted, that's because the jokes are on them; Frasier and Niles are forever having the air let out of their cappuccino-stoked pretensions."[5] Looking at each character and how they developed will reveal the lengths to which the creators went to ensure that these characters were vibrant enough to find an audience, even if two of the main characters were elitists.

FRASIER CRANE, THE INSECURE NARCISSIST

There are any number of descriptors for Frasier Crane that are given directly by other characters, including "lovably pompous," "pushy," "tough," "fussbudget," "pretentious," "resilient," "snippy," "sarcastic,"

Three Cranes: Martin, Niles, and Frasier. *NBC/Photofest;* © *NBC*

"huffy," "vain," "resourceful," "tenacious," "conceited," and "optimistic."

Creators, critics, and writers who addressed the show seemed to enjoy finding new ways to describe the character. "Elegantly pompous."[6] "Intellectual blowhard."[7] "A pompous, deluded buffoon."[8] "Snobbish, arrogant, conceited, and pretentious."[9] "A pomposity, but a vulnerability, a lovableness, but at the core of the character is a person who's trying to do the right thing."[10] Grammer himself describes Frasier as "flawed and silly and pompous and full of himself" but "genuinely kind" and "totally vulnerable."[11]

The list could go on, but perhaps the best list of descriptors comes from writer David Isaacs, who, when recommending that screenwriting students try to define a character, asks for ten words to describe that character. Isaacs notes that because characters should be complex, some of their words should appear contradictory to one another. His example was Frasier Crane and his ten words were: caring, proud, witty, intuitive, honorable, hedonistic, competitive, analytical, sophisticated, and dedicated.[12] This exercise proved so useful and promising for understanding characters that we decided to complete lists for all the main characters. Our list for Frasier Crane varies somewhat from Isaacs's but also provides an accurate picture of Frasier Crane: pompous, proud, cultured, intellectual, assertive, competitive, earnest, ethical, witty, romantic. The wonderful thing about these lists is that you can start to see contradictions that are real, that are human, that help to make the character more than just a caricature of unvarying, exaggerated attributes.

Sometimes the best conflict for a story can come from within the same character. David Isaacs cites the first-season episode "Call Me Irresponsible" as an example where a character's own traits are at odds. Frasier is an indulgent man who enjoys the pleasures of life, but he's also a deeply ethical man with boundaries about what is right and wrong. Thus, when his romantic desires for a woman run afoul of his professional ethics, he is unable to pursue the relationship that both he and she want.

Grammer had to make an adjustment from playing the *Cheers* Frasier to playing the *Frasier* Frasier. James Burrows says, "When I was directing the pilot, I kept saying he's got to be more emotional, he's got to be more like Sam, and we were all in agreement." Grammer had to become a "new Frasier" who was still recognizable as the character fans enjoyed on *Cheers*. This Frasier Crane is central to the action of his own show instead of the broader side character on *Cheers* who is less vain (though far, far from humble) and more grounded. This was necessary, Grammer believes, because "I am the glue of the show. The action takes place around me. . . . I give it a center, some reason to be."[13] One thing that does remain true is Grammer's interpretation of Frasier Crane as an intellectual who is so flawed that he is also an everyman.[14] As much as he is defined by his elitist airs and attitudes, fans can also identify him as a man desperate for a proper love life. A committed romance is constantly pursued, but rarely reached for Frasier Crane.

FRASIER AND RELATIONSHIPS

Frasier begins with Frasier Crane leaving his wife and moving to a new city, and closes with him moving to a new city, but also chasing after a woman. He never gives up that hope for love. Frasier is constantly dating and searching for love but never really has a woman he dates for multiple episodes throughout the series. He does face a few times where he is so discouraged he wants to give up, but mostly he just keeps on trying. He falls fast and quickly, but he also finds fault just as quickly. It is possible that he is afraid of commitment.

Writer Joe Keenan states Frasier is "always looking for the perfect woman, and his definition of the perfect woman was often a superficial one, a trophy catch."[15] Grammer notes there were two defining aspects to his character, the first being he was a "responsible psychiatrist and would be loath to do anything unethical."[16] The second perhaps explains all of Frasier's romantic actions, "that he loved Diane [from *Cheers*] fully, which has defined the way that he loves in every relationship he's had."[17] While the show beautifully demonstrates the mending of Frasier's filial relationships, his romantic relationships result in more than a decade of ups and downs. Mostly downs.

In the Season 9 episode "Don Juan in Hell Part 2," Frasier has just broken up with a woman his family really liked in order to pursue another woman who is in many ways not a good match for him. However, he gives up pursuing her when her ex-husband returns to win her back and Frasier counsels her "to give him a second chance." Frasier comments, "It was the noble thing to do . . . although my honor won't keep me warm at night." Frasier takes off on a solo road trip, claiming, "I just need a little time alone." However, on this trip, explained as physical manifestations of his unconscious, we see Frasier with the women with whom he had his most serious relationships: Nanette, his first wife from college; Diane, his fiancée from *Cheers*; and Lilith, his second wife. Or, as the episode puts it, "the slacker, the barmaid, and the icicle." Together the four discuss and examine why Frasier cannot seem to make a relationship work. Lilith points out, "It's that quest for perfection which ultimately defeats you, because the perfect woman does not exist." And with this comment, Frasier's mother appears. Frasier's mother best explains his relationship difficulties, saying, "You've spent your whole life trying to replace me, but it's completely understandable. I was your first love."[18] To Frasier, his mother was perfect and no one ever compares. He is, after all, a Freudian.

Grammer, after playing Frasier Crane for seventeen years but before he knew when *Frasier* would wrap up, shared these thoughts: "In terms of *Frasier*, I have found a character and created a character that is memorable, even in terms of our culture. And I realize that's quite an accomplishment. But the day will come when he has to go and I will bid him a fond farewell and think of him as kind of living on somewhere in some world where he's still doing his best to be as good a man as he can be."[19] In the end, Frasier Crane's journey on the show is not so much achieving a new stage of life, which we see all the other characters manage. Niles and Daphne are married with a new child, Martin and Ronee are married, and Roz is the new station manager. Yes, in the finale Frasier is taking a new job in San Francisco and pursuing a love interest in Chicago, but that does not carry the same weight of the others' accomplishments. Frasier's accomplishment is mending his relationships with his father and his brother and finding an honest, nonromantic love with Roz and Daphne that had been missing desperately from his life. That is his capstone, not starting a new chapter in a new city but closing his perfected life in Seattle.

NILES CRANE, THE LONELY ELITIST

Frasier's fussy, pompous, kind, fastidious little brother, played perfectly by David Hyde Pierce, becomes a crucial character on the show. Perhaps even *the* crucial character. If you watch the first season note that Niles is much more of a peripheral character. He's still funny, but he doesn't drive the show the way his relationships with Maris and Daphne do in subsequent seasons. The first season is much more about Frasier and Martin, and from the second season on Niles's failing relationship with Maris and adoration of Daphne become key to the show's success.

Casting two talented actors who are so similar in physical appearance that they can portray actual brothers was too perfect to pass up. But, far more than a physical appearance, Pierce added to the show his incredible acting ability. Pierce, in an ideal coincidence, studied at Yale University just as Niles did. However, rather than studying psychology, he studied classical piano before switching his focus to acting[20]—and fans of comedy everywhere should be grateful he made that change.

But apart from Yale and an affinity for classical music there are few similarities between Pierce and Niles. Pierce has said he would not like Niles in real life: "I think I couldn't stand him. I remember people like him at school and never really hung out with them—people for whom their world is the only world."[21] During the early seasons of the show, Pierce claimed, "We don't dress alike, we have very different tastes. I'm not a suit person. I have to borrow from wardrobe when I have to go out and attend something. I'm single and not obsessed over any maids."[22] Even John Mahoney noted the chasm separating Pierce and Niles: "Some of us are more like our characters than others, and David couldn't be more different from Niles. When I watch David being so fussbudgety and playing that character and I know what he's really like, I find it very very funny."[23]

As different as he is from the actor who portrays him, Niles was written with the purpose of being Frasier—but just a little bit more, "a Crane who hasn't been exposed to life, like Frasier was in Boston."[24] Pierce agreed to play Frasier's prissy brother, Niles, before even seeing a pilot script, resulting in serious concern when he first received the script:

> "I got it the night before the read, and I thought, 'This is terrible,'" he recalls. "As I read it I thought, 'They've written two of the same characters!' Then when we sat down and read it [at the table read], it all became clear. They came up with an even weirder version of Frasier to make him seem more . . . normal."[25]

This character quality not only was entertaining, but allowed for the growth of Frasier's character. Grammer explains, "The beauty of finding

David, is that we got to keep Frasier. Because David is the old Frasier. My Frasier is somebody else now."[26] Appropriately, Pierce prepared for his new role by watching Grammer from early episodes of *Cheers* to know how to play Niles.[27]

To say Pierce steals scenes is an understatement. His acting is a work of both comedic and dramatic art depending on what is called for in a scene. No matter the scene, no matter if he is the center of focus or off to the side, watch what he's doing and it is usually something perfect for the scene. His portrayal of Niles has been described as a "piece of precision engineering—physical and verbal comedy played to equal perfection and hitting their marks every time."[28] Pierce comments on the joy he finds in playing Niles: "There's just something about that character that the writers tapped into. A combination of whimsy, intelligence . . . I'm not an actor who loves to do a lot, but my favorite thing is to get a perfect line. It's magical, and they do that again and again for Niles."[29] Pierce tells an early lesson in comedic performance that helped him know how to deliver those perfect lines: "I can vividly recall telling a joke in, like, second grade and realizing it was funnier if I didn't laugh. I've been deadpan ever since."[30] Pierce's ability stood out even to guest actors. James Patrick Stuart, who played Guy in the iconic "Ski Lodge"[31] episode, praised Pierce's performance: "It was like going to the symphony and watching the lead violinist. His timing was impeccable. He rode that audience like a pro. He knew the exact moment they were ready for that reaction."[32]

In attempting to boil down the essence of Niles Crane, we settled on these ten adjectives: compulsive, meticulous, pretentious, analytical, ostentatious, submissive, loyal, clever, lonely, and endearing. "Loyal" may seem an odd choice for a character who famously spends years pining for Daphne while married to Maris before eventually getting a divorce and marrying Daphne. But Niles never instigates the separations with Maris and he fights against the divorce until Maris acts in unbearable ways. He would have remained lonely in a broken marriage out of loyalty if Maris had not forced him out of it.

Due to more than a decade of growth, the Niles we see at the finale is definitively not the same Niles we first met in Season 1. At the beginning of the show Niles is a very snobbish, unexposed, and submissive-to-the-point-of-being-weak character. Through the years we see him begin to become a stronger (as he stands up to Maris and later Mel) and more confident character (particularly when he begins dating Daphne).

When viewers first meet Niles he is decidedly lonely. He's in a bad marriage with a distant wife and his filial relationships could charitably be described as weak. Through the eleven years viewers spend with him he strengthens his relationship with his father, exposing him further to a more blue-collar world. He maintains and grows his friendship with Frasier. And, perhaps most unexpectedly considering the antagonism the two first display, he even allows Roz to become a close friend. His character easily faces the most ups and downs, heartbreaks and joys of all the characters. Through it all he maintains all his compulsive little quirks, as Frasier once comments, "I'd forgotten what a weird little person you are."[33]

Niles Crane is a slight fellow with a "strong chin and swimmer's build" and "abnormally well-developed calf-muscles" and is "slim-hipped." He has self-proclaimed "delicate features" and is "fine-boned" with "congenitally short hamstrings" and "problem follicles." He has panic attacks and narcolepsy when extremely stressed and is known to hide underneath a piano for comfort. In a sign of either his frail back or the girth of Maris's luggage (or both), Niles has been known to throw his back out when he carries Maris's makeup case. Of course, since Niles also threw out his back while adjusting the seat in his Mercedes, he undoubtedly has a problematic back. He has "shy kidneys" that are "unusually small" yet has "no cough reflex, and excellent bladder control." He gets nosebleeds when he violates his ethics, such as when he lies, and faints at the sight of his own blood (despite having attended medical school). He gets seasick easily and was sensitive as a child and an easy target for bullies. He suffered from bed-wetting until he was twelve or thirteen years old and was given strict doctor's order to stay out of sunlight as a child. In his youth he was a runner-up National Spelling Bee champion.

As a compulsive habit, Niles wipes down his chairs with a handkerchief before sitting. Niles has no physical coordination whatsoever, a trait the writers happily paired with Pierce's gift for physical comedy. Christopher Lloyd admits, "No one knew what a great physical comedian Pierce was."[34] However, luckily they found about it "thanks to executive producer Casey's then 7-year-old son, Brendan, who suggested during the first season that it would be funny to see Niles bang his head on something. They cooked up a scene in which pencil-limbed Niles struggled to hop up onto a kitchen counter, only to crown himself on the stove hood and ricochet off the refrigerator. Pierce, 36, performed the stunt so deftly that the writers have slipped him more slapstick."[35] Scenes of Niles attempting to catch a banana, or being delirious while on allergy medication as he ruins an entire table at a restaurant, or is given a five-minute scene with no dialogue were written in as if dedicated solely to Pierce's physical ability.

Despite the character's lack of coordination, Niles does play squash frequently with Frasier—leaving Martin to remark, "You've got to wonder what goes on, on that squash court"[36]—and takes a kickboxing class. Late in the series he also discovers he is a fair marksman. And on one occasion, he miraculously makes a half-court shot at a basketball game, earning him the nickname "Half-Court Crane." Although he states he does not lift, he at one point attempts to join a gym but isn't sure "whether aerobics or weight training is the quickest route to 'buff'!"

From his introduction in the pilot episode, Niles is almost never out of his suit. Only toward the later seasons, particularly once he and Daphne get together, do we ever see him in more casual clothes (and even then, they are not terribly casual) as he wears more sweaters and polos. In one episode we see Niles buy jeans (just buy, never wear, as jeans are a middle-class item of clothing); however, this is also a reaction to his troubled relationship as he is refusing to process the idea of Maris kicking him out of their house. Niles's high-end clothing is so synonymous with his character that showing him buy a pair of jeans is a sartorial representation of him slowly breaking down while dealing with the end of his relationship.

One inconsistency with the character is his cooking ability. At times Niles cannot cook (usually for a scene with Daphne helping him prepare a meal), but at others Niles is an excellent chef and can even "identify a sauce from a great distance." In terms of his palate Niles is a pretentious, picky eater with refined taste. When Niles questions Daphne if she thinks he is pretentious, she yells back at him, "You'd eat a worm if I gave it a French name!"[37] His pickiness is not completely unwarranted, as he is allergic to a number of things, such as (but not limited to): cumin, scallops, nutmeg, oat bran, wheat germ, carob, parchment, mites, rose hips, and Jerusalem artichokes, and he refuses to eat bacon "because of the nitrates." Whether his eating habits are out of pickiness or necessity, such fastidiousness gives us great monologues, such as this request for filet mignon, which encapsulates his character so well: "I'd like a, a petite filet mignon, very lean—not so lean that it lacks flavor, but not so fat that it leaves drippings on the plate. And I don't want it cooked—just lightly seared on either side, pink in the middle; not a true pink, but not a mauve either, something in between. Bearing in mind the slightest error either way, and it's ruined."[38]

His refined palate expands with his relationship to Daphne as she exposes him to new cuisine, such as fast food, resulting in him eating curly fries at the Tacoma Mall, and enjoying places like "Burger-Burger-Burger" with meals of "two chimichangas and a You Ain't Nothin' But a Corndog," leading Niles to exclaim, "All for less than four dollars. Where has this food been all my life?" To this Frasier replies, "On the end of a coroner's artery scraper! What the hell has happened to you? You've devoted your whole life to developing your standards, only to succumb to the fast, the cheap and the tasty."[39] Despite Niles's refined eating habits, he faces a heart issue in Season 10, resulting in immediate heart surgery, ultimately giving him a new outlook on life.

Niles constantly obsesses about his social standing and how he is seen. When his divorce from Maris takes a toll on him financially, he is forced to switch from his beloved Mercedes-Benz to an "old hatchback." Niles claims, "I was petrified someone I knew would see me driving this humiliating car! It looks like some buggy derailed from a carnival ride, except this has no safety features."[40] This is not the first time Niles has been forced to drive a hatchback. Back in Season 3, while having his car serviced, all that is left by the rental agency is what Niles refers to as a "hunchback." When he is corrected by Frasier that it is a hatchback, Niles snobbishly replies, "Well, there's a novel idea: name the car after its most hideous feature. I presume it was a toss-up between 'Hatchback' and 'What's that odor coming from the floor?'"[41]

This fear of becoming a social exile is a continuous theme throughout his separation from Maris. Niles is concerned he is being "relegated to B-list charity events. Grubby little theatre companies and last year's diseases." Frasier tries to comfort him by explaining that Maris is "better connected and has more money" than Niles. However, a notable trait of Niles's is his inability to accept negative truths: "I know what happened. My invitation just got lost in the mail. No—it's not so far-fetched. It could have been missorted . . . or a stamp could have fallen off . . . or it could have been stolen by my mail carrier. Ho-downs are catnip to postal workers!"[42] While attempting to throw a party on the same night as

Maris, he finally accepts what is happening when he breaks down, saying, "No one wants to come to my party!"[43]

Niles marries two dominant women, Maris and Mel (Dr. Melinda Karnofsky), and later marries a much different type of woman with Daphne. Niles is very submissive when it comes to all women and really just wants their acceptance and approval. Even when it comes to his sister-in-law, Lilith, whom he basically despises, he still seeks her approval and friendship. Years prior, Lilith had snickered during his wedding vows at what Maris had said, and Niles felt slighted. But as soon as she apologizes, everything is fine and he wants to be friends with her. "Oh, Lilith, thank you! Oh, this bad blood between us has gone on far too long! Next time you're in town, we'll have dinner, just you and me!"[44] Jim Mock, a professor of marriage, family, and human development, identifies an aspect of Niles's character that explains much of his relationship with Maris, but also this reaction to Lilith. Niles was bullied, a nerdy, smart kid, but "probably the kid that never got the girl. And so when he finally gets the girl, later on, it's too scary to do anything to upset the girl because then you could lose her. So you kind of become that wimpy kid again."[45]

However, there is a very strong transition there from how he is when he is with Maris and how he lets her treat him to his final remarks to her in Season 11. As he explains his opinions: "Not yet. I like to know what I want before Maris tells me."[46] His final conversation with Maris comes as she is in jail awaiting trial for the murder of her "Argentine polo player" boyfriend. She continually calls Niles for support and requests. Niles, given his nature, often complies, until he reaches his breaking point, informing her, "I am on your side, but there is a limit because I have a wonderful, pregnant wife, and as far as my attention is concerned, she comes first, always! I will help you through this, but now, you have to help me by saying goodbye."[47]

The character of Niles Crane was created seemingly just by chance. But what an unexpected gift to television he became. From his fantastic lines and deliveries to his physical performance, he is simply captivating throughout the entire show. But more than just entertainment, his character tugs at our heartstrings and pulls us along on his journey through life and romance. Truly, Niles Crane is the most endearing snob.

MARTIN CRANE, THE CRANKY AVERAGE JOE

Martin Crane is a grumpy man whose character softens immensely throughout the series. Played by John Mahoney, when viewers first meet him in the pilot episode he is arriving at Frasier's apartment to move in. All we know of Martin Crane at this moment is what his sons have said about him: he is not close to either of them; he does not get along with Niles's wife, Maris; and he can no longer live alone due to an injury. Martin hobbles into Frasier's apartment with his ever-present cane in hand, wearing a blue plaid shirt and simple gray jacket. Notably, in contrast to Niles's suit and Frasier's sweater vest with white button-up shirt, Martin is indeed wearing a blue-collar shirt, a visual symbol of their cultural divide.

Summing up Martin into ten words, we chose: principled, blunt, abrasive, hardworking, blue collar, sentimental, rigid, simple, proud, and competent. From the beginning his blunt and abrasive sides are obvious, but some qualities, like his sentimentality, are revealed in small doses throughout the series.

Martin is an army veteran who fought in the Korean War, a fact that is referenced and used as a setup for many jokes throughout the show's run. He then spent more than thirty years on the police force, becoming a homicide detective. Martin was shot while attempting to stop an armed robbery at a convenience store. The injury left a bullet in his hip, resulting in him being unable to return to work and forcing him to walk with a cane for the rest of his life. Also, his injury requires him to have a physical therapist, giving us Daphne.

Martin and Daphne have a bickering-old-married-couple rapport mixed with a father-daughter relationship. They squabble over his physical therapy yet bond while rolling eyes at Frasier's pomposity. They are two of a kind trapped in Frasier's elite world. In the series finale, Daphne has just had a baby and is upset at missing Martin's wedding, saying, "I feel like it's me own dad getting married."[48] In a curious coincidence resulting in something of an on-set paternal relationship, Mahoney is originally from Manchester, England (home to Daphne Moon), and at times would help Jane Leeves with her accent.

Across most of the episodes, Martin is a deeply moral man and it is often noted that he passed his code of ethics onto his children. But Martin's moral code does seem to flip-flop at times. He will refuse to help in certain situations, such as when Niles needs parking tickets removed for Maris: Martin tells him he won't help and says, "I think the law should be the same for everyone."[49] Conversely, he tries to trick Niles into writing a prescription for him rather than go to his doctor, which Niles says would violate his own ethics. Although he is a very ethical man, Martin at times adjusts his morals to benefit from a situation.

One other odd inconsistency in his character is Martin states he never had a brother, but a later-season episode centers on an estranged brother of Martin's, Walt, to whom he hasn't spoken in years. Of course, as this brother is never mentioned again (despite Martin getting married, a scenario likely to solicit an invitation to his brother who lives in the same city), he might as well not have a brother.

In terms of characteristics that never vary, Martin loves sports and can often be found sitting in his Barcalounger watching a game or heading off to Duke's bar to watch sports there. He is accepting of everyone and forms a strong relationship with Roz, connecting with her immediately, referring to her as "one of the guys." He is also particularly hardworking and hates that his hip injury forced him into retirement. In Season 9, Martin returns to work as a security guard for a building.

Easily, Martin is the smoothest of all the Crane men when it comes to women. Although hesitant to begin dating again after his hip injury, throughout the series he is seen casually dating multiple women, even attempting, but ultimately failing, to juggle two women at the same time. As Frasier and Niles both struggle with romance throughout the series, they often (reluctantly) receive dating advice from their father. Martin has two significant relationships in the series, Sherry and Ronee, both of whom he wanted to marry. After having multiple marriages herself, Sherry did not want to get married again, and their relationship ended as Martin realized that he did want to get married again. It isn't until many seasons later in Season 11 that Martin meets Ronee. After Frasier and Martin compete for Ronee's attention, it becomes known that Ronee has her eyes set on Martin. The two are engaged a few episodes later and married in the series finale. This was not the first time Frasier and Martin were interested in the same woman. In Season 3 both pursue a police officer, and yet again the woman chooses Martin over Frasier.

While Martin ends the series happily married to his new wife, Ronee, there is absolutely no doubt of how much love and affection Martin has for his first wife, Hester. Martin and his sons mention her in reverence and in the highest esteem. In Season 4, all three Crane men are arguing about the fact that none of them like the women in their lives. Martin is upset at Frasier and Niles for not being more welcoming to his girlfriend Sherry, while they point out how little Martin cared for their respective wives, Lilith and Maris. Frasier boldly exclaims to Martin, "Oh, why don't we just face facts? I mean, since when has any of us ever—from Sherry to Lilith to Maris to Diane—has ever been able to pick one woman that the other two could stand the sight of?" It is then that Martin drops the proverbial mic as he yells back, "I picked your mother,"[50] ending the argument and causing Frasier to sheepishly back off, admitting defeat.

Martin and Hester met over a crime scene, as Martin was a homicide detective and Hester a forensic psychiatrist. To commemorate their initial meeting, every year on their anniversary, Hester would make "gingerbread cookies with the legs kind of bent and the head kind of crooked." Learning that this style was an homage to a crime scene, a shocked Niles hilariously comments, "We thought they were dancing."[51] Although Hester refused Martin's initial proposal, the two were married after she became pregnant with Frasier. They were happily married for more than thirty years, although their marriage was not without its ups and downs. It is revealed in the Season 1 episode "Beloved Infidel" that Hester had an affair with a family friend during a particularly difficult time in their marriage. As Martin tells Frasier, "Don't hate your mother for this. I wasn't the easiest person to live with back then, and she had plenty of reason to do what she did. Luckily we were able to put it behind us."[52]

Martin is the opposite of Frasier and Niles—he is down to earth and unpretentious. Frasier and Niles often belittle Martin. They assume they have a higher intellect than him. Season 4 episode "The Two Mrs. Cranes" involves a hilarious role switch in which, to help Daphne let down a former lover, she pretends to be married to Niles, while Niles pretends Frasier's home is his own, Frasier is merely a guest staying there as he is separated from his wife, Maris, who is impersonated by Roz as she arrives at the apartment. Martin emerges from his room unaware of the situation and is quickly informed by Frasier what is happening: "I think for this evening it would be best if you just excused yourself. You see, it involves quick thinking and improvisational skills, and a knack for remembering details." Martin sarcastically quips, "Oh, I never used any of those skills as an undercover cop."[53]

Remarkably, just as Pierce is nothing like his character Niles, Mahoney is nothing like his own character. Rather, as it turns out, Mahoney is actually more like Frasier and Niles. Mahoney clarifies just how different he is from his character. "Oh, yeah, I'm a real culture vulture. I have a master's degree in English, I'm a great reader, I love classical music and the opera. That's another great thing about playing Martin. It's so much fun to go outside yourself."[54] Regardless of this difference, Martin is a complex and vital character, and one that could only be imagined being played by Mahoney.

Of course, Martin moving into Frasier's apartment is not disruption enough for this series. He had to bring his best friend, Eddie, to live with him, too. Eddie would provide the perfect cap to many scenes in *Frasier*.

EDDIE, THE SCENE-STEALING TERRIER

One of the most famous dogs on television, Eddie is the pooch that helped set the show apart from many other sitcoms at the time. The "character" of Eddie was written into the show because the creators were informed by rating research that a dog would bring in viewers.[55] Eddie was hilariously introduced into the series on the very first episode, as an unwelcome invitee into Frasier's home when Martin insists his dog stay with them. Martin emphatically claims, "But he's my best friend!" Frasier refuses by saying, "But he's weird! He gives me the creeps! All he does is stare at me."[56] At this point it is unknown to the audience exactly who this Eddie is. A title card with only the word "Eddie" appears and then the screen fades back in on a dark apartment, lit by the glow of the television screen. The camera is on Martin sitting in his chair eating a sandwich with sauce dripping onto a napkin tucked into his shirt. The camera slowly pans left to the couch where we see an uncomfortable-looking Frasier. The slow pan continues until we are shown an adorable Jack Russell terrier perched on the couch staring directly at Frasier.

In a series that had numerous running gags through its run, Eddie's penchant for staring at Frasier was one of the first to be introduced. As a few examples of how it continuously popped up, consider the following. In the second episode, Frasier complains, "Dad, I can't read my paper, Eddie's staring at me."[57] A couple of episodes later, Frasier waxes on even longer directly to Eddie, "What is so fascinating about me? What is

Moose as Eddie. © *NBC; Photographer: Alice S. Hall; NBC/Photofest*

it? Do you imagine I am a large piece of kibble? Am I some sort of canine enigma?"[58] In Season 3 Frasier wonders why Eddie still stares: "My darling, I would have thought that old fascination would wear off by now."[59] In the fourth season, Frasier attempts a staring contest with Eddie: "It's time he learned what it's like to be stared at all the time. Bring it on, Buster, you got nothing. You can't touch me, I'm—Gah! It's like his eyes turned into sorcerer's pinwheels and started spinning!"[60] And in a tenth-season episode Martin begins to wonder if Leland Barton, one of Hester's old research partners, may have actually been Frasier's father. Eddie sitting and staring nonstop at Leland is one of the clues that cause Martin to be suspicious.[61] Perhaps one of the most interesting parts of this long-running joke is that it was carried off by two different dogs.

A dog named Moose (1990–2006) played Eddie for Seasons 1–6 before he retired. For the remainder of the series Eddie was played by Moose's son, Enzo (1995–2010). So similar in their appearance, they had played the same dog before—both playing Skip in the 2000 film *My Dog Skip*, with Moose as the older Skip and Enzo playing the younger.[62] A female Jack Russell named Folie, though dubbed Mrs. Moose on set, also served as an occasional stand-in for Moose.[63] Although Enzo was bred into the showbiz world, Moose was not. Moose was born and bred in

Florida but was given up by his owner due to his unexpectedly rambunc-tious/rowdy nature. Moose was eventually given to the organization Birds and Animals Unlimited,[64] which provides animals for roles in films and television.[65] Moose was cast by creators Angell, Casey, and Lee for *Frasier* and was put to work on one task—to stare. Moose's trainer, Mathilde DeCagny, worked to perfect this skill, stating, "You have to get him so focused on you that they won't notice any other distraction."[66] The reward for doing the trick was a specialty liver treat, "Bil-Jac," that was imported to Los Angeles.[67] To get Moose to stare for the length of time he did was an amazing feat, considering the typical nature of Jack Russell terriers to be very hyper, nearly uncontrollable dogs. Due credit, then, really must be given to trainer DeCagny for her ability to know exactly how to train Moose and her work in the timing of his tricks for filming. Pierce praises DeCagny and her ability, stating, "The dog isn't great, it's the person making him do these things who's great. Moose is a wonderful dog, but it's Mathilde who makes him so great on the show."[68]

Even DeCagny acknowledges that she has to have a very large role in the dog's performance. "He's usually really good. But he's on his own out there. Everybody else is an actor, but Moose is a dog. I'm orchestrating the whole thing and I have to remind him what to do."[69] The writers even gave her a brief bit of on-air recognition in the Season 7 episode "Out with Dad": Frasier remarks to his date regarding an opera performance, "Of course the finest Gilda ever sung was by the great Mathilde DeCagny." It's a subtle shout-out as few would know the name of Eddie's trainer, but it is a shout-out nonetheless.

Despite the incredible but basic trick that always merits a laugh, eventually just staring wasn't enough. Series creator David Lee explains their need for more tricks, but also their hesitation to rely too much on Eddie: "People wanted to see him do more. We didn't want to just do a show about a cute dog, but we couldn't resist, and so we started giving him more and more to do."[70] Tricks were gradually added, such as running out and jumping on the side table wearing deer antlers to pose for a Christmas photo or modeling an endless array of outfits and costumes because, as Martin claims, "He looks good in hats. He's got a hat face!"[71] or, with a tilt of the head or a perfectly timed bark, adding just the right accent to David Hyde Pierce's incredible physical acting in "Three Valentines." It must have been a great gift for directors to cut a close-up of

Eddie giving a "trademark quizzical stare" to add one last laugh to a scene.[72]

Eddie was a fan favorite and reportedly received more fan mail than any human on the show.[73] He was so immediately popular that Moose appeared alone on the cover of *Entertainment Weekly* in December 1993.[74] Moose even has an "autobiography" book, titled *My Life as a Dog*, that was really written by Brian Hargrove, a television writer and playwright who also happens to be married to David Hyde Pierce.[75] Moose's popularity was acknowledged in a 1999 *Simpsons* episode. As Marge is taking a tour of Hollywood, she says, "According to my map, this house is owned by the dog from *Frasier*."[76]

Mahoney describes what kind of dog Moose was: "It's not like working with a dog. He's the most un-doglike dog that I've ever known, inasmuch as he's been trained all his life to only do things when he's ordered to do them, when he's rewarded, so he has no spontaneity, except around his trainer, whom he loves."[77] Mahoney also says, "It's like working with another actor as opposed to working with another dog, except he's shameless in the scenes he steals."[78]

Despite being a fan favorite, working with an animal would clearly have its ups and downs on set when filming. Jane Leeves, who had many of the scenes with Moose, explains some of the issues/frustrations that arise during filming: "He's a dog and sometimes doesn't want to do what he's told, and it can be frustrating. I get the brunt of it because I tend to be in most of the Eddie scenes and nobody else has the patience for working with him."[79] But, despite that frustration, she recognizes that "people love that damn dog. There's not an event that we go to where they don't bring him up. So what are you going to do?"[80] Mahoney also admits, "I do get angry sometimes. He's hard to work with when he doesn't get his trick right. I work and work all week long rehearsing and getting these lines down, you concentrate on your character, try to remember your lines, and Eddie screws up, and you get a half hour of waiting for Eddie to get it right."[81] Grammer also says that it would take twice as long to finish a show when Moose had a scene. "It's not a hardship, you know, it just takes longer. He doesn't always get it the first time and we have to stop and go back."[82]

It has been reported that Grammer did not like to be upstaged by a dog. But really, it seems more as though he didn't want the dog to be praised for being an actor and for his performance because he was just a dog. Grammer explains, "Acting to me is a craft, not a reflex. It takes years to master, and though it does have its rewards, the reward I seek is not a hot dog."[83] However, even when explaining that he doesn't mind Moose, Grammer does seem to present an undercurrent of objection: "Moose is just a dog. He's a funny dog. I've had no objection to him at all. When it works, I'm very pleased. . . . I'm really fond of animals as a rule. But it's been fun to fan the flames of the rumors about me being the W. C. Fields of my generation."[84] Regardless of his feelings, Grammer did thank Moose in his 1994 Emmy acceptance speech: "Most important, Moose, this is for you," said Grammer.[85]

4

DAPHNE AND ROZ

You're smart, and nice looking, and fun to be with.

DAPHNE MOON, THE LOVABLE ECCENTRIC

Daphne (played by Jane Leeves) is Frasier's live-in housekeeper and Martin's physical therapist who manages to very quickly integrate herself as a member of the family. Daphne is the most eccentric of the characters, and that is reflected in the ten words we chose to describe her: warm, empathetic, quirky, giving, hardworking, intuitive, charming, patient, stubborn, and flexible. She does manage to be both stubborn and flexible—she'd have to be growing up with eight brothers and living with the Crane men. If she wasn't both she'd either be completely run over and shouted down or she'd have had to move out.

Aside from being a talented physical therapist, she is skilled at darts and billiards, thanks to her brothers, and can shoplift a frozen turkey between her legs. For a time as a child she raised show rats. As Daphne explains, "I mean purebred rats, as in Siamese or Himalayan or Husky. My most prized one was an Andalusian Blue named Lady Prissy—and she wasn't sick a day in her life, so don't go blaming all rats because of a few bad apples!"[1] When Daphne was twelve she starred in a television show in England, as she explains, "It was quite popular in its day, maybe you've heard of it? 'Mind Your Knickers'? It was about a group of high-spirited, ethnically diverse twelve-year-olds in a girls' private boarding school."[2] Although she does cook frequently for the Cranes and often helps Frasier and Niles with their own cooking, Daphne is often described as a poor cook, particularly when she makes traditional English cuisine. Niles eventually tells her, "Well, you're not the best cook in the world. In fact, you're not very good at cooking. At all."[3]

Daphne's fashion style evolves throughout the show. In the beginning she appears in very odd outfits with a baggy style, portraying a "sexy housekeeper look: skintight leggings, leotard tops, baby-doll dresses and granny boots—all topped off with a perky ponytail."[4] When we first meet Daphne, she appears for a job interview at Frasier's apartment in a short floral dress, black tights, and a ruffled cardigan complete with a thick black choker and a large black scrunchie holding her hair back. She sits down on Frasier's couch and begins to search in her oversized bag for her resume. In doing so, she pulls out a short-handled broomstick, a glass goblet, a sponge, and a few other items while the camera shifts to Frasier's baffled expression, until she finally pulls out her folded-up resume. This display earns her the rarely used but perfectly appropriate nickname, "Mary Poppins." However, she slowly evolves into form-fitted attire. This evolution does coincide with the natural trends of clothing at the time, but we see her dress significantly differently from the start of the show to the end of the show, whereas Frasier and Martin stay essentially the same.

Daphne claims to be "a bit psychic." Although this is often the butt of jokes, she does have accurate knowledge of things she wouldn't know otherwise at times, and this ability is used as strong plot points in a few episodes. In Season 9, we learn the background behind why Daphne thinks she is psychic. Niles tells her he doesn't believe she actually is psychic because there is no actual scientific evidence. Daphne hires a scientist to test her abilities. When the researcher asks when she first suspected she had psychic abilities, she tells them: "Oh, years ago, when I was a little girl. Grammy Moon first saw the gift in me. See, I was a girl in a house full of boys, which I hated, until Grammy told me that only Moon women had second sight. She had it, her mother had it and so on. After that, I noticed I could sense things before they happened, sort of like a secret power. Anyway, it's just always been a part of who I am."[5] Niles realizes the importance of her believing in her abilities stems from her coming to accept herself as a young girl and does not ask for the results.

Although mentioned frequently in the first few seasons, her psychic abilities are downplayed considerably through the progression of the show. The most notable instance of her psychic visions comes in Season 6 when she questions whether to accept Donny's proposal of marriage. Martin sees Donny buying an engagement ring for Daphne. While debating with Frasier whether they should tell her, she overhears them and is ecstatic. However, after a psychic vision, Daphne believes she is meant to be with someone else. She confides in Niles about her vision of an unknown man, and he encourages her to turn down Donny's proposal when he asks. Of course, Niles does not really believe her vision but rather is using this as a means to break up Daphne and Donny so he might have a chance to be with her. When Frasier realizes what Niles has done, he convinces him to do the right thing, and Niles explains to Daphne that he thinks her "vision" is a manifestation of her fear of commitment and that she should say yes to Donny. Donny proposes and Daphne does say yes, all while Niles watches the moment looking heartbroken. However, the show toys with all our hearts and emotions as after the engagement Daphne tell Martin, "I just had that vision again. Only this time . . . oh, that's a bit scary. My mystery man standing with some sort of dragon."[6] The scene then fades out to Niles's apartment where he is opening a gift he had received from Roz—a small statue of a dragon.

Daphne comes from a large family of eight brothers: Simon, Stephen, Nigel, Michael, Billy, Peter, David, and Reginald. We meet Simon and come to know him well, and in the finale we also meet Michael and Stephen. Daphne does not get along with her mother, Gertrude, and for the first half of the series is often seen on the phone arguing with her or trying to get off the call, until she arrives in Seattle and lives with Daphne and Niles for much of the last few seasons. Daphne is much closer to her father, Harry, despite him being a neglectful drunk. Her father makes a short appearance on the show when Niles unsuccessfully attempts to get Daphne's parents to reconcile their marriage.

Throughout the series, Daphne often tells rambling stories about her family and long-winded tales describing her childhood. She delivers these fantastic monologues that are so ridiculous, it's amazing Leeves could ever deliver them without laughing. Despite this, Daphne is often in the shadow of Niles (Pierce is such a force), but she can hold her own against him. Leeves really deserves more credit than she has received as a comedic actress, particularly for handling those monologues so well.

However, despite being played by a British native, Daphne's accent was the subject of much debate. The character Daphne is from Manchester, England, while Leeves is from Essex. Leeves explains her own accent versus Daphne's: "I have a standard British accent and Daphne has a Mancunian accent, since she's from Manchester. It's like the difference between a traditional American accent and a southern accent. A Mancunian accent is more working class. I'm so used to slipping in and out of it, but sometimes my accent has gotten us into trouble on scripts because the words don't come out the way the writers envisioned. For instance, I was supposed to say a joke once that ended with the word duck, but with the accent, it didn't sound funny, so they changed it to elephant."[7] Leeves claims the specific accent she had on the show was the producer's idea and she worked with an accent coach to create an accent that "sounded like I'd grown up in Manchester but had lived in the States for a while."[8] Although *Frasier* is given a hard time for her accent being inaccurate, it was important that American viewers be able to understand her accent.[9]

Daphne is quite a character with all these quirks. Leeves enjoyed all the leeway the producers gave her in establishing the character's history. She states, "I think it helps the characters because they become more of a

Niles and Daphne. *NBC/Photofest; © NBC*

part of you because it's your own creation. . . . I told [the producers] Daphne would have eight brothers and that would make her comfortable living with all of these men and that she's a caregiver. She thrives on taking care of people, and [I told them about] her insecurity about herself and her feeling she's not good for much else. I think that stops the character from being the sweet, simple girl who does everything for everybody. I think it's the flaws in people that make them the most human and easy to identify with."[10] With all these various quirks, perhaps Frasier sums her up best when he says, "The woman is like an artichoke. You just peel away one astounding leaf after another."[11]

ROZ DOYLE, THE SASSY PRODUCER

The character of Roz was named after a real person named Roz Doyle who worked on *Wings* with the producers, Angell, Casey, and Lee. The real Doyle died of breast cancer in 1991 at age forty-nine. Casey explains the effect her death had on all of them: "We were crushed. It was absolutely gut-wrenching for all of us."[12] In her honor, they named a character on their next series after her, played by Peri Gilpin. However, the character had yet to be fully developed when they began the show. Gilpin described developing Roz as a character, stating: "It was wide open. She could be so many different things, and much to their credit, they were very honest about it from the beginning. They said they weren't sure who she was, and that they were going to play [with the role]. I loved that Roz was not a stock character, I didn't have to slip into some kind of slot and say, 'Oh, here's how I deliver my lines and here's what my function is.' They really took it slow and let somebody come out of the booth."[13]

Eventually they created a memorable character that steals more than a few scenes. To describe Roz Doyle's essence, we settled on the following ten words: strong willed, uninhibited, assertive, brash, snarky, accepting, dependable, competent, dismissive, loyal. As usual with these lists, there are attributes that seem contradictory, but that is true to human nature. An individual can simultaneously be loyal to one's friends and dismissive of others.

Roz is a booming presence that at times puts Frasier back in his place, particularly when it comes to his radio show. The radio station is her domain, and she is more the master of it than Frasier. She is vital to the success of his show, although he often does not even know how much she does. In a Season 5 episode, Roz, after finding out from Frasier that it's ratings week for his radio show, begins to panic. Frasier comments, "Oh Roz, you do this every year, you convince yourself we'll have a disastrous week with no good callers, but our listeners always come through in the end, don't they?"[14] As Frasier begins his opening monologue on the show, we are shown Roz scrambling with callers as she manipulates and goads them into giving her more interesting and complicated issues to put on air, "Hey, Career Change, I've got a bed-wetter holding. When you say 'trapped,' is it possible you feel you are a woman trapped inside a man's body?" and "Hey Bed-Wetter, I've got a transsexual in crisis, you gotta beat that. Have you ever wet a bed with anyone else in it? A hooker, a stripper, or maybe your best friend's wife?"[15] As she announces the doubtlessly ratings-inducing callers to Frasier, he gives a smug look without having the slightest notion that she created the scenario for him. However, Frasier does take time to acknowledge and thank Roz for what she does. In Season 6, after returning to his radio show he tells his listeners,

> I realized I have a lot to feel grateful for; grateful for my listeners who trusted me with their problems; and grateful for the person whom I most trust. It's not an exaggeration to say I put my career in this woman's hands every day. And she never lets me down. She shoulders many responsibilities here, and in her personal life, with a grace and skill I admire more than she'll ever know. I'm proud to call her my friend: my producer, Roz Doyle.[16]

It simultaneously makes this monologue more and less special that Frasier had to speak extemporaneously because he had planned to make a self-congratulatory speech. It would have been nice if he had planned to praise Roz, but making a speech on the fly also means there is less chance of artifice in his thoughts.

Roz has a great career, is great at her job, and is not ashamed of her sexuality. She unapologetically worries about aging and her appearance. Gilpin comments on who Roz is: "Roz is very good at what she does and very happy doing it. She's needed, she's appreciated, she has a great time at work, she's in just the place she wants to be, she's ambitious and wants to move up at the station, but it's so good where it is now that she's very happy."[17]

Roz and Niles. *NBC/Photofest;* © *NBC*

Roz is originally from Wisconsin, and her mother, who appears once on the show, is the state attorney general. She has one sibling, her sister Denise, who appears two times on the show (with disconcerting inconsistencies between the two appearances). She loves her family and loves to visit them, but gets frustrated at their expectations of her as she complains to Frasier, "Well, every year I go to my reunion. My relatives crowd around me and I answer the same questions. No, I'm not married. No, I don't have any kids. Yes, I still have that tattoo. No, you can't see it. It would just be so nice if I could at least say I have a great career."[18] Frasier counters by pointing out how she stands out among women with her career and all that she has done. "You know, Roz, ten years ago KACL didn't have any women producers? You're a pioneer. You've won awards. You help people."[19] In a popular culture world that well represents housewives and stay-at-home mothers, Roz stands out as a forceful, uninhibited career woman.

Roz quickly becomes known on the show for her dating and sexual pursuits. In Season 1 Frasier questions Roz, "Why is it that every time we try to have a serious discussion, we end up talking about your sex life?" She easily replies, "Because I have one."[20] Peri describes Roz's unrestrained nature: "She's also happy running around and meeting guys and going where the wind blows. I don't think she's ever had one judgment about a guy. There's no one who hasn't been good enough."[21] Roz truly feels no remorse in living an unattached, free life. When after Roz holds and nuzzles an adorable puppy, she hands him back to Frasier, he asks her how she can "just toss him aside after such a tender display of affection?" She remarks, "I can do it with men, too."[22]

Her very active sex life is used for many jokes, particularly by Niles. But she dishes it right back to Niles and teases him about his snobbery and pretentiousness. Truly, no one can bicker and insult like Roz and Niles. Gilpin describes their dynamic and relationship: "Niles is a much more exaggerated version of Frasier, who she can barely tolerate when he gets pompous and pedantic. Niles is that much of a hard-core snob, and that's offensive to her. But I think that she sees he has a vulnerable side, so the swipes are acceptable. He usually gets her too. Somebody has to jump in before it gets violent."[23] Roz and Niles's relationship evolves over the eleven years, from Niles forgetting they've even met "three or four times" in the first season to the final season when Niles has a breakdown in Café Nervosa and begins undressing and it is Roz who defends him. A waiter says he's going to call the cops, causing Roz to announce, "The hell you are! This man's tips alone have probably paid for all the pot you'll ever smoke. Just back off, cowboy! And that goes for the rest of you, too. . . . Okay, listen up! My friends and me are going to back out of here, nice and easy. As far as any of you are concerned, this never happened. And if any of you decide to be a hero and call the police . . . trust me, I will find you!"[24] This protective action is a far cry from Roz and Niles in their initial friendship, filled with jabs such as when Frasier, intending to discuss a closing restaurant, asks Niles, "Oh, Niles, guess what thriving Seattle night spot is closing its doors?" and Niles responds, "Roz, you're moving."[25]

Regrettably, Roz is a part of two unsuccessful storylines in the series, her pregnancy in Season 5, and her sleeping with Frasier in Season 9.

Halfway through the show Roz has a child on her own after getting pregnant during her brief relationship with a twenty-year-old college student whom she met when he was a waiter at Café Nervosa. (The fact that he was twenty was made clear as she explains, "Well, of course he is not a teenager anymore! He had a birthday three weeks ago!")[26] She gave birth later in the season to a girl, Alice May Doyle. Although Alice appears on occasion and is referenced frequently, she ultimately plays a very insignificant role on the show. Perhaps, this is because a child in the series was never the intention of the creators; as producer Christopher Lloyd explains, the idea came from the NBC network: "It's one of those things because they like doing event shows."[27] The episode when Roz finds out she's pregnant is brilliant, and the one when she meets the parents of the father of her unborn child is hilarious, but Alice becomes part of the pantheon of almost-never-seen children on network television.

The storyline of Frasier and Roz getting together evolved a little more naturally but still never worked or reached a rewarding finale. In nearly every episode Roz is mentioning a new date she has or lamenting that she does not have a date. She has one long-term relationship on the show, Roger, a garbageman. Their relationship serves as an exploration of the class divide between them, as Roz, although she adores him, is embarrassed by his job. But that relationship comes to a sudden close in Season 9 when the audience is informed that Roger ended the relationship because "there's no more fireworks." Frasier and Roz are very close, becoming extremely good friends and colleagues and often relying on one another for support. Following the breakup from Roger, Roz is upset and turns to Frasier for comfort, which eventually leads to them sleeping together. A Roz-Frasier pairing had been toyed with in seasons before[28] but never fulfilled. Until now. Terrified of this ruining their relationship, Frasier follows Roz to Wisconsin as she attends her family reunion. The two discuss everything and clear the air, and the moment is rarely brought up again until the finale as Roz says good-bye, humorously saying, "You've always been just like a brother to me. Which is weird, I know, because we slept together, but . . ."[29]

Of all the main characters Roz is easily the one who could have been left out. She's not family by birth or marriage, but she integrates herself so fully in each of the characters' lives, *Frasier* would never have been the same without her. She and Daphne become best friends, most likely because they are the only two constant women in the Crane men's lives.

Roz is invited to be the maid of honor in both of Daphne's weddings. Roz and Martin are also extremely close as they both seem to be cut from the same cloth. Roz is often invited to Martin's poker games, when his own sons are not. After meeting her, Martin comments to Frasier, "I really liked your friend Roz. . . . Nice gal. Why don't you ask her out? She's great-looking and she can really hold her liquor."[30] She could have easily just been Frasier's producer, and left at that dynamic, but thankfully Roz grew to become a close member of the Crane clan.

Part II

Under Analysis

The cast of *Frasier*. © *NBC; Photographer: Chris Haston; NBC/Photofest*

5

THE EVOLUTIONS ARE TELEVISED

Why is it so easy to love our families, yet so hard to like them?

The characters audiences met on September 16, 1993, in "The Good Son" are not the same characters to whom they said good-bye on May 13, 2004, in "Goodnight Seattle." Obviously their names are the same, and unlike many shows there are the same five actors who made up the core cast in the beginning, but each character evolved considerably from where they began. And, most significantly, the relationships also evolved naturally. When watching the eleven-year journey, the difference from Martin and Frasier's fight in the pilot episode to tears being shed that they won't be living in the same city anymore is earned, but when those two extremes are held up in contrast it is striking how differently the characters interact.

Peter Casey argues that one of the reasons the show was successful is exactly because it did allow characters to change. "I think the key to that kind of longevity is having characters that don't stay the same, that evolve over a period of time and change as we all do. With that change, hopefully new avenues of comedy open up." Another creator of the show, David Lee, says that the key to a high-quality television show is: "Interesting characters in compelling relationships. That's the bottom line of every successful show, much less a sitcom. Interesting characters in compelling relationships."

While all the characters have unique interactions, the two core relationships that drive *Frasier* are Martin-Frasier and Niles-Daphne. One of the major gulfs that initially separates those characters is undeniably class. Frasier and Niles attempt to ooze upper-class sophistication, while Martin and Daphne happily settle into middle-class comforts. Their different preferences in tastes, social activities, and attire are indicative of their contrary worldviews. The separate spheres in which they operate are, at the start of the series, too distinct for the characters to find common ground. This is much more evident with the Martin-Frasier dynamic in the early years, but once Niles and Daphne finally get together their class differences are a primary point of conflict in their early relationship.

In addition to the Frasier-Martin and Niles-Daphne dynamics, other character interactions are worth exploring. Frasier and Niles are cut from the same cloth but clash outrageously. Roz definitely operates in a separate world from the other four characters, particularly after Niles and Daphne get together, but she is also a key character in the show and shares individual moments with the rest of the cast.

FATHER AND SONS

The differences between Martin and his sons are instantly apparent when seen on the screen. The wardrobe department does an excellent job of infusing the characters' nature into their outward appearance. Niles is always in his suits, Frasier either his suit or sweater, while Martin has some variation of flannel shirts or T-shirts and plain slacks or sweatpants. Their tastes in food similarly symbolize their divide: beer and chips versus wine and foie gras. Of course, the differences go well beyond their tastes in fashion and food; as writer David Isaacs notes, their vocations also put them at odds: "It's easy to see that Martin is built to contrast with Frasier and Niles. The sons are both psychiatrists, trained to scrutinize every bit of human behavior. Martin is a cop, trained to survey a situation and act quickly and decisively."[1]

This dynamic is very clear from early in the show. As John J. O'Connor notes in his review when Frasier first started airing, "Beneath the silly haughtiness ("I need routine," Frasier insists, "It is the magic that is me") are two intelligent middle-aged men desperately trying to position themselves in relation to their own lives and that of their aging parent. They are rather uncommon characters in a terribly common predicament."[2]

Very early on it is made clear that Frasier does want a better relationship with his father and this is one of the reasons that he lets him move in. Just as clearly, he's not very patient about it. In only the second episode, after another argument, Frasier tells Martin that the situation of him living there might not be working out. Martin wisely informs Frasier, "Look, you want us to forge some great father-son relationship, to make some connection. Well, that kind of thing takes a couple of years, not a couple of days, doesn't it? You're the shrink."[3] This is one of the few acknowledgments from Martin that he expects his relationships with his sons to change. Frasier and Niles more often voice this goal or act in ways to try and improve things. For example, they both go ice fishing with Martin with the explicit goal of hearing him say "I love you."[4] And, after much complaining, he does, and it's a genuine breakthrough for their relationship.

While there are many more episodes that highlight the relationship of Martin and his sons, one of the greatest symbols of their differences, their initial frustrations with each other, and their final acceptance of each other is Martin's chair. Yes, the chair. Martin's old, decaying, dirty, held-together-by-duct-tape chair. The only piece of furniture that Martin brings with him when he moves into Frasier's apartment becomes a visual touchstone that defines both characters. The working-class recliner stands in stark contrast to the upper-class furnishings that surround it in Frasier's apartment. Across eleven seasons, the iconic chair in the midst of Frasier's decor becomes symbolic of the defining conflict between Frasier and Martin. Frasier's evolving relationship with a piece of furniture follows the progression of the broken father-son relationship that is present in the pilot episode but healed by the series finale.

Undeniably, Frasier and Martin are two poles in a class conflict that is explored—sometimes symbolically, oftentimes explicitly—across the series. Claude Lévi-Strauss argued that in myth or narratives you can find oppositions or binaries that represent the conflict in a society, and as narratives explore how to mediate and resolve these conflicts, cultural or social models are taught.[5] Applying this theory to television, Victoria O'Donnell identifies a few examples of how the upper-class/lower-class binary is presented in *Frasier*, including Frasier's love of opera and Martin's fondness for football games or Frasier's taste for wine contrasted with Martin's preference for beer.[6] Another symbol of this binary is Martin's Barcalounger, which is a decidedly working-class piece of furniture in both form and function, dropped into Frasier's apartment, which is decorated as "a high-end spectacle."[7]

Further demonstrating the conflict between Martin's and Frasier's decorating styles, in the pilot, Frasier's explanation to Martin of his eclectic style is met with an eye roll and an indifferent "It's your money."[8] Perhaps more than Frasier's impassioned defense of his mismatched furniture and objects, Martin's reference to cost explains Frasier's choices. Designer pieces are priced at a point that even the upper middle class would be strained to purchase them. Part of the appeal of the designer brand is not the functionality of the pieces, but the conspicuous consumption and class status implied by owning them. And, in instances such as when Martin's chair is the only comfortable seat Frasier can find in his apartment when his back is hurt, they are sometimes not as comfortable or functional as furniture targeting middle- or lower-class consumers. When Frasier argues for his "eclectic style" by saying if you've got really fine pieces of furniture, it doesn't matter if they match they will "go together," he's actually arguing that as long as you are rich and can afford to buy these pieces, everything will go together. Designer pieces will naturally make a consistent declaration of Frasier's class, even if the style doesn't make sense to Martin's blue-collar sensibilities. In the end Martin turns Frasier's logic back on him; when his son protests that Martin's chair doesn't match anything in the apartment, Martin offers a sarcastic "I know. It's eclectic."[9]

Frasier's distaste for the chair becomes such a known aspect of his character that it can serve as the unspoken setup for a punch line. In the Season 4 episode "Four for the Seesaw," Frasier and Niles meet two women who design kitchens. Beth and Laura had expected Frasier and Niles to be bored with their vocations, but Frasier and Niles insist they are keen to "debate the merits of downdraft cooktops and ceramic backsplashes." To keep their conversation going and try to ignite a romantic relationship, Frasier invites them up to his apartment to see his kitchen. When walking through the apartment Beth pauses and declares, "And there's the chair. Wow. He wasn't kidding."[10] Whatever derogatory description Frasier provided is left to the viewers' imagination, as it occurred sometime after we see Frasier and Niles meet the women at the bar and before they enter his apartment later that evening. Without Frasier's established contempt the dialogue doesn't elicit the laugh.

Despite his loathing for the recliner, Frasier knows the importance the chair holds for his father and therefore he not only endures its presence in his apartment, he actively ensures its continued existence on more than one occasion. These acts reveal the love for his father that runs deeper than their frequent disagreements or Frasier's predilection for elegant furnishings. In a Season 2 episode, the chair is accidentally left at the curb outside the apartment complex by a dim-witted handyman who was supposed to take it down to storage while Frasier attempted to purchase a newer recliner for his father. By the time they attempt to retrieve it, the chair is gone. Frasier goes on his radio show and asks his audience to be on the lookout for "a runny split-pea green and mud-brown striped recliner with the occasional spot of stuffing popping out from underneath a strip of duct tape."[11] Eventually, after significant effort and some personal shame, Frasier is able to track it down and bring it home.

And, in a Season 9 episode, the chair is actually destroyed. While Frasier's apartment is recarpeted, the chair, which has been moved to the balcony, catches on fire and falls, landing right in front of Martin and Daphne on the sidewalk below. Martin is furious, and Frasier is troubled and apologetic that this happened, knowing it is ruining any of the progress he has made in his relationship with his father in the previous eight years. However, later Frasier explains, "I contacted a master builder, showed him some photographs, and had him duplicate it. As for the material, I tracked down the original manufacturer, and once I got them to admit they made it, I had them reweave it!"[12] In the end, Frasier admits that, ironically, the re-creation of Martin's chair is now the most expensive piece of furniture in Frasier's apartment. Frasier has made an aesthetic and financial sacrifice to make his father happy. And though Frasier denies it in this episode, it will be revealed in the series finale that the chair has also increased in emotional value.

In Season 10, the first step of Frasier reclaiming the apartment as his own private space occurs when Daphne marries Niles and moves out of Frasier's apartment. In the series finale, Martin is remarried and is now moving out of Frasier's apartment, returning the bachelor pad to his son for the first time in eleven years. There are two subtle callbacks that bookend the series and Frasier's relationship with Martin's chair, one through a line of dialogue, the other through an unexpected and most likely unrecognized guest appearance. In the pilot, when a worker, played by Cleto Augusto, first brings the chair into Frasier's apartment, Frasier decries its invasion into his space. When Niles moves a chair to makes space for the Barcalounger, Frasier yells at his brother desperately, "Niles! Niles! Niles, be careful with that! It's a Wassily!" In the series finale, eleven years later, Cleto Augusto returns as the delivery man to remove the chair (wearing the same outfit as in the pilot), and Frasier's caution this time is a somber "Be careful with it" about Martin's chair, not about any of his designer furniture. It is only after the chair is gone and Frasier wistfully looks over his apartment that he makes the decision to move to a new city. For years Frasier had treated the chair as a representation of his home not being his own space, but when it is gone he knows it really is no longer the home he's known for a decade, and he is ready to move on. One of the defining binary conflicts of the series, Frasier's snobbishness versus Martin's blue-collar lifestyle, has been resolved.

Perhaps the most perfect evidence that Martin and Frasier have reached a different state in their relationship comes with contrasting dialogue from the pilot and finale. In "The Good Son," when Martin asks Frasier if the reason Frasier took him in was guilt, Frasier replies:

> Of course it is! But the point is, I did it! I took you in! And I've got news for you—I wanted to do it! Because you're my father. And how do you repay me? Ever since you've moved in here it's been a snide comment about this or a smart little put-down about that. Well, I've done my best to make a home here for you, and once, just once, would it have killed you to say "thank you"? One lousy "thank you"?[13]

The scene ends uncomfortably with Martin walking away and pointedly not saying anything to Frasier. In the series finale, Martin's last line of dialogue comes right after Frasier announces he is moving to another city. Martin tenderly puts his hand on his son's face and says, "Thank you, Frasier. For . . . well, you know."[14]

BROTHERS

In an unexpected twist, the writers developed the character of Frasier's brother Niles and chose to make him very similar to Frasier. David Hyde Pierce describes his first encounter with the character Niles:

I met with the creators of the show and Jeff [Greenburg] and they said "well we think we're going to have a brother. We know that Frasier is a Freudian, so Niles is a Jungian and we know that Frasier went to Harvard, so Niles went to Yale and that's kind of all we know." And I remember that was it and then I got the part and I remember when I got delivered the script the first time because I read it and I thought, "This is stupid," because they'd written two of the same character. Why would they do that? Which is why I don't write or produce television shows. It was a good idea. [15]

A show with a pretentious lead and an equally, if not more, pretentious brother to play off him created a new dynamic rarely, if ever, explored before. Ken Tucker of *Entertainment Weekly* claims that their relationship is the first of its kind on television and the unexpected strength of the show. He states, "In the only real innovation of the new television season, Niles is also a prim intellectual type. Two opera-loving, egg-head heroes in one show—unprecedented in TV history, I believe. Every scene between Frasier and Niles is just about priceless. These similarly dour, thin-haired brothers, united by blood and their common contempt for the mass culture in which they're forced to live, are at once the most hilarious and poignant siblings on television." [16] If the strength of the show is Frasier and Martin's relationship, then Frasier and Niles's relationship perhaps highlights its creativity. It is brilliant of the writers to go that direction when it would be expected to do just the opposite in writing a new character.

This unique relationship also helped the actors, as Pierce explains: "One of the strengths of *Frasier*, in the writing and the performance, was that the characters were three-dimensional so you could build on them. That certainly happened with the brothers. On the page, they were in conflict. We both instinctively as actors brought the other side of that as well. I think that's why the show had such legs, why it was such fun." [17] As series producer Maggie Blanc puts it, "This relationship of the brothers is so peculiar. Everyone relates to them, whether you're in that kind of hemisphere or not." [18] And it was something of an accident that their relationship ever became what it was. David Lee says, "The idea of *Frasier* was a man coming to terms with his father later in life. And that was the heart of the show. And it was originally the relationship we wanted to build the show around. But what happened was that the character of Niles started to emerge as also an interesting part of the mix and that the three of them were an interesting dynamic to explore together."[19]

The Crane brothers are fantastic, competitive best friends but rivals, who will do anything for one another. They need and rely on one another as they are two very good psychiatrist brothers who need help themselves. Through various flashbacks and stories told throughout the series, we know that Frasier and Niles were very close in their childhood. Multiple times, Martin mentions how it was just Frasier and Niles together growing up, without other friends. In the episode "The Friend," Frasier realizes he has not made any new friends since moving back to Seattle when he needs someone to attend an event with and Niles is unavailable. He then goes on to try and make a new friend throughout the episode. When asking if he has lost his "knack for making friends," Martin points out, "Well I hate to bring it up but you never were very good at it. It was always you and Niles ever since you were kids."[20]

It's obviously perfectly normal for two brothers to be very good friends and playmates, but their childhood adventures were not necessarily the stereotypical roughhousing of young men often seen in popular culture. Sure, they got in trouble with their parents, for example, when they burned down the garage, though as Niles notes it was not because of playing with matches or sneaking their dad's cigar: "Well, between Frasier and his Bunsen burner and me and my mosquito repellent in retrospect it was unavoidable."[21] They performed Shakespearean plays together, which did lead to them stealing a skull from the school lab for the Yorick scene. But that bit of boyhood thievery wouldn't catch up to them for several decades. They wrote a series of books together titled the Crane Boys Mysteries, in which they were "two plucky lads who used their keen psychological insights to solve crimes brought home by their detective father." They even attended prom together, though Frasier argues that their dates canceled and they went stag together, to which Niles replies: "In retrospect, yes, we should have canceled the horse-drawn carriage, but hindsight is 20/20."[22]

Despite their strong bond as children they grew apart as adults, particularly as Frasier was in Boston and spent most of his time at Cheers. From the first episode it becomes clear they do not speak very often, even though Frasier has been back in Seattle for months, as they are discussing issues regarding their father that have been going on for some time but are new to Frasier. In the Season 3 finale, "You Can Go Home Again," which takes place almost entirely as a flashback, we see a conversation when Frasier has just moved back to Seattle. Frasier sits in Café Nervosa when Niles walks in; Frasier sees him and asks, "Niles, aren't you going to join me?" Niles looks a little bothered and replies, "Oh, well, I would, but I have a routine. I come in every day, order coffee and spend some quality time . . . with myself, you understand." Frasier continues to push, saying, "Niles, I've seen you once in the last two years,"[23] revealing just how different their relationship was from the time Frasier spent in Boston from how we have come to know it. This is a strong contrast with their final exchange on the finale as Niles is saying good-bye to Frasier before he leaves for a new city: "I'll miss the coffees." To which Frasier perfectly replies with, "I love you."[24]

Their separation while Frasier was in Boston may have led to Niles becoming even more picky and pretentious and Frasier learning to be less so. When explaining the character, the producers told Pierce, "Niles is Frasier had he never gone to Boston and been exposed to Cheers."[25] When Frasier returns and their relationship grows, he easily falls right back into the pretentious snooty behavior with Niles. The two attend operas and plays together; they obsess over fine dining and preparing peculiar meals. They delight in their spa retreats and bathing products. And of course, with their love of sherry and wine tasting together, where else can you hear conversations such as Frasier asking Niles, "Oh, by the way Niles, if you were stranded on a desert island, what would you choose as your favorite meal, aria and wine?" Niles responds with, "The Coulibiliac of salmon at Guy Savoy, 'Vissi d'Arte' from *Tosca*, and the Coutre Roune Chateau Neuf du Pape '47." This causes Frasier to sneer, "You are so predictable."[26]

Unfortunately, the show does constantly jab at Frasier and Niles in regard to their close friendship and time spent together, especially from Roz. At one point it is mentioned by a dinner guest, "You get the one you get the other."[27] Even when Frasier's friend Woody from Cheers comes to visit, he feels sorry for Frasier as he says, "Well no offense, but look at your life . . . you hang out with your brother."[28] This idea of their need for separation is particularly emphasized when Frasier realizes he has not made any new friends since moving back to Seattle two years ago. Frasier decides he wants a new buddy to do things with as he feels he keeps "falling back on Niles."[29] The episode continues with him attempting to befriend someone whom he really has nothing in common with. In the end, Frasier returns to have coffee at Café Nervosa with Niles, and the pair discuss their current fashion dilemmas. Why is it constantly brought up as such a horrible thing that they are such close brothers and friends? After all, siblings are the ones whom we will know the longest in our lives. Why would their close friendship be anything but celebrated? Despite the constant cynicism toward the friend, the two brothers share a close friendship and are without a doubt each other's best friend.

While Frasier and Niles have a strong and unbreakable friendship, what is a sibling relationship without the rivalry? And, similarly, we know through stories told throughout the show that this rivalry also dates back to when they were kids. As Martin explains, "Boy, you and Niles— it's been the same since you were kids. If one of you has something, the other one always has to have it too. I had to buy two Balinese lutes, two découpage kits, two pairs of lederhosen. When you finally moved out of the house that was one embarrassing garage sale."[30] In classic Freudian fashion, the brothers blame their rivalry on their need for attention from their mother. When they discuss where their rivalry first began, the first thing they competed over, Niles answers, "It'd have to be Mom. We were always jockeying for her time and attention."[31]

While embarking on the ill-fated attempt to write a psychology book together in the episode "Author, Author," Frasier and Niles lock themselves in a hotel room in order to get the work done. Their plan does not go well and results in them bickering and fighting so much that we see Niles lying on the bed with Frasier on top of him holding his neck in a choke hold, as Niles yells, "My God, my God, I'm having a flashback: you're climbing in my crib and jumping on me!" And Frasier yelling back, "You stole my mommy!"[32] The sibling rivalry runs very deep. Both of them acknowledge they thought the other was their mother's favorite, until Frasier points out, "Well, isn't this ironic? Both of us thinks the other one is the favorite when in fact neither of us was."[33] But that realization does not stop them from competing with one another in all aspects of their life.

The two share in equal parts rivalry and love with one another—they are each supportive of the other, yet endlessly envious of each other's achievements, and attempt to one-up the other. Examples of such instances are consistent throughout the show. For example, when Niles is named president of their wine club, Frasier starts his own wine radio show. However, Niles specifically prevents members of the wine club from calling in.[34] As children they competed over their IQs and were told by their mother they were only two points apart. In reality, Niles scored a much higher result than Frasier and when this truth is made known, both of them study all night in hopes of appearing more intelligent than the other.[35] And when Niles gets his own culture column in a snooty magazine, Frasier tries to create a culture radio show (a plan that backfires, naturally).[36] Niles constantly does not get recognition as a psychiatrist like Frasier does when he wins SeaBee Awards for his radio show. This causes Niles to take jabs at Frasier's "pop psychiatry"[37] by saying, "This nomination is just one more signpost on the low road of celebrity which my brother has chosen for himself. . . . I'm still in the minority who believes that psychiatry is a noble profession that is tarnished by such things as popularity contests, not to mention a bouncy little radio program."[38] However much Niles tries to belittle Frasier's work, it is clear the insults come from a place of envy, as Niles is frequently trying to parade his recognition in psychology journals and his own SeaBee nomination as a guest psychologist on a radio show.[39]

Just as they bicker over who was their mother's favorite, the two constantly compete for Martin's approval and affection. This is best displayed in the episode "The Gift Horse," in which Frasier and Niles have agreed upon a spending limit for Martin's birthday present. Niles comments, "Oh, I'm so glad we agreed to rein ourselves in this year." And Frasier agrees, "Finally to do away with our annual contest to see who could give dad the most lavish gift." It quickly becomes apparent that Niles has gone over the spending limit with his gift of a membership to a beer club. This sneak attempt is matched by Frasier as Niles learns of his new gift—a pair of binoculars. However, Frasier is bested yet again as Daphne reveals Niles has purchased season football tickets as well.

Both agree to stop trying to get better gifts, but we quickly see an escalation in their competition to give their father the best present. Suddenly Martin announces, "You and Niles, you go overboard trying to find these great presents for me and I've got to be honest, it's always made me kind of uncomfortable. . . . So this year, I just wanted you to know . . . I'm over it! So, go crazy, you only turn sixty-five once!" With this, Frasier knows the one gift he can get Martin that will beat Niles, the one thing he's asked for—a big-screen TV. Assuming he has won the competition, Frasier gloats to Niles only to realize Niles has managed to beat him as he purchased Martin's horse from when he was on the police force and put him up at nearby stables for him to visit anytime. Martin is stunned and touched at the gift and tells them, "I love this horse, it's the greatest present I've ever gotten." In that moment, knowing the effect those words would have on Frasier, Niles tells Martin, "I think I may have misled you. The horse is from me *and* from Frasier."[40] Their rivalry can get extreme at times, but their familial ties will always unite them. As Pierce comments, "Frasier and Niles could go at each other hammer and tongs, and yet they still loved each other as brothers."[41]

When the brothers aren't competing against each other, they are collaborating on some over-the-top venture, which usually ends in a disaster. Easily some of the most hilarious and best-written episodes center around failed endeavors between Frasier and Niles. When the brothers try to write a book in Season 1, it is the first of many, many, failed ideas they have, including opening a new restaurant (Les Freres Heureux), going into private practice together, countless dinner parties (there are five different episodes featuring a joint dinner party as the main storyline), trying to raise money for their former school, attempting to run a caviar business, and producing a play with their idolized Shakespearean turned Sci-Fi TV actor, which ultimately ends in fire sprinklers and injury. Although it takes the brothers years to realize their plans always ultimately fail, Martin is always ready to point it out. When they plan to buy a restaurant, Martin says, "Don't tell me you two are seriously considering doing a dumb-ass, idiotic thing like buying this place,"[42] and he tells them later, "You two can't work together."[43]

Despite their competitiveness, their endless bickering at times, and their inability to execute realistic dreams, they always forgive each other in the end, and their relationship is always just fine. The two never have a serious falling-out or an episode of one not speaking to the other. It would have been easy to have gone that route for dramatic effect, but thankfully, the series never went in that direction. Although they do not have nearly the ups and downs of Martin and Frasier's relationship, their relationship also comes full circle. In the very first episode, as they are reconnecting, Niles tells Frasier, "Remember what Mom always said: 'A handshake is as good as a hug.'"[44] They hug as their final good-bye in the finale.

NILES AND DAPHNE

Interestingly, Frasier never has a long relationship story on a show bearing his name. He has relationships here and there over various episodes, and his past marriage to Lilith is often mentioned, but the relationship storylines belong to Niles. Throughout the series Niles has three considerable relationships—Maris, to whom he is married, separated from, gets back together with, and ultimately divorces. Then there is Mel, with whom he has a relationship and marries quite briefly before getting divorced. But through all this Niles was infatuated with Daphne, which is the love story that the audience roots for. A *New York Times* reviewer writes that they were "the only potentially appealing relationship in a show that is all about ghastly marriages, unfriendly divorces, bad one-night stands and other examples of love gone awry."[45] Daphne and Niles begin dating at the beginning of Season 8, get engaged and married in Seasons 9 and 10, respectively, and end the series having a baby boy in the finale.

Their story is a "delicately choreographed courtship."[46] It is the heart of the show; the anticipation of their evolving relationship is the driving long-term narrative. The will-they-won't-they dynamic is a classic trope of sitcoms—successful series from *Cheers* to *Friends* to *The Office* have used it to drive stories and, more importantly, keep invested viewers returning from week to week. Of course, the "will they" often occurred either during a ratings sweeps month or as a season-ending cliff-hanger, to respectively drive up ad rates or keep viewers coming back next season. Yes, Frasier and Martin's storyline is crucial and a main focus throughout the show, but the Niles-Daphne relationship is the most endearing element of the show.

However, writing in their storyline is a tricky thing to do considering that for a large portion of the show (Seasons 1 through 5) Niles is married to another woman, Maris. The writers are able to weave in this infatuation with Daphne without making him look like an adulterer or creepy. As the audience you are able to know and understand that Niles loves Maris and is very loyal to her, yet you know it is a terrible marriage and he is quite unhappy in it. He finds joy in being around Daphne yet still fights for his marriage. It's a difficult balance, but the writers navigate it very well, if sometimes allowing Niles an aside that is perhaps a touch too lecherous.

Jane Leeves and David Hyde Pierce. *NBC/Photofest;* © *NBC*

When the series begins, Niles is with Maris and for him his love for her is simple and safe as he describes their relationship: "It doesn't burn with the passion and intensity of a Tristan and Isolde. It's more comfortable, more familiar. Maris and I are old friends. We can spend an afternoon together—me at my jigsaw puzzle, she at her auto-harp—not a word spoken between us and be perfectly content." Moments later, he describes feelings for Daphne in a very different way, as he says, "I can't get her out of my mind. When I look at Daphne she stirs a passion in me I've never known before."[47] Daphne is the opposite of Maris in almost every way, in her appearance, her nature, and how she makes Niles feel. Maris is high society; Daphne is not. Maris comes from a wealthy family and has never had to work; Daphne often has to worry about money. Maris is cold and selfish; Daphne is warm and caring. Maris is consistently having work done to alter herself physically; Daphne rarely comments on her own appearance. Maris is at times helpless; Daphne is the one who gets things done. Pierce describes some of their differences: "Maris is tight, Daphne is loose. Maris is short, Daphne is tall. Maris is manipulative and difficult, Daphne is friendly and open."[48] Pierce continues on to describe why Niles would be infatuated immediately with Daphne: "I think she's just such an exotic flower to him, and she's so beautiful and it's so unusual for him to be treated by a woman with such friendliness that he's overwhelmed by that openness because Maris is so manipulative and difficult."[49] Jane Leeves explains Niles's obsession as being a result of the different lives they've lived, that Niles has never been around someone like her. Leeves says, "She is the complete opposite of anything he's ever known. She's grounded and down to earth, and that's just not the sort of person he's used to. She's not out for herself like everybody else, she's there to help others. And it turns him on to see her rooting around under the sink and fixing things."[50] Their differences in social class are perhaps what makes her so appealing to Niles.

However significant their relationship came to be for the show and the audience, it was not necessarily a part of the original pilot, as the moment Niles meets Daphne does not occur until Episode 3. Pierce explains, "When Jane and I worked on the first episode, we talked about how that might be fun, and then it appeared in the script. So someone's psychic."[51]

The series continues to explore the one-sided infatuation, as Niles adores Daphne from a distance, never able to get too close. Niles, unfortunately, introduces Daphne to many of her boyfriends. In Season 1, she dates Eric, a waiter at Café Nervosa, a place Daphne only started going because Frasier and Niles go there. In Season 3, she dates Joe, the construction guy, for many episodes. They were introduced because Niles dropped a chair in Frasier's apartment, scratching his wood floor, and they called Joe, whom Niles had recommended, to fix it. Despite Niles's efforts to foil their date, Niles eventually does encourage Daphne to go out with him. And in Season 6, while dealing with his ever-long divorce from Maris, Niles switches divorce lawyers to Donny, who then meets and spends time with Daphne because she has to testify that Niles has never been in love with her. Daphne and Donny then begin dating and become engaged toward the end of the season. Of the entire series, few scenes hurt as much as watching Niles being forced to watch Donny propose to Daphne as she cries with happiness.

Daphne is eventually told how Niles feels about her by Frasier in the middle of Season 7, while she is engaged to Donny. Frasier, who is on medication for his back, accidentally informs her, "Niles . . . he's crazy about you!"[52] This knowledge changes how she looks at him beginning in that same episode when she sees Niles for the first time and she tensely says his name as she welcomes him to Frasier's apartment. This is a clear signal to the audience that there is a new shift in the dynamic. In the episode "Big Crane on Campus," Daphne and Niles are cooking in the kitchen as Niles prepares a meal for his new girlfriend Mel and acting as if the preparation of a sauce is an important and difficult medical procedure. It is a hilarious scene in its own right but becomes extra meaningful as we catch the first glimpse of Daphne having feelings for Niles. Niles burns his hand, and she quickly comes to aid him and begins caressing his hand tenderly as she does so. Martin walks in, and she jumps as if she has been caught and runs off.

As the momentum builds on their relationship, Daphne seems unable to fully admit her feelings. In the Season 7 episode "The Dark Side of the Moon," her emotions come pouring out as frustration and anger. As Daphne is torn on whether she should tell Niles or not, shortly before her wedding, she tells Frasier the truth and he encourages her to tell Niles. Frasier always meddles in things, often to their destruction, but this time you desperately want him to meddle. As Daphne prepares to tell him, Niles returns home having spontaneously married Mel. Realizing she lost her chance, Daphne continues her plan to marry Donny. However, the night before the wedding Frasier tells Niles how Daphne feels and Niles confronts Daphne saying he would leave Mel for her. (Again, a scenario that should make him seem like a horrible person, but given his character through the entire series, it plays as endearing.) The two share a kiss and although Daphne tells him she loves him, she says she can't go through with it, claiming, "I can't! Donny is a dear and wonderful man, and I made a promise to him. And Mel. You made more than a promise to her. And we're supposed to forget that? And for what? We have no idea how we'd be together. For heaven's sake, we've never even been on a date." Hurt, Niles hides away from the wedding the next day in the family Winnebago; however, Daphne joins him in there as she leaves Donny at the altar for Niles. As they prepare to drive off, Niles tells her, "Fasten your seat belt, Daphne." Daphne responds, "Fasten yours, Niles."[53] This is the first time we hear Daphne call him Niles by her choice, and it is amazing what a name can do after years of hearing her say "Dr. Crane." Of course, Jane Leeves gives a perfect delivery, and David Hyde Pierce gives the perfect reaction to the moment. Through the next four seasons their relationship grows from dating to marriage, and the series ends with them having a baby, named David.

The reception of Daphne and Niles finally getting together was mixed. While the series built all the way to that moment for seven full seasons, there is, as with any couple finally getting together on a television show, the question of "what now?" As one reviewer from the *New York Times* writes, "Part of the problem, of course, is that happiness just isn't as amusing to watch as frustration, misunderstanding and self-pity. (I am surely not the only person to feel this way; the *Frasier* writers appear to be dying of boredom with their new subject matter.)"[54] Unfortunately the story may have been distracting and turned many fans away. Ken Tucker of *Entertainment Weekly* writes regarding Daphne and Niles being together, "This has even been a very good season of *Frasier*, as far as both the jokes and the acting are concerned. The patter is snappy, and it's truly a wonder that both Grammer and David Hyde Pierce as Niles manage to find endless permutations of witty fussiness. But I'd also be lying if I didn't admit that, had I not looked at a bunch of recent episodes to write this piece, I wouldn't have been aware of its continued quality, because that silly Niles-Daphne subplot has driven me away."[55]

What is unique to television is its ability over years to portray relationships between characters. Wendy Lesser argues, "What television thrives on, and what almost no other medium can use to quite the same degree, is the stretched-out unconsummated relationship."[56] This is not a requirement for television shows but a common practice on many. Of course if a show is built on the premise, the question of what happens next if two characters do get together has given rise to what is called the "Moonlighting Curse." The term comes from a CBS TV series, *Moonlighting*, which aired from 1985 to 1989 about a pair of private detectives (Bruce Willis and Cybill Shepherd) and was a combination of drama, comedy, and romance. The sexual tension between the two main characters, David and Maddie, was the driving force of the show until the end of the third season in the episode "I Am Curious . . . Maddie," when the two characters got together.[57] Ratings declined in the fourth season and took a nosedive in the fifth.[58] Many attribute the loss of interest to the fact that the two main characters did, however briefly, get together, thus causing loss of interest in their storyline. Although this correlation cannot be proven, the accepted truth of it generated the "Moonlighting Curse"— referring to two characters on a show in which the audience has investment in their relationship, but the show loses viewership as the characters get together. Television history is populated with couples and shows that have fallen under this curse—Nick and Jess (*New Girl*), Castle and Beck-ett (*Castle*), Brennan and Booth (*Bones*). And ones who have managed to survive it and continued to thrive as a show regardless—Ross and Rachel (*Friends*), Penny and Leonard (*Big Bang Theory*), Sam and Diane (*Cheers*). So where do Daphne and Niles fall among this curse?

For some it was the questions of "How long can we be expected to tolerate the relationship? And if it ends, what can possibly follow?"[59] While we cannot deny that the seasons following Daphne and Niles get-ting together took a drop in quality and entertainment (they are our low-est-rated seasons in the opinionated compendium of episodes in this book), we don't blame this shift on their relationship, but rather other factors in the writing.

The relationship once they are together is not perfect. *Frasier* explored the conflict that happens after having a seven-year infatuation with some-one and finally bringing the couple together. When the couple first gets together, Daphne struggles with Niles's affection. She loves how he treats her, yet is afraid she can't live up to his expectations and as a result, she overeats. Daphne goes away to a spa specializing in weight loss to be treated for her eating habit. While there she is treated by a therapist, Gloria, who helps her understand why she cannot control her eating. Daphne explains to Niles the reasoning: "You told me all these stories of how you pined for me for seven years. How I'd been your unattainable dream. How could anyone live up to that? Gloria thinks I was terrified of letting you down, of not being perfect, so I ate. And ate. And, apparently, ate."[60] Niles tell her that he never cared about the weight she gained, that he never noticed, but this is symptomatic of the problem. Niles, as a psychiatrist, is unable to analyze himself. It is impossible for him to see that he has built Daphne up too much, that he isn't seeing the real her. This idea is a crucial theme of the show—two very talented psychiatrists who cannot see the problems in themselves, despite their belief that they can.

Niles has to figure out how to not always see Daphne as perfect. Having been in love with the idea of a relationship with Daphne, he is struggling to adjust to the reality of a relationship with her. As Frasier puts it, "You were never in love *with* her, you were in love *at* her."[61] Funnily enough, the major breakthrough in their relationship comes from Niles finally criticizing something about Daphne, something viewers haven't seen before. Niles tells Daphne that he does not like her cooking.

Upset by what he said, Niles tries to comfort Daphne, saying, "Oh, I'm sorry, darling. I just want to show you I see you the way you really are."[62] And it is from this moment that Niles continues to love Daphne but begins to see her as a real person with flaws rather than just the fantasy.

The Daphne and Niles relationship is able to explore very relatable feelings and issues found in all relationships. Yet it also portrays a very beautiful presentation of love, as Frasier comments to Niles, "I hope one day to love a woman the way you love Daphne."[63]

6

SET DESIGN

So what do you think of the place? Is it everything you imagined it would be?

WHY SETS MATTER

When Kate, one of the coauthors of this book, moved to New York in her early twenties she quickly discovered just how much popular culture had lied to her. Having seen countless TV shows and films set in New York City displaying gorgeous apartment interiors, nothing was more disappointing and frustrating than learning that every apartment shown was a cruel, cruel lie about the size and quality one can actually afford. Sure, you can intellectually acknowledge that the apartments seen on TV shows and films are unrealistic for anyone outside of the upper class, but the presence of those settings is so pervasive in entertainment it is difficult to truly divorce your expectations from the constant display of luxurious New York living spaces. That is, of course, until, reality forces you to see what is actually affordable.

The truth is the sets of television shows, even more than film sets, become intimately familiar to viewers who watch them week after week, or, if bingeing through a streaming service, for hours on end. We let the sets into our lives just as we do the characters, usually without us being aware of it. Although viewers may not pay close attention to the spaces around the characters, everything appearing on-screen is important and considered. Every series' set is done in particular ways to help establish a connection with the audience and to reveal characteristics of the people who live there. Diana Friedman says, "The sets of situation comedies aren't just a collection of random props that surround the actors; they're statements of style. They're designed to convey a particular mood, to both reflect and enhance the personalities of the people who live in them—just like anyone's home."[1] The importance of the relationship between a set and characters is particularly clear with Frasier's apartment.

Amazingly, right now the set design on *Frasier* is more than twenty years old, and yet it is somehow still current. It still fits today's style and trends (well, perhaps the wood color is a little outdated . . .). In the time we've worked on this book, when *Frasier* comes up in our conversations with others, one of the most common reactions we have received is some acknowledgment of the "great apartment." The apartment was designed more than two decades ago, but is still admired and talked about because what the set designer, Roy Christopher, created amounts to a timeless perfection.

There are numerous articles online discussing Frasier's apartment, how well designed it is, and how enviable it is. It consistently is included in lists of "Best Apartments on TV." Naturally, some of these articles were written during the era the show was airing, from 1993 to 2004. However, many have been written in the ten-plus years since the show ended, continually praising the design of the apartment. One can quickly find an article from 2013 titled "7 Lessons from *Frasier* on Home Decor, Living and the Finer Things in Life,"[2] or a 2011 commentary: "Of all the fictional homes that are part of our pop culture, the muted color scheme— injected with pops of vibrance through art, the formal edge to a contem- porary space, and the great flow make Frasier's apartment one of the ones I'd most like to call home."[3] In 2014, Joe McGauley wrote: "Say what you will of his many faults, but Frasier Crane, from *Frasier*, knew just what he was doing when he bought a place in Seattle's Elliott Bay Tow- ers. The luxurious three-bedroom, [three]-bath spread with killer views of the Space Needle is without question one of the finest fictional bachelor pads ever conjured up."[4] These are just three examples of dozens of praises sung regarding Frasier's apartment. Even the cast loved the apart- ment. Peri Gilpin gushes, "Isn't it just so striking? Now everyone wants Roy to do their apartments."[5] So iconic was this apartment that the living room was re-created for an exhibit at the Museum of History and Industry in Seattle in 2012—years after the show went off the air.[6]

So why does this apartment consistently stand out over endless others seen on-screen, more than twenty years since its debut? The apartment hardly changed over the eleven-year run of the show. No large furniture pieces were switched, aside from a random episode in which Martin's chair was removed or covered for a party, or the disastrous attempt on Frasier's part to buy Martin a new chair and get rid of the old one.[7] Over the years an object here or a knickknack there was moved, and the side table's accoutrements would be updated, to show this was a home the characters lived in and was not merely a stagnant set.[8] The only addition of note was the Chihuly glass bowl appearance in Season 5, which was so subtly done it hardly felt like a change at all. So, again, why do people love this set so much?

Is it the space? The layout of the apartment, featuring one main living room, a kitchen, balcony, three bedrooms, three bathrooms, and a half bath, is stunning.

Frasier's Seattle apartment. *NBC/Photofest;* © *NBC*

Is it the decor and styling? The tans and browns seen throughout, the sleek and modern, yet just comfortable enough lines, are striking.

Is it the objects scattered on available spaces? Everything from a Chihuly vase to African art makes an eclectic but sophisticated space.

Is it that upon first glance, you can instantly feel as if you know the type of person who lives there? An individual with taste, but who wants there to be no doubt he has better taste than you, *or* who is so provocatively demonstrative of his taste, it borders on tacky.

Clearly, it is all of the above. The combination of all these factors coming together results in a space that, although only seen through a screen, starts to feel like home. A viewer begins to establish a personal connection with a place, and the set is an invitation into Frasier's elite world. In particular, Frasier's apartment evokes "an atmosphere of luxury and refinement that is rarely seen on situation comedy sets. And indeed the museum-quality paintings and pieces of iconic furniture don't just serve the script; they also make a larger statement. For millions of viewers each night, they defined the perfectly modern style of a sleek sophisticate."[9] Perhaps Christopher sums up why this apartment is so beloved when he says, "It was all for a man who had money, taste, and style."[10]

The set design is particularly crucial on a show like *Frasier*, which features very few scenes shot on location and consists of mainly just three sets: the KACL radio booth, the Café Nervosa coffee shop, and of course, la pièce de résistance—Frasier's apartment. While there are other spaces shown throughout the series with enough frequency to become somewhat familiar—particularly Niles's apartment at the Montana in the latter half of the series—and sets for when the characters visit a store or a bar or some other location as a setting, every single episode has a scene in Frasier's apartment. This is significant. This allows the audience each week (or every twenty-two minutes of bingeing) to have a connection with that living space. Returning somewhere familiar not only becomes a habit, it becomes a comfort, to the point that you want to return week after week, or with each episode.

Christopher explains another reason for the praise and love directed toward Frasier's apartment at Elliott Bay Towers as he says, "Sets work when they reflect the character of the show that lives there. I've done a lot of shows with stunning sets that don't click with the public as much because they don't like the show. In this case, people love Frasier and people feel like this is a place where Frasier would live—and a place they'd like to visit."[11] The set of Frasier was featured in magazines such as *Metropolitan Home*, *Redbook*, *TV Guide*, and *Entertainment Weekly*, and the producers received fan letters for the set alone.[12] When discussing our research for this book, some people have told us they literally sought out exact pieces of furniture from Frasier's living room. Whatever the reason may be for this show connecting so well with audiences, one thing is certain—this apartment is beloved and has become the standard of great television apartments.

THE STRUCTURE OF THE APARTMENT

The producers of *Frasier* approached Roy Christopher, one of the most famous production designers in the television industry, to design the look of the series. Christopher's work in television goes back to *The Dean Martin Show* of the 1960s and includes design work on such famous series as *Welcome Back, Kotter*; *Murphy Brown*; *Wings*; and *NewsRadio*. Of set designing, Roy has said, "I'd like to teach designers how to read a script, how to break it down, how to think. What they're really paying for is your mind. They want you to be able to take verbal stuff, written stuff, and translate it into verbal terms—that's an art. Open your mind to that. Read a poem and paint it."[13] Ken Levine, a television producer, director, and writer who has worked on many series—and one of the only individuals to have written the Frasier Crane character in three separate series (*Cheers*, *Frasier*, and a guest appearance on *Wings*)—refers to Frasier's living room as Christopher's masterpiece.[14] Considering the length and quality of Christopher's career, this is no small compliment. Christopher himself says he has received more attention for his *Frasier* set than for any other show he's worked on.[15] It seems that those working on the set enjoyed creating the apartment as much as viewers enjoyed taking it in. While still working on the show, Christopher stated, "It was a great thrill to design this set because you're given a leading character who is so sophisticated and so worldly and has such exquisite tastes that for myself and the original set designer, Sharon Viljoen, and for Ron Olson, who's our current set decorator, it's been a joy to bring to life the world of Frasier Crane."[16]

Frasier's apartment set was built on the same soundstage at Paramount Studios that housed the set of *Cheers*. It includes three bedrooms, three and a half baths, the main living room with a balcony, and the kitchen. The living room is the heart of the show, and is the main setting in nearly every episode. Also frequently used is Frasier's kitchen; however, a lot of liberty was taken with the layout of this kitchen, as the large appliances and structures often changed with no explanation—sometimes there is an island, sometimes not; the oven on occasion moves from the island to the side, and so on. Toward the back of apartment of what viewers see as the left hallway are Frasier's and Martin's bedrooms, both only shown a few times throughout the series. Frasier's luxurious master bathroom is complete with a massive tub, wood-paneled shower, lounge chair, and a Rothko painting hung over the toilet. Down the right hallway is Daphne's bedroom, which is only seen a few times and most heavily featured in the episode "Daphne's Room," in which Frasier clumsily and inadvertently keeps invading Daphne's privacy.[17]

The set immensely aided the writers and crew in their storytelling. As Peter Casey states, "Frasier's condo was stylish and contemporary with multi-levels and lots of doors and hallways to provide us with a multitude of exits and entrances."[18] This is key for a show that involves lots of hidden conversations and characters unexpectedly entering and overhearing. Perhaps more importantly for the director and crew, the way the set was designed allowed great flexibility for the camera shots. Typically a sitcom like *Frasier* will use four cameras, but angles can be limited by the set in use. On *Frasier*, the set was built with movable parts to allow needed shots to be easily taken. For example, as Levine explains, "The wall leading to the kitchen can swing in and you can get a camera way up into the set."[19] This allows the couch, which is angled away from traditional camera positions, to be filmed straight on.[20] To get other side angles shooting across the living room there were "ports" built into some of the wall pieces: "These are sections that can slide out allowing cameras to peek through from the other side of the wall."[21] Also, a false wall could be brought in to cover an absent wall where the camera and studio audience sat if they ever needed to shoot from the back of the set to the front.[22] Essentially, no matter where the actors stood or what direction they were facing, the set allowed the proper angle for a good shot of an actor's face.

Viewers who tuned in to the character's appearances on *Cheers* would have seen a different living space for Frasier. There we saw the home he shared with his wife, Lilith, filled with warm colors, a brick wall, and curved lines giving a cozy feel. This was a home meant for a couple rather than the bachelor pad Frasier strives for in Seattle, full of shades of tan, a skyline, and straight lines. The new apartment in the Elliott Bay Towers was purposefully given a very different feel than his life in Boston—a direct contrast from a family home to his new bachelorhood. In Seattle he is starting over, and the easiest way to portray that is visually in the space around him. "To symbolize that Crane had left his stuffy, pretentious life in Boston behind to start a new (and equally pretentious) life in his hometown, the show's writers—Peter Casey, David Angell and David Lee—decided to give him a 'design sensibility,' and moved him into an airy, stylish bachelor apartment."[23]

The space is Frasier's dream home. He just left what had become a very unhappy life, moved across the country to Seattle, and created his ideal environment, with everything he wants, just the way he wants it. Producer Christopher Lloyd explains, "Everybody has a dream house where he'd live if he finally extricated him- or herself from whatever current situation they're in. Frasier got out of a marriage that wasn't working. He leaves a stuffy, traditional house in Boston and moves into a fabulous penthouse apartment with all the space he ever wanted."[24] Frasier, in a way, retakes control of his life by having his apartment just the way he wants it. A similar representation is seen in Niles's evolving aesthetic choices, as explored later in this chapter. Of course, to introduce conflict in the pilot, Frasier's space is invaded by two very different people, Martin and Daphne, and he has lost control of his space. In contrast, eleven years later, it is when Martin and Daphne move out that Frasier feels the effect of his empty apartment and decides to move to San Francisco.

THE VIEW

Frasier's apartment is filled with the best that designers have to offer, yet the crowning feature of his apartment might be the balcony and its view. To almost every guest, Frasier points these out, as it is a mark of status for him to see such a skyline from his apartment. Frasier is so enamored with his view he even tries to use it as a means of impressing Martin when he first moves in, saying, "Dad, what do you think of the view? Hey, that's the Space Needle there!" Martin replies curtly, "Oh, thanks for pointing that out. Being born and raised here, I never would have known."[25]

While he is pretentious about it, undeniably the view is unreal—quite literally. There is no building in the city that has that view, or could possibly have it. It is actually an image taken from a "craggy cliff" in Seattle.[26] The skyline backdrop cost around $50,000 to $60,000 to create. The production sent a crew to Seattle to take photos and select a view. After getting all the necessary approvals from the producers and the studio, they sent the chosen view to Paramount to process and create the backdrop. As if preparing to film a pilot episode wasn't intense enough, they didn't know if the skyline backdrop would be ready for the show or how it would look, as the backdrop is forty feet wide and twenty feet tall. As a precaution, they built canvas Roman shades for the windows that could drop down and cover the nonexisting view in case the backdrop wasn't done in time.[27] However, it was completed, and the day before filming the pilot they put up the backdrop, lit it, and it looked beautiful.

Frasier continually takes great pride in this view, perhaps reflecting his inner self, as it has been said, "Those living in glass houses will look outward instead of inward."[28] Frasier is constantly concerned with how he appears to others and often uses his view as a means of impressing someone. In the episode "Three Dates and a Breakup," Frasier is enormously pleased with himself for having a date for each night of a three-day weekend, as he tells Roz, "I have a date this evening. And I've got a date tomorrow night. Oh, and let me check my calendar for Sunday. Oh yes, another date!" Frasier begins his date ritual for each woman with the exact same preparation. He turns on classical music, begins to dance just a little for himself, and then dims the lights. As each woman enters the apartment they all comment on the view by saying: "Oh, I can admire this view for hours," "Oh, what a lovely view," and "Wow. Even more stunning than I remembered." Then Frasier hands them a glass of wine and toasts, "To . . . possibilities."[29] Frasier constantly throughout the series uses this view as an attempt to impress dates and visitors.

Having such large windows in the apartment, aside from having the view, allows for the appearance of more space without actual space. This idea became particularly prevalent during the mid-twentieth century as a solution to small houses, resulting in "compactness with the illusion of spaciousness,"[30] for those who couldn't afford more space but wanted the illusion of it. Frasier can afford a great apartment, but the large windows make his apartment feel even larger and grander. Adding further to the expense and elitism of windows is the difficulty for architects in managing their proportions. Windows have, for centuries, been believed to be a key demonstration of an architect's competence.[31] Additionally, as Sandy Isenstadt, professor of the history of modern architecture at Yale University, explains, "Windows are a special challenge for design professionals. They are uniquely positioned both inside and outside and thus subject to the rule of two realms."[32] This reinforces how well Roy Christopher designed this apartment.

While the use of the balcony may be as a symbol of Frasier's status and wealth, or at times merely a tool to move characters offscreen and out of earshot, the high point of the show's use of the balcony is as a space for individuals to have complete transparency. There characters can bare their secrets, confess something, or have a place for their most vulnerable discussions. The large windows in and of themselves equal transparency—everything is open, perhaps leaving characters to feel more comfortable having conversations in that location. The balcony itself is a space existing outside the confines of Frasier's inner apartment. It is connected to his living room, yet separated by large glass windows, leading to a space in the open air. While the space itself is wide open to the outside, it is perhaps the most private space in the whole apartment, aside from the bathrooms; but even there, poor Daphne gets spied on by both Frasier and Freddie in two different episodes, and multiple characters get walked in on.[33] The balcony is exposed and transparent yet simultaneously private from listening ears. While there, characters are able to speak freely without fear of being overheard, even though they can be seen.

The most candid and vulnerable conversations in the whole series take place through these glass doors, on the balcony. These moments are sprinkled throughout the series and always feature a character speaking with what they believe is frankness. Comically, when Frasier's new station manager, Tom, confesses his romantic interest in Frasier, it is on the balcony (Frasier misinterprets and believes he is interested in Daphne).[34] When a politician Frasier has decided to support confesses his most closely held secret to Frasier, that he believes he was abducted by aliens years ago,[35] they are alone on the balcony.

More seriously, an emotionally exposed Lilith suggests resuming her relationship with Frasier, confessing she found his letter and wants him back in her life, while a distraught Frasier is forced to tell her that he wrote the letter over a year ago and no longer feels that way.[36] Daphne's recognition of her feelings for Niles most concretely happens while she stands on the balcony thinking Niles is ready to confess to her his own feelings.[37] And it is the setting of real moments of vulnerability and emotions, such as when all the Crane men stand on it as Niles throws away his wedding ring as a symbolic acceptance of the end of his marriage to Maris.[38] This is one of the most powerful moments on the show. Edward Gardiner perfectly summarizes this moment:

> There's just such a strong emotional connection to all the characters that we can't help but feel moved and affected by their fates. In one of the most poignant moments in the entire 11 seasons we see Frasier, Niles and Marty bellowing their romantic woes to the whole of Seattle over quiet, melancholic laughter. The scene works so well because it's the characters at their most vulnerable and honest. We're suddenly there with them, empathizing, rather than standing back as a separate party admiring the surface.[39]

The final balcony moment of the series is Frasier admitting to Martin and Niles that he is scared to leave Seattle to start his new job in San Francisco, as he says, "I'm happy for myself. And scared too. But it's a good scared." Perhaps as Frasier steps outside he is able to look inwardly on himself, just as many of the other characters do on that balcony.

THE MONTANA

A strong contrast to Frasier's sleek, high-end preferences is Niles's "grand over the top style."[40] Niles's taste is mostly displayed as he moves into his own apartment, the Montana, during his separation from Maris. A major continuous storyline throughout the series is the on again/off again marriage between Niles and Maris, ultimately ending in his divorce being finalized in Season 6. Due to his financial struggles with the cost of divorce lawyers, Niles is forced to economize to the point of subletting his beloved apartment at the Montana, a necessity that becomes apparent when Niles is forced to pack his own lunches. "My God, is this your lunch? A bologna sandwich? And a fruit cocktail?! Oh, Niles. You see what these lawyers have reduced you to?"[41] The divorce from Maris represents not only financial failure to him but also many of his failures in life. Living at the Montana means so much more to Niles than just a nice apartment, or having financial means; it also means he's made it. He's achieved something. When he first moves to the building he exclaims, "I have some wonderful news. I just signed a lease for an apartment in one of the most exclusive buildings in Seattle."[42]

The apartment itself is a massive, gorgeous space, with dark wood floors and paneling contrasting the light beige furniture. For Niles, everything is overstated wealth, everything is heightened.[43] This is an extremely different style from Frasier's, as it is much more classical and ornamental than his brother's streamlined, modern apartment. We see soft curves compared to Frasier's harsh lines, dark colors versus light, and more pillows and scattered trinkets than Frasier's uncluttered and organized home. There are no windows in his main living room, and we learn there are three floors featuring a library, study, separate kitchen, gift-wrap room, and multiple guest rooms. Both Frasier and Niles surround themselves with antiques; however, they are very different kinds. Where Frasier tends toward exotic, pre-Columbian objects, Niles leans toward tapestries and Renaissance style. Impressively so, both brothers express their pompous and pretentious lifestyles in very different ways.

Niles's apartment situation becomes a means to explore and showcase the chaos in his life. He wants to break free of Maris, but doesn't want to leave the comfort and luxury he has come to find with her mansion and wealth. He eventually decides that leaving her is better than staying, and gives it all up. Moving into the Montana highlights a moment of independence for him, as if he is finally taking control of his life, rather than constantly being dominated by Maris. As Niles declares, "Frasier, ever since I was a little boy I have walked by this building and wondered what sort of people could live in such a magnificent place. . . . Getting in here after Maris dumped me proved that I was not a complete failure." Unfortunately, as the divorce negotiations are dragged on by Maris, Niles begins to lose that control, as he can no longer afford to maintain his current lifestyle.

Due to this, Niles is forced to move into the cheap and low-end Shangri-La Apartments, which showcases his will to break free of Maris's hold. Staying at the apartment gives him a newfound sense of power, as he embraces the lower-class, Shangri-La lifestyle for a time. He pretends, even to himself, that he's just fine and integrates with the building's community. But he reaches his breaking point when he reclines in the lounge chair provided by the building and Martin says, "I'd be happy here myself—this is my kind of place." This causes Niles to howl, "Get me out of this hell hole!" Despite his best efforts, the Shangri-La is not who Niles is, nor who he wants to be. His identity is attached to his home.

Niles wants to leave the Shangri-La and knows his easy way out of there is through Maris, who, with his apology, will take him back. But if he does that he's giving up so much more than not having to live at the Shangri-La. Although he goes as far as actually calling her, Niles resists begging and rather just informs her of his new address. Niles still express-es concern for how to live at the Shangri-La, which leads Frasier to tell him, "You know, Niles, perhaps this place is the price you'll have to pay for your freedom," to which Niles confirms, "Well, it's worth that."[44]

Where and how you live affect how you act and behave. As Niles moves from the Montana into the Shangri-La, his actions change as he begins skipping his wine events to go to a Ping-Pong tournament at the apartment complex. He invites Frasier and Martin to stay one evening as "the guys in D building are bringing over a six-foot sub and they've rigged the pinball machine so it's free play all night."[45] He even changes his style of clothing, as he is seen wearing a Hawaiian shirt that was left at the apartment by the previous tenant (who, given the clues, committed suicide), rather than his usual collared shirt, designer tie, and suit jacket.

Similarly, Frasier matches the decor of his home in what he wears, while Martin and Daphne tend to look somewhat out of place in the designer style of Frasier's home. However, Martin matches his Barca-lounger, and when Frasier sits in it or stands near it he looks out of place. What a man is wearing should match his décor; what is in your home affects the way you dress, the way you act. Architect Otto Wagner claimed,

> A man in modern traveling suit, for example, fits in very well with the waiting room of a train station, with sleeping cars, with all our vehi-cles; yet would we not stare if we were to see someone dressed in clothing from the Louis XV period using such things? . . . It is simply an artistic absurdity that men in evening attire, in lawn tennis or bicy-cling outfits, in uniform or chequered breeches should spend their life in interiors executed in the styles of past centuries.[46]

As the divorce finally is settled, all Niles wants is to return to his home at the Montana. However, due to a sublease tenant, he is forced to stay at the Shangri-La. Tragically, at the same time, his eternal pursuit of Daphne is halted by her dating his divorce lawyer, Donny, leaving him spiraling and distraught. Niles desperately wants the comfort of his home at the Montana. Clare Cooper Marcus explains, "A home fulfills many needs: a place of self-expression, a vessel of memories, a refuge from the outside world, a cocoon where we can feel nurtured and let down our guard."[47] After seeing both Maris on a date and Daphne with Donny at a restaurant, the nightmare of seeing your newly ex-wife and dream girl each with another man in one location, Niles falls down on the couch in Frasier's apartment, pathetically exclaiming, "Frasier, I wanna go home." It is then finally, at this lowest of moments, that Frasier takes action and works out having the tenant leave the apartment early. As he first walks through the doors, returning home, Niles says, "Oh . . . I'm home. Oh, I can already feel the last four months dropping away."[48] The scene cuts to the Montana living room, which is a comfort of familiarity to both Niles and the audience.

THE CITY OF SEATTLE

Frasier accurately uses names of locations, facts about the city, and even a few famous local people to help portray Seattle. Visiting and filming in Seattle was something Grammer wanted for *Frasier*, claiming while he was on *Cheers* the cast and crew bonded with Boston and became closely associated with the city. Grammer argues that being on location "reinforces the show in my mind. It gives it credibility."[49] Despite this goal, the series only filmed on location in Seattle once, for the hundredth episode. This was probably for the best as many of the weaker episodes vary from the established structure and format, including this special episode. For the episode, the actual mayor of Seattle, Norm Rice, played a guest role, in which Frasier celebrates the thousandth episode of his radio show and the day is declared "Frasier Crane Day." While filming there, Mayor Rice did actually declare "Frasier Day" for the city.[50]

However, the original location planned for the series was not Seattle, Washington, but rather Denver, Colorado. Soon after that decision, the state of Colorado passed a law that many felt discriminated against the LGBT community, resulting in the decision to switch the location of the show. With this, the producers chose to go as far west as they could, landing in Seattle. This proved to be the better choice. Creator Peter Casey explains:

> Seattle was pretty cutting edge at that time. It was the center of the grunge scene, the coffee revolution was taking off, it had a great arts community, and their restaurants were exploring new and exciting cuisines. All in all, it was fertile ground for Frasier and an inconvenient schlep across the country for the *Cheers* gang. We didn't have a problem having Lilith visit because she was his ex-wife and they shared a son. It was organic. The other characters would take some fancy footwork, but after the show established itself that first season, we didn't have a problem doing one *Cheers* character a season.[51]

The show often highlights things significant to Seattle, such as mentions of the sport teams (although this unexpectedly dates the show as the NBA's SuperSonics are no longer in Seattle), the Monorail and Pike Place (both seen in the hundredth episode), the opera, the Elliott Bay Book Company where Frasier likes to shop, and of course Chihuly glass sculpture.[52]

There is a Season 2 episode that highlights the pride Seattle natives have in their hometown. In the episode "The Botched Language of Cranes," Frasier offends the entire city when he tells a caller on his radio show that she should move to a new city to find the change that she needs, as he says, "Certainly there are far easier places to cheer up than this dreary, soggy old city of ours." Naturally this upsets many, including his old rival, Derek Mann, who writes in his column the next morning:

> Yesterday, I heard him advise an unhappy young woman that she could magically cure her depression simply by leaving Seattle. I know it would cure my depression if the Seattle-hating Dr. Crane would take his own advice and leave town as soon as possible!

Frasier continues to make it worse as he has a hard time apologizing for his advice and unknowingly rants on the air, saying, "Never in my life have I heard from such a bunch of whiny, provincial crybabies. I swear to God, this entire city has lost its tiny, rain-addled mind!" Ultimately, we know Frasier loves the city of Seattle as he states, "I do not find Seattle a depressing place to live. It would take more than clouds to obscure the beauty of her landscape and more than drizzle to dampen the warmth and good fellowship that makes Seattle the only place in this bad old world that I care to call home."[53]

In one of the greatest salutes to the city's identity, the producers created one of the major sets as a coffee shop, Café Nervosa, where all the characters spend a large portion of their time. As Frasier explains, "Nervosa is more to me than just a place for coffee. It's my refuge, my sanctuary for contemplation." And Niles claims, "Nervosa is my haven, my cocoon."[54] The choice to do a coffee shop was appropriate as Seattle was quickly becoming synonymous with coffee. This was also practical for the series to not be lost in *Cheers'* shadow, as Angell explains, "We certainly didn't want to do a bar, for obvious reasons."[55] In preparing the set of Café Nervosa, Christopher relates that they went around Seattle and took pictures of coffee shops and designed from there.[56] For production they had three different sets for Café Nervosa, depending on where the characters sat: a small set, medium set, and large set, which allowed for different scenes to take place all throughout the café.[57] This was a significant point to the set because just as in real life, you would not always be able to sit at the same table every time, no matter how regular a patron you were.

More than simply providing a setting for action, well-designed and decorated sets accent the characters, highlight the comedy, and reveal themes for a series. Grammer thought that the set was historically significant and a great example of how a set "integrates into a show and almost is a character in the show."[58] Roy Christopher and the rest of the production team created one of the most perfect blends of form and function in the set for *Frasier*. From the layout to the furniture to the objects, careful attention was paid to ensure that everything on camera elevated the storytelling without detracting from it. These added layers of meaning can be appreciated by students of design, but aren't required to be known for the comedy to be enjoyed. This is a delicate balance, one that has perhaps never been more perfectly achieved than on *Frasier*.

7

CURATING THE SPACES

You know, every item here was carefully selected.

SET DECORATION

While the structure of the set of Frasier's apartment was a brilliant design, the decoration of the apartment was equally powerful. When placing objects in your home to fill your life, you don't want just the product, you want everything with which it is culturally and personally imbued. You want all it can represent—the history of the object, the narrative of where it came from, the fantasy portrayed in the advertisement. Beverly Gordon, a professor of design, explains, "The material goods that are an integral part of consumer culture—are an embodiment of a desired experience."[1] Frasier references his beloved Coco Chanel couch multiple times throughout the series,[2] and he essentially buys into the idea that he has put himself into the class and lifestyle associated with Coco Chanel's atelier in Paris by owning this object. Television audiences do the same thing. "Consciously or not, we mimic the decor, colors, and floor plans of our favorite TV homes—if not copying them literally, then using their look for inspiration."[3] With each week or episode viewed, you can claim a little piece of this world and be a part of it. And so we envision ourselves in the set, or surround ourselves with items similar to those seen on the set.

Generally the items in Frasier's apartment are genuine and not built for display. Almost everything seen was something you could purchase, which many viewers did. Sharon Viljoen, the original set designer, said that she found items through sources an interior designer would use for actual clients rather than having objects made in house by the production staff.[4] She created a room to reflect her client's taste, even if this one was fictitious.[5] In doing so, she created a design that was not only aspirational for viewers, but also achievable.[6] Notably, there was a resurgence in interest and sales in Eames lounge chairs, which were frequently seen and referenced by the characters, while *Frasier* was on the air. "When television shows become big hits, they sometimes spawn their own decorating trends." It is impossible to claim a one-to-one correlation between a chair's appearance on a TV show and corresponding sales, especially with a revival of midcentury style around the same time,[7] but some influence from one of the most watched shows on television is highly likely.

Similarly, as previously mentioned, Frasier takes great pride in his couch, stating, "This couch is an exact replica of the one Coco Chanel had in her Paris atelier."[8] Well, "exact replica" is probably not the right phrase; perhaps "scale model" would do better. The original in Coco Chanel's atelier was huge, measuring twelve feet long and four feet deep.[9] Frasier's couch for the show cost between $15,000 to $20,000, with twenty-four yards of suede cloth used to re-create it, based on the Chanel version.[10] Since then that couch has been manufactured to be sold to the public, and Roy Christopher notes, "It's a very popular piece of furniture."[11] Once again, an item from the show influenced design choices among viewers.

So what do these objects say about Frasier as a character? Who is he? What are his tastes? In her book *Sitcom Style*, Diana Friedman argues that Frasier's "museum-quality artwork, custom-made furniture, and high-end decorative accessories show that Frasier is an exhibitionist. He surrounds himself with culture, wealth, and arrogance to hide the mess that is his social life."[12] She continues, "The pad, like its owner, has a haughty, manicured style, with every inch seeming to shout, 'I am sophisticated! I am cultured!' Despite this pretentious declaration, the interior is inviting and serene, made comfortable through a combination of furniture upholstered in smooth leather and soft suede, warm wood accents, and floor-to-ceiling windows that deliver an expansive skyline."[13]

Within the series, Frasier Crane routinely takes great pride in his deliberately designed living space. Frasier explains that his apartment has a carefully selected decor: "It's a style of decorating, it's called 'eclectic.' Well, the theory behind it is, if you've got really fine pieces of furniture, it doesn't matter if they match—they will go together."[14] What Frasier espouses here is not strictly true when it comes to design theory. Of course, there have been debates about a unified decor versus an "eclectic" style for more than two centuries. Significantly, it wasn't until the eighteenth century, when Robert Adam developed the concept of wallpaper matching the upholstery, that the idea of establishing a unified look between the fixed and movable objects within a room became a trend.[15] Prior to Adam, most rooms contained family heirlooms that were passed down and naturally mismatched because of all the contrasting trends through which the family's previous generations passed. But what Frasier has on display are anything but heirlooms handed down from his father. Indeed, Frasier rejects most objects that Martin attempts to display in his apartment, from bold Christmas decorations, to a painting Martin purchases as a gift, to a mounted jackalope head. Frasier's "eclectic" taste is really a means of justifying his buying of "highbrow" objects rather than pieces with which he has an emotional attachment or an aesthetic appreciation. Thus Frasier uses his decorating style as a means of showing off, bragging to guests about his decor. He prefers praise over sentimental attachment.

While he prefers the praise, Frasier clearly does loves the adornments in his apartment. Sentimentality may not have been the motivation in obtaining them, but it inevitably developed. In Season 11, after years of viewers watching him buy and maintain his collection, Frasier fears losing his belongings due to a lawsuit. He cries as he caresses his objects, "My . . . things, my beautiful, beautiful things. I love them so. . . ."[16] Objects give people a sense of power, even just in ownership. Frasier feels better owning these things and uses his objects as a means of identity and showcasing value in his life. He places considerable personal value in owning things that have been given intrinsic value by the world.

Frasier defines himself (and others) by what is owned, and as the audience we interpret his character from these items. LeGene Quesenberry and Bruce W. Sykes, in their article "Leveraging the Internet to Promote Fine Art: Perspectives of Art Patrons," state, "Television programs that have a demographic of young, educated, and professional viewers have begun to present the sets as integral parts of character development. In shows where the action occurs at home or partially at home, the decor identifies the character."[17] We are given a glimpse of how much the decor within the same space can define a character when a late-season plot takes Frasier into the apartment directly above his. Frasier's rival, Cam Winston, has exactly the same apartment layout and color scheme as Frasier's, but with a distinct decor that helps define Cam as a character. It is immediately clear that it is the same space, but owned by a different type of individual, with a plaid couch, oversized leather chair, draped curtains, large chandelier, many more knickknacks, and lots of plants and greenery along the walls. It is startling and almost upsetting to see an apartment we have become so familiar with this way, but it is exactly what was required to differentiate Cam Winston from Frasier.

Similarly, Christmas episodes allow the apartment to become Martin's space for one time each season. Every year Frasier and Martin battle about style and taste and how many decorations to put up, but Martin generally wins out. As Sarah Pugh writes about the Season 3 Christmas episode, in which Freddie is coming and Martin really goes all out for his grandson, "It's also the first time in the series we see Martin's true love of decorating for the season. A great visual is Frasier walking into his own apartment, barely recognizable under the colored lights and plastic figures adorning the usually pristine space."[18] Frasier wants his decorations tasteful and understated; Martin wants them loud, bright, and tacky, and these preferences define each of their characters.

How important objects and decor are for defining a character is never better showcased than in the Season 8 episode "The Great Crane Robbery." In this episode Frasier attempts to find a new style of furniture to redecorate his apartment. There is, yet again, a new owner of KACL, Todd Peterson, one of the "brightest stars of Silicon Valley" and "one of the youngest members of the Fortune 500." Todd arrives in a typical Silicon Valley uniform of casual pants, a polo shirt, and a candy bar in hand—a striking contrast to Frasier's buttoned-up image with a suit and tie and briefcase. After Todd admits he knows nothing about culture because he has spent his life behind a computer, he asks Frasier to help him, stating, "You can teach me to have as much taste and style as you." Always willing to give the "gift of Frasier," Frasier jumps on this opportunity. Frasier invites Todd over to his apartment to build a friendship, but with the ultimate goal of also gaining a syndication contract for his show through their relationship. After seeing the apartment, Todd offers to buy it from him. Frasier laughs, telling him, "My humble home is not for sale," but informs him a unit below him is available. Todd immediately rents the apartment, thrilled to be neighbors with Frasier. However, when Frasier arrives for Todd's housewarming party, he sees that Todd has duplicated Frasier's apartment exactly, minus Martin's chair. This emphasizes how unique and sentimental the chair is compared to all the other furniture that can easily be duplicated by someone with money.

Rather than upset his new boss, Frasier, with his eyes on the potential syndication deal, decides to change his apartment instead, claiming, "Perhaps I'm being too hasty about which of us should be doing the changing. Perhaps I'm holding on too tight to my possessions! Décor is, after all, a fluid art!" Eight seasons into the show, we know this is a very un-Frasier-like comment. However, we are given a montage of Frasier trying out

Martin and his beloved chair. © *NBC; Photo: Justin Lubin; Photofest*

new furniture in the apartment, which really highlights how perfectly his previous furniture unified the space. This montage also showcases how accustomed we have become to his style after eight seasons of watching. The space has become so familiar to us that anything different feels off and we are immediately aware of it.

In the montage there are five different furniture styles tried out in the apartment while "Classical Gas," a guitar anthem from the 1970s, is heard. Finally, in an empty apartment, devoid of all furniture and decor except for Martin in his chair, Frasier is frustrated that nothing is working, exclaiming, "I give up. I've tried a million combinations. I even had early Byzantine mingling with mid-century Danish! The only furniture that looks good in my apartment is my own!" Yet again, Martin knows best as he says matter-of-factly from his infamous chair, without looking up from the newspaper, "Well, I could have told you that three loveseats ago."[19]

The important part of Frasier's apartment and decor style is that it is his own. His choices and his style reflect himself; it is his and his alone. When Todd comes and mimics it exactly, it is flattering to have someone appreciate and want the same style, but it also feels like the loss of an identity. To some it can seem frivolous to place so much emphasis on what you wear, what you surround yourself with, and what you purchase, but it is not frivolous at all. We project who we are—our identity—in what we put on our body, what we place in our homes, and what we spend our money on. As professor of architecture, Clare Cooper Marcus declares the "house as a mirror of self."[20] Frasier may choose a high-end lifestyle, and want items that only come with a designer label and dismiss anything else, but that's a part of his identity. That is who he is, and to have someone else copy it identically takes away a piece of his identity as it has been established on *Frasier*.

OBJECTS IN THE APARTMENT

The objects and decor of Frasier's apartment are meant to stand out, to be discussed—by characters and viewers—to play a strong role throughout the show. Scenes in the apartment serve as an ever-present reminder of Frasier's tastes and claims. "The designer furniture that surrounds Frasier in his new life is as deliberately chosen and arranged as a still life and serves to enhance the cultivated image he projects."[21] Nothing is there by accident. Friedman explains, "In fact, behind the scenes, among producers and television executives, the sets of shows receive as much attention as scripts, actors and costumes do. Decor, paint, and artwork are all building blocks that are used to enhance the show's fantasy and fiction."[22] Viljoen declares that "each object was meticulously selected."[23] Nothing was there without reason. Knowing this, we can understand a lot about Frasier's character. But first we must be aware of each object.

Frasier's apartment is a treasure trove of iconic and high-end designs by famous designers. Throughout the series, these designer names are tossed about among the characters with effortless ease, but how does that translate in prime-time television to a national audience of varying social classes? Christopher Lloyd argues why it worked so well, saying, "Some viewers do understand the names bandied about. Generally we find people understand these references much more than most writers think they do. Even if they don't, they get the idea he's talking about something that's quality."[24] The specificity of the reference is also always funnier than an abstraction, even if the specific reference is unknown. Saying a wine is a "Piechoné Logeavie" is funnier than saying it is a "fine wine" even if someone is not a winebibber. Objects on the show are rarely introduced to give their context and meaning to the viewers, but rather they are just there, or stated by name in a conversation, and you are expected to either know or assume they are of value.

As if playing a game to see how many references they could make, the show weaves designer names casually in everyday dialogue. Within the first three minutes of the pilot episode, Frasier utters the line "I am not a piece of Lalique."[25] Lalique refers to the delicate glassware by French designer Rene Lalique, most famous for his art nouveau pieces in the late nineteenth to early twentieth century. Those with the knowledge of what Lalique is understand Frasier is saying, "I am not fragile." However, given the context of the scene and previous dialogue by Roz of avoiding criticizing Frasier, even without knowledge of hundred-year-old French glassware, a viewer can follow the conversation just fine. These layers of meaning can make the show more powerful, particularly with multiple viewings, but do not detract from the overall humor and comprehension of the show.

Jokes are continually made in reference to artists and their work throughout the series. In the Season 3 episode "The Focus Group," Niles is ranting to Frasier about an incident that took place while attending a gallery opening the night before. He explains that while discussing pointillism he made a "rather emphatic point" and "lost the grip on [his] canape and found that it became airborne," landing on a painting. The owner of the gallery then demanded reimbursement for damage to the painting, to which Niles hilariously argues, "How he could notice a fleck of foie gras on a Jackson Pollock is beyond me."[26] This joke is funny given Pierce's comedic delivery, and the phrase "fleck of foie gras"; however, it is funnier when one knows Jackson Pollock employed a paint-splatter technique for his paintings.

While often the design and art references are just dropped in with no significance other than being mentioned, from time to time they are used as a means of establishing status or worthiness of individuals. In Season 1, Episode 11, Frasier is trying to find a new doctor for Martin but is unsure of whom to choose. When trying to persuade him to consider a doctor in his building, it is only when Niles mentions the doctor has "a Lichtenstein hanging in his office" that Frasier agrees he is worth going to, saying, "Ooh, Lichtenstein. He sounds perfect."[27] Roy Lichtenstein, a twentieth-century painter famous for his style of pop art, is not an artist one would presume fit Frasier's oeuvre; however, recently two Lichtenstein paintings have sold for over $42 million each at auctions.[28] The high financial value of the art makes it understandable that Frasier would suddenly trust the doctor more, as it is an indication of class, not taste. Probably as much for the wordplay as to reveal anything about Frasier, viewers do learn that Frasier owns a Lichtenstein himself, as he mentions that an art restorer "saved my life last year when Eddie licked my Lichtenstein!"[29]

The financial value of these objects truly becomes apparent when learning about the cost of building and decorating this set. In 1993 it cost $250,000 for the architecture and building of the set.[30] Adding in the furniture, objects, and artwork (many of which were just rented), the total cost comes closer to one million dollars,[31] and therefore, if the set was dressed, there was a twenty-four-hour guard.[32] Roy Christopher says, "We had an ample budget. *Frasier* was a very unique show and I always told the people working on it don't use this as a template for the future because I don't recall the word budget ever being discussed on *Frasier* in eleven years."[33]

To appreciate the decor more fully, here are the outstanding, more recognizable pieces with their 1993 purchase prices:

- The Eames lounge chair and ottoman, rented from Herman Miller, $1,500 to $3,200.
- The Wassily chair by Marcel Breuer, $1,395
- A Nick Berman Design Floating Ball side table, $2,250
- The Pastoe curved sideboard, $3,200
- The lamp by Le Corbusier, around $2,200
- An original Chihuly sculpture in Season 5, about $60,000
- Replica of Coco Chanel's couch, $15,000 to $20,000
- Steinway medium grand piano, most likely around $100,000

Objects that are identifiable but difficult to price:

- A Rothko painting in Frasier's bathroom
- An iconic Rauschenberg print from the 1970s in the hallway
- The vase painting by American film art director Jack Otterson
- Viljoen also designed an armchair and coffee table similar to ones designed by Emile-Jacques Ruhlmann.
- A "weird little frog sculpture"[34] next to the fireplace. Christopher described the object as "a humorous touch to the set. We call him 'Froggy.'"[35]
- And finally, the countless African and pre-Columbian objects displayed throughout his apartment, an eclectic collection that demonstrates that Frasier has traveled widely[36]

Many of the African and pre-Colombian objects are placed in custom-made geometric inset shelves.[37] Personalized touches are placed throughout the apartment, such as a picture of Freddie on the cabinet next to the front door that was updated with new pictures of the actor who portrayed him.[38] As for the books seen on Frasier's shelves, "the volumes in the bookcase are highbrow types. A staffer was allowed to go on a spending spree at local bookstores. The CDs, however, are random."[39]

While all these objects were placed in Frasier's apartment with intention, a few select items stand out in meaning through the series. The Chihuly sculpture casually appears, unannounced, in Frasier's apartment on the stand next to the fireplace three episodes into Season 5. It is in a prime location easily seen from most camera angles as it rests prominently in the background. The multicolored sculpture of brown, orange, yellow, green, and purple glass is rarely mentioned.

The sculpture was designed by artist Dale Chihuly for the show when the cast and crew filmed on location in Seattle for the hundredth episode and were invited to a reception at the Lake Union Studio of Glass. [40] The Chihuly original is worth approximately $60,000[41] and was reportedly wrapped up after every day's filming and would not appear on set until time to film. [42] However, this piece is significant not only because of its worth as another piece of Frasier's eclectic art but also because Chihuly glass art has become synonymous with Seattle. As Quesenberry and Sykes explain, "The art, including the Chihuly vase, represents the status of the owner and nods to the sophistication of the audience, many of whom recognize Seattle as a leading force in the world of glass sculpture."[43] Having such a sculpture on set would have to have been a deliberate tribute to the city. Even when it goes completely unmentioned for the majority of the series, the Chihuly rests in Frasier's apartment, visible in most every scene, silently and effortlessly representing the city of Seattle.

Objects also reveal character—you can infer facts and traits about people from the objects around them. From Martin's recliner, championed by the middle-class man, we can infer his social class, as well as the value of his television, based on its position of prominence. From the very first episode, we see Frasier has a beautiful Steinway medium grand piano in his apartment. From this one would assume he must play the piano or be the type of person who would aspire to play the piano. As it is also a very expensive object, we again assume he must be able to afford one.

Incidentally, the piano was a last-minute addition to the set by creator David Lee. In an interview, Christopher states that the set was all designed and being built at the mill when Lee called, wanting to add a piano. The original design had the room ending before the piano area, so the set was going to have to be redesigned to make room for a piano. Christopher's response was simply, "Whoa, okay!"[44] Despite the added difficulties, Christopher describes it as a blessing as he was able to make the set larger and create the see-through bar area connecting the kitchen to the living room. [45] In interviews, Christopher has a very steady, monotone voice when describing the set; however, as he begins to retell this story it becomes clear he recalls the stress and emotion this moment created.

What inspired this need for a piano in the apartment? The producers realized two of the main stars had piano training,[46] with Grammer a talented musician and Pierce having studied classical piano at Yale University[47] before switching and pursuing acting.[48] With this much talent and training between two "brothers," it seemed like a golden opportunity to have scenes involving playing the piano. The use of the piano ranges from funny setups, to continuous gags, to heartfelt family moments. The piano was used outside of the show as well. In breaks between filming, Pierce could at times be found sitting at the piano, softly playing "an opera aria from memory" as he studied an open script.[49] Interestingly, the piano was the one object from the apartment that Grammer took with him after the show finished.[50] He claims it was "a nice memento."[51]

CHAIRS

Easily the most significant object of design for the series, even with all the notorious designer items, is the Barcalounger. Martin's old, duct-taped, striped recliner, so infamous on the show that it could qualify as a character. The chair is shown in nearly every episode, mentioned even when it is off camera, and known already to new characters before they ever see it. Without this chair's presence, the show would have lost so much. As viewers, we are used to seeing Martin's chair in its regular spot facing the TV in Frasier's apartment. However, before the recliner arrived, an ultramodernist and sleek Wassily chair had filled the spot, seen briefly in the first episode before making room for Martin's chair.

The two chairs could not be more opposite visually, in materials and in what each chair represents historically and culturally. They embody the extremes of high-class design and middle-class America. Somewhere in the middle of the two styles is the Eames lounge chair and ottoman, also owned by Frasier. This chair can be seen throughout the series placed next to the balcony windows and occasionally when Frasier reclines in it (Martin almost exclusively sits in his Barcalounger). The Eames chair combines the sleek modern style of the Wassily with the comfort and recline of the Barcalounger. Each chair plays a major role in the world of design and to understand the significance of each chair it is instructive to briefly explore the history of chairs in general, as well as the evolution of chairs in society.

Chairs—these crucial yet at times underappreciated objects are a part of daily life. An object so abundant in our culture has naturally been analyzed, overanalyzed, examined, and reexamined countless times to invent the "ideal" chair for society. These objects rose in status and have become "important markers of stylistic and technological shifts"[52] because "architects and designers who want to be considered important have to have designed at least one successful example to demonstrate their credentials."[53] There are many different kinds of chairs for all aspects of life: work, home, lounging, eating, and so forth, that result in chairs coming in different shapes and sizes, although all have the same function—to be sat upon. There is one theme that is agreed on and sought after—is the chair comfortable? Ideally, a chair will be comfortable and look good, providing function and form. This is not always the case, as seen by Martin's chair, which is extremely comfortable but is a visual nightmare. Mahoney says the chair was "a godawful fabric but it's extremely comfortable. Everybody sits on it. When we rehearse, it would take an act of Congress to get the grips or cameramen out of the chair. If I had a secret room, I would love it. It's truly the most comfortable chair I have ever sat in."[54] Christopher calls it "the most enjoyed piece of furniture on the set."[55]

Although difficult to pinpoint exactly, it is believed that the first "chair" in the form we are familiar with today dates back to at least the ancient Egyptians. Whenever they began, the known evolution of the chair is a fascinating journey that could, and does, fill many books. For our purpose we'll focus on the twentieth century, particularly on three particularly iconic and influential chairs of the time, which happen to be the three chairs featured on Frasier—the Wassily, the Eames lounge chair and ottoman, and the Barcalounger.

In the book *Iconic Designs: 50 Stories about 50 Things*, which selected fifty iconic designs of objects throughout history, the chosen chair design was the Wassily, although the Eames lounge chair was also recognized as an equally significant iconic chair. In the book, Clive Edwards, a professor of design history, describes the factors and differences between iconic chair design versus any other chair design, and particularly why they stand out. He theorizes that the major distinction is that iconic chairs are often looked at just as much as they are sat in, meaning the emphasis on the aesthetic is just as crucial as on the form—they are as much works of art as they are functional tools for our bodies. He continues, stating these iconic chairs reflect a number of facets, such as the chair's "production, materials, cultural references, and points of distinction."[56] Iconic chairs must simultaneously fulfill a comfortable function and act as a status signifier. In regard to Frasier and his two iconic chairs, the Wassily and the Eames lounge chair and ottoman, both are utilized by Frasier in these ways—he does sit on the chairs, but they are a means by which he establishes his cultural and economic status to those who enter his apartment. However, these chairs are only significant to those who are aware of the social cachet that they hold, which is perhaps one reason Frasier frequently announces his furniture by designer name, implicitly noting its significance.

Before Martin came and disrupted his new bachelor life, Frasier had his apartment perfectly decorated to his taste, including a Wassily chair where Martin's recliner ends up. Frasier's use of the Wassily chair would be a very conscious, deliberate, and expensive choice, as it was one of the most famous designs by acclaimed designer Marcel Breuer. Breuer, a modernist, architect, and furniture designer, was an avid chair designer and theorist and ultimately theorized that a chair should and could be designed in such a way that the structure would gradually diminish so eventually one would feel as though floating on air.[57]

Breuer began designing chairs that could evolve in that direction. The ideal material for such a task was steel, as it would be strong, inexpensive, lightweight, and easily portable. Ideally, the furniture was to be light and airy, and according to Breuer the key to such a chair was that it "neither impedes movement nor the view through the room."[58] This is a strong contrast to Martin's Barcalounger, which demands the attention of the viewer's eye. This portability of the Wassily is clearly accurate, as shown during "The Good Son" episode, when even delicate Niles is able to whisk the Wassily up into the air seemingly effortlessly.[59] This is contrasted in a later season when Niles declares, "You know I don't lift!" as he and Frasier attempt to move Martin's bulky chair only to drop it suddenly, scratching the floor.[60]

Breuer designed the Wassily chair around 1925–1926, and in terms of design, the chair literally shifted the style of furniture forever. Breuer single-handedly revolutionized the modern movement with his tubular steel furniture style, but also with manufacturing, as the chair was created to be mass produced. The charming mythology of this chair is related by Breuer:

At that time I was rather idealistic. 23 years old. I made friends with a
young architect, and I bought my first bicycle. I learned to ride the
bicycle and talked to this young fellow and told him that the bicycle
seems to be a perfect production because it hasn't changed in the last
twenty, thirty years. It is still the original bicycle form. He said, "Did
you ever see how they make those parts? How they bend those handle-
bars? You would be interested because they bend those steel tubes like
macaroni."[61]

From then, Breuer began experimenting with tubular steel, noting the
power of bending it rather than having points of welding, ultimately
creating the first Wassily, originally named the *Clubsessel* and "B3."
However, afraid of the criticism he might receive, he did not tell anyone
about his design. Another student at the Bauhaus, Wassily Kandinsky, the
Russian painter and art theorist, happened to see the chair in Breuer's art
studio one day and greatly admired it, which led to others' interest.
Breuer goes on to casually confirm, "A year later, I had furnished the
whole Bauhaus with this furniture."[62] The chair was later marketed as
Wassily, named after Kandinsky, when it was reissued in the 1960s.[63]
   Stripped down to just its skeletal frame with a thin layer of leather for
the seat and the back, which are angled to be slightly reclined, the chair
offers the most minimal support for the sitter. The leather is available in
shades of black, brown, red, and surprisingly, a tricolor option that resem-
bles cowhide.[64] The end goal is apparent—the illusion of just floating, a
frame of "lines in space without mass."[65] Design historian and one of the
curators of the *Marcel Breuer, Furniture and Interiors* exhibit at the
Baltimore Museum of Art in 1981, Christopher Wilk, talks about "the
sense the chair gives of the seat and back being suspended above the
ground—or, more correctly, floating within a network of lines and planes.
The sitter never touches the steel framework of the chair."[66] Edwards
notes that the chair's "materials are a metaphor for modernity, technical
progress, efficiency, and standardization. The chair argues for modern
design and its virtues, and is often seen as modernism exemplified."[67]
Though the exact design of this chair has undergone slight changes from
its original prototype to its re-issues throughout the years, the version
seen in Frasier's apartment would be essentially the same as Breuer's
groundbreaking design.
   However iconic and revolutionary the chair was, it may not be the
most comfortable. Breuer himself described his Wassily chair as "me-

chanical" rather than "cozy,"[68] and it has been compared to an "exercise machine."[69] Yet, despite "being seen as ergonomically challenging for many, it remains a classic design that links the material object to the impalpable ideals of modernism. In this sense the chair is no longer just a chair, it is a symbolic representation of an idea."[70]

Regarding its cultural impact, not only was the design of steel chairs nonintrusive in appearance and portable, they were also very easy to clean, which made them popular in doctors' offices. A key part of the modernist agenda with steel furniture was hygiene, the steel itself being particularly easy to clean, as well as unobstructed by fabric or upholstery. This is the exact opposite of the dirt-gathering capabilities of Martin's chair. When Daphne tries to clean the Barcalounger with a new super-powered vacuum, the vacuum sparks and breaks down, causing Frasier to note that "the Dirt Scourge 2000 is no match for the dirt pile 1957."[71]

In its few appearances, the Wassily easily fits the rest of the decor without any distraction; it is hardly noticeable and does not stand out. Martin's chair, conversely, sticks out instantly to both the audience and characters. When Gil Chesterton arrives at the apartment for the first time to attend a party, he praises Frasier's taste before seeing the chair. "The palette is pure, subtle elegance! The detailing . . . well, it's inspired! And the furnishings . . . Oh, dear. Is that a chair?"[72] In all likelihood, very few members of the audience knew a detailed history of the Wassily. But when Martin first has this chair delivered, Niles removes Frasier's chair to make room for Martin's, and Frasier yells, "Niles, Niles, Niles, be careful with that, that's a Wassily!"[73] From this, the audience learns the name of the chair but also infers that the chair holds intrinsic value even without knowing a history of chairs.

EAMES LOUNGE CHAIR AND OTTOMAN

More than six decades after its initial creation, the Eames lounge chair and ottoman is still one of the most revered designs. The chair came about with the design world's rejection of the machine aesthetic and a turn toward nature. The dream of "sitting on air" was over, and the advances in technology brought about new innovations in design. Husband and wife Charles and Ray Eames experimented with the new technique of molding plywood, hoping to improve the standard lounge chair.

The result is an expertly crafted, ultracomfortable lounge chair. Charles Eames said that he wanted to design a modern chair that had "the warm receptive look of a well-used first baseman's mitt."[74] The chair was produced by Herman Miller in 1956, and the response was immediately and overwhelmingly positive.

Somewhat ironically, given Frasier's disdain toward anything for the masses, the Eames lounge chair made its debut on national television. On March 14, 1956, NBC's *Home Show* hosted by Arlene Francis featured Charles and Ray to discuss their new chair design.[75] To merely say the lounger is popular is quite an understatement as it has been the subject of documentary films, books, plays, *New Yorker* cartoons, and museum displays, and is featured in the permanent collections at New York's Museum of Modern Art and the Art Institute of Chicago.[76] The chair itself was also the sole subject of an exhibition at the Museum of Art and Design in New York and a book-length catalog in 2006, for the fiftieth anniversary of the initial design and release.[77] The chair has also been featured in many films, such as *Tron Legacy* and *Closer*, as well as other television shows aside from *Frasier*, such as *Gossip Girl*, and knockoff versions have been seen in films and television shows such as *Iron Man* and *House*.

The chair is designed to mold and comfort the body, a sharp contrast to Breuer's chair aspirations of sitting as if nothing is there. "The lounge chair consists of three shells—the headrest, the backrest and the set— each made from five fused layers of plywood plus two layers of Brazilian rosewood veneer. . . . Unusually, too, the upholstery was attached to the chair seat by a zipper."[78] When reviewing the *Eames Chair* exhibit in 2006, *New York Times* writer Roberta Smith described the chair: "With its thick tufted cushions and slightly insectlike structure of three curved, laminated wood shells, it was a strange if not ungainly combination of forthright Modernist structure and unapologetic creature comfort."[79] In regard to the aesthetic look of the chair, you can create your own as the chair and ottoman come in a variety of leathers, veneers, and two sizes.[80] The chair was "conceived to provide welcoming comfort to the body."[81] It is indeed so comfortable that even Martin liked the chair. Eleven years after forcing his beloved Barcalounger into the apartment, Martin finally sits on the Eames chair for the first time. As he does so he remarks, "Mmmm, well this is pretty comfortable. I would have been okay with this."[82] Frasier can only stare at him in horror. Ironically, given that

Martin finally sits in the Eames chair and notes how comfortable it is, when Frasier hurts his back the only place he is able to get comfortable in the apartment is Martin's chair. Niles is horrified that Frasier is sitting in the chair, but Frasier confirms how enjoyable it is and adds, "You know, and when you sit in it, you don't have to look at it."[83] But in regard to the style of the Eames chair, Smith eloquently continues, "Sometimes a chair is just a chair. But sometimes it is more: a luxury item, a symbol of authority, a refuge for mind and body, a design landmark."[84]

Not only is the chair comfortable, but in the design world, it was an instant success and almost immediately "became an icon of American design."[85] The perfect mixture of comfort and modern design, "a cross between a Mercedes-Benz and a Barcalounger, the Eames lounge chair was hailed as innovative from the start and also as a kind of alien."[86] It claimed elite status, and was desired by the elitists themselves, everyone from "captains of industry, college deans, modern-art collectors or architects."[87] However, appropriately for the show and Frasier himself, the chair is frequently linked and promoted as the ideal chair for psychoanalysts. Frasier does not have his own practice throughout the show, aside from the one failed attempt in Season 11, so he does not have his own psychiatrist office in which to have the chair. However, in Season 10 he does take on Kenny, the station manager, as a patient and gives him therapy from his own home. As he does so Kenny lies on his Coco Chanel couch, while Frasier pulls up the Eames chair and reclines fully to listen and take notes as Kenny talks. Interestingly, the one time Frasier has an official, private-practice therapy session that isn't portrayed with humor is also one of the very few times we see him sitting in his Eames chair.

Even though the chair is hardly emphasized throughout the series and Frasier is only seen sitting in it a handful of times, the chair was noticed by viewers, and the impact was an increase in sales that is credited to the hit show.[88] Sharon Overton argues, "Frasier helped fuel a renewed interest in the classic icons of mid-century design, such as Eames and Wassily chairs."[89] As a personal anecdote to demonstrate the impact television shows can have on individuals, Kate has a colleague who has owned an Eames chair for many years and admitted he purchased one without knowing anything else about the chair, simply because he saw it on *Frasier*. He claims the chair provides a heightened sense of confidence and level of luxury to his life, a classic case of when popular culture meets consumer culture.

THE CHAIR

Within this masterpiece set of high-end design, it is Martin's chair that catches the audience's eye, becoming what Christopher calls "the most famous thing in the room" that is filled with work from some of the most iconic designers in history.[90] Many workers behind the scenes acknowledge the effort that went into establishing Martin's chair as an eyesore. Christopher seems to take a particular delight in discussing this "crummy chair," saying that all the early chairs they looked at were too classy, because they really were looking for "a piece of crap" chair and noting that there "wasn't really anything awful enough on the market" for what he and the producers had in mind.[91] Two of the producers, Peter Casey and David Lee, explain that they not only had an especially ugly chair built for the show, they beat it up and made sure it was extra dirty, to contrast to Frasier's clinically clean, modern living space:

> *Peter Casey:* Roy Christopher brought in a huge book of fabric swatches to pick for the chair. And, as hideous as that particular fabric is right there—understand that this book of about a thousand swatches were just variations of that exact same pattern—

> *David Lee:* We didn't think it was bad enough so we added the dirt and the duct tape.[92]

With varying-sized stripes of puce green, dirt brown, and rust red, the chair unavoidably becomes a centerpiece of an apartment that is largely decorated in neutral tans, creams, and shades of beige. Frasier calls the chair a "beer-stained, flea-infested, duct-taped recliner," an "old relic," and an "atrocity" that "blight[s] the environment." Conversely, Martin calls it a "comfortable place to park my fanny" and "the old throne."

Always cognizant of how much the setting can reveal about a character, Christopher took particular delight in inserting Martin's chair into Frasier's carefully designed apartment. The designer said he loves the moment Martin's chair is first brought into this perfect apartment because the contrast says everything about the relationship between Frasier and his dad in one visual. Quesenberry and Sykes discuss this dichotomy as they write, "In *Frasier*, the Eames chair is as much an indication of Frasier Crane's identity as the prosaic recliner is an indication of Martin's identity. It also illustrates the chasm between the two characters regarding education, incomes, experiences, and desires."[93] Frasier ultimately allowed the chair in his home, because he understood it was something Martin needed, yet it is all he gives him decorwise. Martin points out during a fight between Frasier and himself, "I mean look at it, there's nothing of mine around this place except for my chair and you've taken pot shots at that right from the start because it doesn't fit in with your frou-frou knickknacks!"[94] Aside from clothing, the chair, compared to the rest of Frasier's apartment, is the only visual opposition between Martin and Frasier representing their respective social status.

Martin's only concern for the placement of his chair is expressed with the blunt question, "Where's the TV?"[95] Martin wanting it pointed right at the TV is not insignificant, as recliners are synonymous with the invention of the television. Television is decidedly a fixture of mass culture and Frasier values intellectualism and style, so a chair designed to recline in front of a television is antithetical to his decor. The fact that Martin often enjoys casual meals in the chair while watching sports only makes the chair a greater disruption to the type of life Frasier envisioned for himself when moving to Seattle—a life of wine tasting and reading rather than beer swilling and cheering. Further adding to the lower-class aesthetic of the chair is the fact that Martin has patched holes and tears in the fabric with duct tape, what he calls his "re-upholstery kit."[96]

As a centerpiece of the main set on the show, it was natural for the chair to become a touchstone. There is a moment of sadness in the series finale when the chair is wheeled out of Frasier's apartment, something that Tina Fey was inspired by while preparing the finale of her long-running sitcom *30 Rock*:

> We watched a lot of classic TV finales in the writers' room leading up to it at lunch or a break. And as the weeks got closer and closer to ours, it got more emotional. I remember [writer] Tracey Wigfield was crying when they wheeled Frasier's dad's chair out of the apartment. One of the things we learned from them was that it's okay to give your characters an opportunity to actually say goodbye to each other in the body of that episode. You don't have to worry if that's cheesy.[97]

Despite Frasier's endless disdain toward the chair, we know he understands how much it means to Martin (as evidenced by his replacing it when it is accidentally destroyed), and we can see over the course of the series that the chair has come to mean something to him. He may not like the chair, but he has an emotional attachment. As it is being removed from his apartment in the series finale, he calmly states, "Uh, be careful with it,"[98] a strong contrast to the pilot episode when he was begging Niles to be careful with his Wassily.

Objects on TV are not always about the aesthetic but also about what they represent. A closer look at the objects can reveal other meanings, as we "ask for consideration of who the object was made for and why, and for an analysis of the uses and role the object plays in its culture."[99] Why did Frasier want each object? Frasier takes such pride in his "stuff." Material wealth signifies true elitism to him, and he values the cultural significance of each item. Furniture is identified with different classes, such as a Barcalounger being linked with the working class. Not only is this link established with Martin and his chair, but the writers are able to turn it into a ten-year running joke even though it is also a very significant, emotional object. Martin's chair in Frasier's apartment provides the perfect visual for the social, cultural, and economic divide between Martin and Frasier.

SENTIMENTALITY TOWARD OBJECTS

In contrast with Frasier's preference for designer labels and costly objects, Martin loves his chair because of comfort and emotional attachment. His nostalgia for the piece is revealed in a monologue when Frasier attempts to buy a new chair for his father. His father insists he wants his old chair back, and when Frasier challenges him, Martin replies:

> I want the chair I was sitting in when I watched Neil Armstrong take his first step on the moon. And when the U.S. hockey team beat the Russians in the '80 Olympics. I want the chair I was sitting in the night you called me to tell me I had a grandson. I want the chair I was in all those nights, when your mother used to wake me up with a kiss after I'd fallen asleep in front of the television. You know, I still fall asleep in it. And every once in a while, when I wake up, I still expect your

mother to be there, ready to lead me off to bed. . . . Oh, never mind. It's only a chair. [100]

Martin's emotional appeal reveals that his love of the chair is rooted in emotional connections and nostalgia, not in the value a designer's name may add. Martin finds Frasier's tastes to be pointlessly costly, as he demonstrates sentimental attachment to things, while Frasier lacks such emotion about his possessions. To him, his objects are a means to separate him from the "common man" and signify his elitism.

Frasier's predilection for choosing a quality name over his own connection to art is established early in the first season. In the sixth episode, titled "The Crucible," the plot revolves around a painting Frasier has purchased from Martha Paxton. While the series is never hesitant to reference artists from the real world, in this case Paxton is purely fictional, but we are told she is "one of the nation's premier artists." Frasier argues that although the expensive purchase was impractical, it "feed[s] the soul," explaining, "I look at it every day and there's not a moment when I do that I'm not uplifted by its beauty." When he has the opportunity to host Martha Paxton in his home, Frasier waxes eloquent about the impact the painting has had on his life, "The way you insinuate the palette but never lean on it, you capture the *zeitgeist* of our generation. It is the most perfect canvas it has ever been my privilege to gaze upon." However, when Paxton reveals that she did not paint it, that she has never seen it before in her life, Frasier cannot even bring himself to call it a painting anymore, instead only calling it "this . . . thing." Daphne argues that she liked the painting when she first saw it, even before she knew who the painter was, but Frasier is now disgusted with it, not only because he paid for a forgery, but because he has lost the cultural cachet associated with owning an original Paxton. For Frasier, but not for Daphne or Martin, the painting lost all of its aesthetic appeal when it lost the cultural value of a famous artist's name. In the end, unable to return the painting to the unscrupulous gallery where he purchased it, Frasier hangs the painting in his bathroom. [101]

An inversion of this plotline is played out several seasons later, but still reveals Frasier's obsession with the cultural value of a decorative piece rather than his appreciation of any artistic merit. While in Season 1's "The Crucible" Frasier adores a painting that he believes is by an elite artist, in Season 7's "A Tsar Is Born" Frasier suddenly cherishes a previously loathed clock when he discovers it may have been passed down from a royal family. Frasier, Niles, and Martin are shocked that they are interested in the same television show, *Antiques Roadshow*, as Niles deadpans, "I'll just go outside and see if the world has ended." When it is announced *Antiques Roadshow* is coming to Seattle, Martin digs up a small bear statue with a clock in its belly to be appraised. Frasier and Niles are embarrassed that their father thinks the clock might be worth something, and when he asks if they want to be on camera with him while it is examined, they lament, "We can't be seen on TV with that hideous thing." But when the expert says the clock was made for Tsar Alexander II, Frasier and Niles immediately make their way into the camera shot. Upon their return home, Frasier places it in a prominent place for display (it had previously been in a box in Martin's closet). Martin acerbically recognizes that "it doesn't look so bad to you guys now that it's worth twenty-five grand." Frasier offers no rebuttal to Martin's comment, which aligns perfectly with Frasier's argument in the pilot of the series—if you have expensive objects, they will go together even if they don't match. Appropriately, as Frasier and Niles think they are descendants of royalty, Frasier begins to wear purple, a color synonymous with royalty. (The end of the episode reveals they are not, in fact, descendants of royalty, much to the brothers' dismay.)[102]

One of the best episodes for demonstrating attachment to an object, even if the execution of the story is only a mixed success, is the Season 11 episode "Crock Tales." Overall, the concept of this episode is enjoyable. One of the last episodes of the series, it features brief vignettes that progressively flash back further into the series' history, but particularly the hairstyles for Roz and Daphne stick out as poor attempts to recapture earlier looks on the show. The episode explores the sentimental value of an object Frasier doesn't really care for, displaying the power an object can have in our lives over the course of eleven years.

As the finale was a two-part, hour-long episode shown back-to-back, "Crock Tales" is the penultimate episode of the series. Through this we are shown just how far each of the characters has come in regard to their relationships with one another; the narrative is scenes in which a small pottery crock played a small part in some way. The episode opens with Frasier cooking a large meal in his kitchen, while talking on the phone with Charlotte, his current girlfriend. When asked by Charlotte what he is doing that evening, Frasier replies, "Oh nothing, really. I'm having the folks over for dinner. Just the family, and Roz. Well, I've done it a thousand times before." This is something the audience knows to be true, countless times we have seen the Cranes, Daphne, and Roz at dinner, coming back from dinner, or scheduling dinner together. But Frasier's line serves as a counterpoint to the final part of the episode, which flashes back to 1993, showing the first dinner the five characters have together. Frasier is cooking; however, Martin, not wanting to eat duck, orders a pizza for his meal. Upset over this, Frasier pulls Niles into the kitchen and says, "I tell you something, this is the last time I try to make a nice dinner for these people!"

The central object of this episode is an earthenware pot. The small, terra-cotta-colored pot easily fits into an individual's hand. The crock is originally a gift from Martin to Frasier after he had accidentally thrown out what he thought was "moldy cheese" but was Cornish Yarg, which is supposed to be covered in mold. In the opening scene, the crock is holding the wooden spoons and spatulas next to the stove, and as Frasier goes to grab a spoon, a large piece of the pot breaks off. Frasier goes to throw the pot away, but he stops to stare at the pot thoughtfully as the camera slowly zooms in and fades into a scene one year earlier of Martin sitting at the dining table, gluing the pot back together, as the year 2003 pops up on the screen. Frasier tells Martin to stop bothering with gluing it, remarking, "It's just an ugly, worthless pot," calling it Martin's "arts and crafts project." The episode continues to travel backward, highlighting the transitions in friendships over the previous eleven years, in total showing seven different times in the characters' history.[103]

In the end, this episode has strained execution, but the idea that a simple crock can become weighted with nostalgia and meaning is a significant one. Particularly, as *Frasier* was about to come to an end, the exploration of how interactions change what and who we care about is a significant theme for a show that featured a character who often demonstrated hollow conspicuous consumption.

8

GENDER . . . AND RACE?

I'm not one to get bogged down in male/female role-playing.

GENDER ROLES

Frasier often used the audience's established expectations of stereotypical gender roles as a well of potential plotlines and comedy from which the writers regularly drew. Frasier and Niles represent very nontraditional males in their interests and tastes: opera, wine, emotions, fashion, and so forth. In contrast, Martin is placed in the role of the stereotypical male with the interests and behaviors of a masculine man: be a gentleman, be a provider, watch sports, drink beer, never show nor discuss emotions. And the women featured on *Frasier* are strong, independent, and at times, dominant over the men. When it comes to Frasier and Niles and the women in their lives, the show often reverses typical gender roles. Dustin Gann explores the masculinity portrayed in *Frasier*, stating, "A sitcom depicting both the public and private life of an educated, single man surrounded by accomplished and independent women highlights the impacts of second-wave feminism and the possibilities of post-feminist masculinity."[1]

As an example of role reversal, in "The Innkeepers," Frasier and Niles open a restaurant together. As things inevitably go wrong, everyone is forced to help out. Niles acts as head chef and must kill and cook eel. Problematically, he is incapable of killing the eels. After a series of attempts swinging a butcher knife inside the tank of eels, Daphne, who was cleaning dishes (as a woman does), loses patience exclaiming, "Oh, for heaven's sakes!,"[2] grabs an eel by the tail, slams its head on the counter to kill it, then hands it back to a stunned (and emasculated) Niles. This moment is just one of many in which Daphne steps up to take control over the Crane men.

In another episode in Season 8, Niles, Daphne, Frasier, and his date, Chelsea, are all driving in Frasier's BMW when it breaks down. Pulling off to the side of the road, they try to figure out what to do. Frasier's solution is: "All right, let's not panic. Chelsea, if you would, please, open the glove compartment. You will find a flashlight and a small toolkit. Reach behind them, and hand me my cell phone. I'm going to call the auto club."[3] Chelsea responds, stating that her ex-boyfriend used to re-store Corvettes and she could look at the engine, and Daphne acknowl-edges she grew up with eight brothers and learned a thing or two about engines. It is only after the two women take over the traditionally mascu-line role of rescuer that Frasier states he and Niles can handle it. Howev-er, he loses all credibility when attempting to pop the hood, he merely pops the trunk.

There is no better example of role reversal in the show than the per-fectly titled episode "My Fair Frasier." Gann explains, "Dating smart and sexy women frequently presents Frasier with a dilemma that previous generations never faced: what happens when the woman has more power and a higher salary?"[4] The episode begins by falling back on classic gender stereotypes before it goes against them for the remainder of the plot. At a department store Frasier is attempting to return a purse he had given to Roz as a gift. Roz, however, hated it and began crying due to her pregnancy hormones, perpetuating the gender stereotype of a crying preg-nant woman who can't keep it together at work.

In another classic stereotype, at the department store Frasier plays the typical male who is poor at giving gifts to women, having picked out the completely wrong purse. Frasier has to return the gift, and the sales repre-sentative grills Frasier on his relationships, asking if the purse was for his wife, or girlfriend. As Frasier explains it was simply a gift for a friend, the sales representative suggests that there is no friend and the purse was for Frasier himself. Growing frustrated, Frasier begins to speak harshly, causing a beautiful and tall blonde woman to come to his rescue: "Excuse me, sir, I couldn't help overhearing, may I help you out here?" The woman speaks to the sales representative, Jill, on Frasier's behalf by saying, "Yes, but a shrewd saleswoman such as yourself knows that this business isn't about rules, it's about relationships. Now, look at this man, cultured, impeccably dressed, well-to-do, exactly the sort of man you'd love to have a relationship with. Now, there's only one thing standing in the way of that relationship, Jill, he's not happy with his purse." As she continues her argument, Frasier steps back to stand among a group of women in the store, setting up the visual of Frasier and women looking on as this powerful woman takes charge of the situation, dominating the scene as the sales representative agrees to let him return the purse.

Frasier is immediately smitten by this high-powered defense attorney, Samantha Pierce. Pierce goes by "Sam," a typically male and more masculine name in our culture. Frasier immediately asks Sam out to dinner as a thank-you for rescuing him. Initially she declines, but ultimately accepts, saying she would love to have dinner with him. Although Frasier does ask Sam out, a close viewing of the scene makes it clear that Sam is the initiator of the relationship. We first see Sam walking into the store as Frasier is speaking to the sales representative. As Sam walks past Frasier, we see her give him a quick but definite once-over, indicating her attraction toward him. She is then the one to initiate contact as she asks if she can help him.

In Frasier's self-centered worldview, he is concerned that Sam will be overwhelmed by his "celebrity status." When disclosing such thoughts to his family, he even states, "When I asked her out, I sensed a bit of shyness which made me wonder if she was perhaps intimidated by my fame." Martin then turns their attention to the TV showing an interview between Sam and Larry King. In the interview, King points out Sam is currently in Seattle to defend the "butcher knife killer," a seemingly important topic; however, the conversation quickly turns to whom Sam has been seen dating recently, such as Kevin Costner, George Stephanopoulos, and Brad Pitt. Despite her being a "noted attorney," a part of what seems to be a high-profile case, King just wants to discuss her romantic life. Would he have asked the same questions if Sam were a man? Arguably, he would have not.

While on their date, after attempting to make awkward small talk, Sam announces she wants to skip dinner to go have sex. Frasier briefly demurs before eagerly agreeing. Yet again Sam takes on the more dominant role over Frasier. Throughout the episode we are shown examples of Frasier taking the more submissive and stereotypical "girl" role. Sam is always being pulled away for work while Frasier is left behind a little bit upset, once particularly because of the meal they never ate that he was in the process of cooking. Frasier feels that something is off in the relationship, to which Niles gently tries to explain, "I might venture a theory at which you're sure to hoot! What may be making you uncomfortable is that for the first time you find yourself in a more submissive role." When Frasier seems baffled by his comment, Daphne bluntly chimes in, "I think what he means is—you're the girl!" Frasier has a shocked look on his face while Niles continues to list reasons why: "How did you two first meet? She came to your rescue. Who initiated the first sexual encounter? She did." This causes Martin to shriek, "She did?! For God's sake, who's wearing the pants in this relationship?!"

The reversal in typical gender roles continues as Sam has to leave for work, and the couple squabbles over Sam always having to leave and saying she will call but never actually calling—the joke is funny because that's how men are often depicted on sitcoms and in popular culture in general. Frasier is a little upset as she leaves, but moments later Sam returns with a giant bouquet of roses for Frasier, saying, "I saw a guy out on the street selling these, I thought they might cheer you up," before she quickly runs off again. Frasier is appeased for the time being with the gift of flowers from her. Daphne points out that this is all typical male behavior portrayed by Sam, saying, "Look, if it's any consolation, I know what you're going through. Women have been putting up with it for generations. Men say they'll call and they don't, or you get a few nice dinners and then the eventual booty call." Frasier is slightly horrified to learn that he has fallen into this role.

The most drastic juxtaposition of male versus female gender roles occurs at a work party for Sam, in which she must leave Frasier to be on a conference call with other attorneys from her firm, leaving Frasier to converse with all the wives, fiancées, and girlfriends of the other attorneys. Frasier effortlessly fits in with them, admiring their own jewelry and chatting about their partners' lack of time to spend on the relationship but always giving gifts. One of the wives, Jennifer, explains, "There's always another trial, but you'll get used to the life. Dates get cancelled, dinners left uneaten but at least you'll get sent plenty of flowers." It is then that one of the other wives, Cindy, sums up what can be considered the theme of the entire episode as she responds, "Oh, Jennifer, he's a man, he won't get flowers."

This causes Frasier to bring up their male and female roles with Sam. "Well, er, look, I'm not one to get bogged down in male/female role-playing, it's just that lately, well . . . the way that you cancel dates all the time and say you'll call and you don't call, and then you have your secretary send me a gift and then when I get upset about it, you think you can buy me off with flowers." Sam calls out Frasier for "whining" as she argues back, "I'm in the middle of the most intense case of my entire career . . . and you're whining about flowers?" Frasier tries to explain how he feels and Sam asks, "Do you want to be the traditional man, and I'll be the put-upon woman?," shrewdly pointing out just how ridiculous the standard gender roles in our society can be.[5]

This role reversal is reflected in the outfits worn throughout the episode. In twenty-two short minutes, clothing and jewelry portray an entire narrative on stereotypical gender norms. Throughout the episode Frasier is often seen in more casual clothes, including a scene at his apartment, in which Frasier is in the kitchen cooking in a blue apron. Sam has short cropped hair and is seen always in a business suit jacket and skirt, being sure to show off her legs throughout the episode. In the following episode, which features a continuation of their relationship, there is a scene out on the streets in Seattle: it is clearly cold as both Frasier and Sam are in large coats. However, Sam is wearing a long trench coat open so she still has her legs on display. In his essay "The Suit: A Common Bond or Defeated Purpose?," Lee Wright describes how the suit is about hierarchy and status, in which the perceived message is equal to if not more important than the overall style of the garment.[6] By wearing a suit, the individual is making a statement of power. In this case, the woman, Samantha, is indeed asserting her power by wearing a female version of the business suit, with a jacket and skirt, yet she still shows off her legs for the male gaze. She is only ever seen in black and red suits, both colors considered to be a symbol of power and assertiveness.

Jewelry comes into play throughout the episode as well. While waiting for his date, Frasier sits on his couch as Daphne walks by, pointing out he must have a "special evening planned." Frasier assumes she knows this due to his "incredible self-confident air"; however, Daphne states she knows this because "your silver collar pin, you only wear it when you've got a hot date." Frasier has specific jewelry he wears for dates; Sam, in contrast, wears at most only minimal jewelry. Accessories continue to play an important part throughout the episode when in a later scene Sam comments how much she likes his tie. Frasier replies, "Oh, as well you should, you sent it to me," even though Sam clearly does not recognize picking out the tie. Frasier then assumes her secretary picked out the tie. Sam confirms it as she mentions "only because he has better taste than I do," emphasizing another stereotypical gender reversal—one might easily assume a secretary picking out clothing for the boss's significant other would be a woman shopping for a woman. Later at the same party Sam gives Frasier a Cartier watch when she feels bad about how busy she has been lately. At first Frasier claims that she cannot just give him a gift to make up for how she has treated him; however, when Frasier sees it is a gift from Cartier he forgives her immediately. When explaining why she is giving him this particular watch, Sam states, "Well, the other day, when we were at the store, you mentioned that you liked something and, well, typical me, I just ran right out and bought it." This reveals that she makes more than enough money to go out and buy a Cartier watch on a whim—for reference, current Cartier watches on their website range from $5,600 to $156,000.[7] Although this episode is from 1997, factoring in inflation, Sam still spent at least a couple thousand on the watch for Frasier. After receiving the watch, Frasier returns to all the other women and proudly shows it off. By the end of the episode, Frasier is at peace with the role reversal in the relationship he experiences with Sam.[8]

Although not as strongly emphasizing gender roles, the following episode does continue to explore their relationship. In "Desperately Seeking Closure," Sam ends their brief relationship after a skiing trip, giving him the "it's not you, it's me" speech. Frasier cannot handle being dumped by her; however, it becomes clear it is less about her and more about the loss of the lifestyle. We know this is continually a goal of Frasier's, as a few seasons later he openly admits, "All my life, I have dreamed of being half of a power couple."[9] In attempts to win Sam back, Frasier chases after her, calls her constantly, listens to her messages on her machine, even goes to find her outside her work. It is all as cringeworthy as it seems. Frasier becomes a borderline stalker in this episode, especially when he listens to her phone messages and then deletes them. But he is not stalking her, but rather her lifestyle. However, patriarchal order is restored at the end of their relationship, with Sam realizing how wonderful Frasier is. Sam tells him:

Halloween role-playing: Roz as Wonder Woman, Frasier as Sigmund Freud, Daphne as Elton John, Niles as Martin Crane, and Martin as Joe DiMaggio. © *NBC; NBC/ Photofest*

I was going to call you later anyway. You see, I think I figured out what happened between the two of us. I panicked. You see, I was starting to really care about you. I thought we might even have a future, even, and, well, it scared me. But the way you pursued me, showing up at the courthouse and leaving all of those messages and now you're here. Obviously, you feel just as strongly as I do. It's funny really. The both of us falling in love so fast and not realizing the other one felt the same way. We should be laughing.[10]

Unfortunately for Sam, Frasier was only using Sam for her social connections. After she confesses to him her mistake and how she feels, he informs her that he likes her, but with perhaps the wrong intentions. Frasier admits to her, "I'm not very proud of this, but maybe I was a little dazzled by the circle you travel in."[11] Frasier did care for the woman, yet he cared more how he could benefit from her. The scenario the writers create around this is humorous, but they could have just left her dumping him, solidifying the role reversal further. On the whole, though, this episode of *Frasier* points out the ridiculousness of such gendered stereotypes of "traditional" male and female roles.

These reversals of masculinity often call into question Frasier's and Niles's sexuality. Gann also states in his essay, "Frasier displays several of the most common homosexual stereotypes: he is single and middle aged, he prefers intellectual pursuits over physical endeavors, his elite education separates him from the masses, and his knowledge of fashion and decor heightens the value he places on appearance."[12] Pierce acknowledges that a lot of their behavior, such as wine tasting and going to the opera, was "seen as gay by a lot of people."[13] And "despite no regularly appearing homosexual characters, plotlines on Frasier routinely highlight the mutability of gender roles, the fallibility of common homosexual stereotypes, and broadening acceptance of homosexual lifestyles."[14] A few times it was even joked that Niles had now become a woman and the news was not a surprise to former acquaintances who had known him.[15] The series features multiple episodes that explore and question all the Cranes' sexuality; however, this is always done as a plot point, and is neither derogatory nor demonizing of homosexuals. The show was progressive for its time in that it did not paint being gay in a negative light, it merely presented the reality that there are gay people in the world. By highlighting that these explicitly heterosexual characters have traits that are broadly, stereotypically seen as indicators of homosexuality, the series undercuts and subverts those same stereotypes. Pierce, as a gay man himself, points out, "It was never jokes at the expense of gay people. We had gay people on staff. David Lee, one of the creators on the show is gay and so, to me, it was always acknowledging the preposterousness of stereotypes."[16] Particularly for a farce episode, homosexuality became another option for misunderstanding who was attracted to whom, not the butt of a joke.

The series most directly addresses the issue of Frasier's sexuality in the episode "The Impossible Dream" in which Frasier seriously questions if he is homosexual or not after having a recurring dream of finding himself in a hotel room bed with his colleague Gil Chesterton. When Frasier asks Martin if he ever thought Frasier could be homosexual, in the perfect display of compassion and humor so typical of *Frasier*, Martin remarks, "All right. Yeah . . . okay, yeah, I thought about it. But no, Frasier, no, I don't believe that. And you know why? Because you would have known by now. Your unconscious or whatever the hell you call it could no more have kept its yap shut than the rest of you."[17] The episode explores Frasier questioning the idea himself, but he is never upset at the notion, merely confused by what his subconscious is telling him at this point in his life.

In the Season 2 episode "The Matchmaker," the series' first episode with a gay farce, Frasier wants to set up Daphne with his new boss Tom by inviting him to dinner at his apartment. Unknown to Frasier, Tom is gay and thinks that Frasier has asked him out. Hilarity ensues as the misunderstanding spirals—Daphne becomes interested in Tom, with Frasier attempting to help her but all the while leading on Tom further. When Frasier discovers the truth he comments, "What on earth could have made him think that I was interested in him? All I did was ask him if he was attached, and then we talked about the theater and men's fashions and oh, my God."[18] Frasier realizes he participates in many interests society has deemed "gay"; however, even with this realization he has no desire to change these interests. Critic Louis Peitzman points out, "The truly amazing thing about 'The Matchmaker' is how casually everyone handles the confusion. OK, Frasier's not thrilled about coming across gay, but he's not horrified either."[19] And neither are Niles or Martin as they each laugh heartily when it is revealed to both of them, and they find joy in the scenario. As Niles informs Frasier of the truth, he tells him, "There's something I have to tell you. Dad wanted to but I won the coin toss."[20] Peitzman continues explaining, "And while Tom's advances are played for laughs, he's not the butt of the jokes. Instead, Frasier's the idiot for ignoring the obvious and leading his guest on."[21] When Frasier finally tells Tom the truth he says, "Don't take this wrong, but it never even occurred to me that you might be gay." Tom immediately replies, "Well, it never even occurred to me that you might be straight."[22] The episode earned a GLAAD Media Award for Best Comedy Episode, given its "lighthearted, inoffensive tone."[23] Homosexuality is used as another option to increase confusion in farces, not as the joke being "someone is gay" as happened too often in earlier entertainment eras.

It is important to note that this episode aired in 1994 addressing a topic that was treated far more conservatively at the time than it is now. In a 2015 interview, Pierce acknowledged this change regarding society, saying, "The way they perceived gay culture, how straight men reacted to it, and the humor around it was completely a product and a reflection of the time,"[24] and suggests those same jokes wouldn't play out the same today.[25] Over the past two decades there has been a clear growth in how homosexuality is perceived on television. The *New York Times* writer Brian Stelter comments, "The cultural battlefield of television has changed markedly since the 1990s, when conservative groups and religious figures objected to Ellen DeGeneres coming out and *Will & Grace* coming on."[26] The power of such a format is that "sitcoms address significant ideas and issues within seemingly innocuous narrative frames."[27] TV has the ability to present ideas before they are truly accepted in culture. Popular culture, particularly television, as it is intimately viewed in our own homes, often prepares society for the next thing.[28] Edward Schiappa, a professor of communication studies at the University of Minnesota, states, "TV and movie representation matters."[29] A study performed by Mr. Schiappa and his colleagues regarding the presence of gay characters on TV found that with such characters there is a decrease in the "prejudices among viewers of the programs."[30] Mr. Schiappa notes, "These attitude changes are not huge—they don't change bigots into saints. But they can snowball." Creator Christopher Lloyd, when discussing his latest show, *Modern Family*, which features a gay couple, notes, "What this is about, really, is how far America has come, not how far television has come."[31]

The lighthearted portrayal of homosexuality is a common theme throughout *Frasier*, as many of the series' best and well-written farces centered around cases of mistaken sexual identity: this was indeed deliberate as Joe Keenan, a writer and eventual executive producer on the show, says:

> I don't know that I had any impact on the characters individually because it's an extremely collaborative form, but I certainly did push the show towards exploring comical, farcical gay themes. I think more than anything, my contribution to that show was to import farce story-

telling into it, because they hadn't done a farce the first season. The
first show I produced was "The Matchmaker," which was a very farci-
cal story. . . . And people liked that episode a lot. It won a GLAAD
award; it was nominated for an Emmy. It became part of the repertoire
of the show that they would on occasion play with farce.[32]

The series goes on to feature three other episodes of mistaken sexual
identity. In the episode "The Ski Lodge," the episode is spent at a ski
weekend at a cabin in which everyone is pursuing someone, with no two
people pursuing each other, including the guest ski instructor, Guy (pro-
nounced Gui), who assumes Niles is gay. Guy even discusses this subject
with Martin, who misunderstands him, resulting in him pursuing Niles,
and questioning, "This is not a delicate subject for you?" When the truth
unfolds, ending with the classic line, "I am not gay, Guy,"[33] Niles is not
upset at the assumption, merely needing to clarify the situation.

In the episode "Out with Dad" it is Martin who is presumed to be gay.
Frasier forces Martin to attend an opera with him as he hopes to ask out a
specific woman. The woman, Emily, is with her mother, who takes an
interest in Martin. Although Frasier and Emily hit it off, Martin allows
the mother to believe he is gay instead of turning her down when she asks
him out. However, Martin is then set up with Emily's gay uncle when
they are invited over to Frasier's apartment. Unaware of the setup, Martin
continues to "gay it up a little"[34] instead of admitting the truth. Martin's
concern in the episode comes not from being assumed gay but from not
wanting to offend their guests.

And in the episode "The Doctor Is Out," we see the most direct example of one of the characters accidentally assumed to be gay as Frasier
finds himself in a relationship with the head of the Opera Guild, Alistair
Burke (played masterfully by Patrick Stewart). While Frasier assumes (or
tries to convince himself) it is just friendship between himself and Alistair, it quickly becomes apparent that Alistair has other intentions. Frasier
continues in the relationship as he loves the social status he is gaining
through his association with Alistair, as he tells Niles, "All my life, I have
dreamed of being half of a power couple, and I finally am! Is it perfect?
No. But it's fun, and I don't want it to end."[35] Frasier ultimately ends the
relationship because he knows he can't give Alistair the relationship he
wants, not because it would bother him for others to assume he is gay.
While there are numerous other gay references and assumptions throughout the show, these are the main episodes featuring a gay farce setup. All

four episodes were written by Joe Keenan and directed by David Lee, both openly gay men.

WOMEN ON FRASIER

As a whole, the show promotes powerful women. Two of the five main cast are women and, considering the show is about a family of father and sons, that is a fairly high percentage. Roz is a very successful career woman, who remains a single mother from Season 5 on, and ends the series being promoted to station manager for KACL. Daphne is a tough Brit who holds her own living with two generally different but similarly strong-willed men.

Roz and another recurring character, Lilith, are both single mothers who are generally praised, not questioned, for the role they're undertaking. This stands out particularly because when *Frasier* premiered in 1993 it was only one year removed from a very loud national conversation about single mothers on sitcoms. Of course, if any criticism had been levied it should have been directed against Frasier, who was what critic Andy Greenwald calls "a deadbeat dad of the first order" because "he moved across the country to get as far away from [his son] as humanly possible without having to use his passport."[36] Of course, that conversation never seemed to have surfaced. But, one year earlier, as Ray Richmond explains, "Anyone who wasn't living in a climate-controlled subterranean geodesic dome will recall the furor in May 1992 that swirled around the birth of a baby boy to neurotic Murphy Brown (Candice Bergen) in *Murphy Brown*. Murph's rejection of marriage proposals from both potential fathers set off a firestorm of controversy that extended clear to the White House."[37] In 1992, while giving a speech to a group Bonnie J. Dow calls "an elite political group dominated by white men," Vice President Dan Quayle spoke about marriage being "the best anti-poverty program of all" before lamenting that "it doesn't help matters when prime-time TV has Murphy Brown—a character who supposedly epitomizes today's intelligent, highly paid, professional woman—mocking the importance of fathers by bearing a child alone and calling it just another 'lifestyle choice.'"[38]

From this pop culture reference embedded inside a lengthy political speech a national debate was born. Quayle's remarks, and remember this is the vice president giving a campaign speech to a political group, became a major story. As Dow enumerates, Quayle's quote made the front pages of the *New York Times* and *USA Today* and was the lead story on the most popular nightly news program at the time, ABC's *World News Tonight.* And for a time, Quayle was peppered at every campaign stop with questions about *Murphy Brown.*[39] *Frasier* producers were unfazed and, though Frasier takes many jabs at Lilith, none of them have to do with her role as Frederick's mother. Similarly when Roz decides to have her baby and raise it herself, it is with the full support of Frasier. Martin does make the ironic observation, undoubtedly a jab at calls for the "good old days" of moral families to which the *Murphy Brown* plot had given rise: "Boy, things have really changed since my day. Back then, if a girl got in trouble, her family would send her away to relatives in another state, and if anybody asked, just lied and said she went to Europe. Then when she came back, they'd raise the baby as a little sister. Not like today—we had morals and values back then."[40]

However, the series does explore the idea of strong women over the more traditionally portrayed stronger men. In the Season 8 episode "Docu.Drama," Frasier is so used to being the boss that when Roz is given her own project and is the boss he has a hard time accepting the role reversal. This isn't necessarily because Roz is a woman, however, but possibly because Frasier seeks to dominate and have total control over all aspects of his life. He does not collaborate well (not even with Niles). Roz was aware of the potentially uncomfortable situation this might create, as she asks Frasier, "Well, actually I was gonna ask you, but I was afraid it might be kind of awkward, you working for me. I mean, you've been my boss for eight years. I just wasn't sure if you could handle it." Frasier, ever the one to assume he is self-aware and can handle such things, replies, "I welcome a little role reversal, I think it'll do our relationship a lot of good." Neither of them handle this shift in power well. Frasier has difficulty letting Roz take control, and Roz equally has a hard time hearing any suggestions Frasier has on the project. Both are wounded by the other's lack of acceptance of the change. The episode concludes with both of them yelling at each other in the KACL booth blaming the other for what they had done; however, both were clearly in the wrong. Frasier ultimately points out, "I'll admit that maybe I was being a little too assertive, all right? But the least you could do is admit that perhaps you were a bit defensive?"[41]

Occasionally the show does simply disregard or belittle women for humor. In Season 2, Frasier helps Roz by praising her work and career but gives her advice and ultimately brings it back to the idea that she needs a man in her life. "Maybe you're just looking for too much from your job. Start exploring other areas of your life. Interests. Maybe a serious relationship?"[42] And in Season 11, Martin refers to Roz as "Frasier's secretary." A dismissive description considering she is his producer and has been for over a decade at this point and in a few episodes will be promoted to station manager.

In Season 6, Frasier and Niles all but ignore Roz and her problem while at the café as they're discussing Niles's problem. Niles is desperate to win the Golden Apron from his gourmet club and must compete by hosting a dinner party. Niles explains how badly he wants to win: "After the year I've been through, I needed something to restore my pride, my dignity, my manhood. That Golden Apron could do it." As Niles is currently living at the Shangri-La during his divorce, he simply cannot host the "cream of Seattle's gourmet set" there. He brings his dilemma to Frasier, who is seated with Roz as Niles unloads his troubles. Frasier takes genuine concern as he says, "Let's give this some thought. Every problem has a solution." Roz argues that it is not an actual problem: "Do you call that a problem? A problem is when your kid keeps you up three nights in a row with colic, and you're so burned out you rear-end a Lexus, with four passengers, each and every one a lawyer, so you'll probably be sued and spend the rest of your working life, if you ever even *get* a job, lining the pockets of four blood-sucking, whiplash-faking fat cats. *That's* what a problem is." Frasier and Niles both ignore her as Frasier simply continues asking questions regarding the rules of Niles's dinner. Roz leaves the table, saying, "Thanks for the sympathy!" as Niles asks, "Sympathy for what?" Frasier dismissively replies, "Oh, I don't know, she broke a nail." Frasier is not wrong, she did in fact break a nail in the beginning of the scene, and the joke of ignoring Roz's problem is funny; however, they are literally ignoring the complaints of a single mother and her legitimate struggle to focus on Niles's frivolous issue.[43]

Despite the strong females on the show it is a strong reflection of the 1990s in how aggressively and inappropriately many of the men treat women. For Kate, the coauthor of this book and young female professional working in a male-dominated office, it is horrifying to watch how the men treat the women at KACL. Frasier's colleague, Bulldog, serves as the extreme male counterpoint to Frasier as the host of a sports show and a quintessential "dumb jock." Gann explains, "Characters like Derek Mann and Bulldog, who exude exaggerated physicality and heterosexuality, remind *Frasier* viewers that traditional masculinity continues to exist within contemporary society."[44] Bulldog is particularly disrespectful, and seemingly that is what his character was written for: in Season 3, regarding the new station manager being a woman, Bulldog asks, "Hey, first things first. Is she baggable?"[45] In a Season 6 episode, after all the employees at KACL are hired back at the station, in celebration Bulldog grabs an attractive coworker as she walks by and bends her over to kiss her. She slaps him in disgust, but that is the end of that. And in Season 11, Bulldog comments regarding a new woman hired in the office, "New chick. So-so face, a little big in the can."[46] However, at times Frasier is just as disrespectful as Bulldog, as there are multiple instances of him hitting on his coworkers,[47] hiring an associate openly with the intent of sleeping with her,[48] and kissing a random woman as he pleases.[49] The nineties must have been such a different time because today many of their actions would end up in sexual harassment complaints.

After ten years the show finally addresses sexual harassment in the office in the episode "The Harassed." Frasier is arguing with his new coworker Julia, a beautiful blonde financial consultant who takes a few minutes of Frasier's show each day to give a stock market update. Despite Julia being a cold and unfriendly woman, Frasier begins to take an interest in her. The two end up in a fight and begin calling each other names: "Magic Eight Ball with a Harvard degree," "half-educated, money-grubbing parvenu," "foreign-speaking windbag," "insecure fraud," "pompous blowhard," "harridan," "know-it-all," "shrew," and "snob." Suddenly Frasier grabs her by the arms saying, "Are you as turned on as I am?," causing Julia to shriek, "What! Oh! Did you just come on to me?"[50] The scene is a deliberate homage to a moment in Season 3 between Frasier and the new station manager Kate Costas (so similar, there's even some of the same insults) in which Frasier is in her office trying to get the promised raise for his coworkers. The two begin arguing and yelling insults back and forth: "arrogant gasbag," "intractable despot," "blowhard," "tyrant," "ass," "shrew," ending with the two sharing a kiss and beginning a doomed relationship.[51]

As a result of Frasier's comment to Julia this time, the entire staff of KACL is required to attend a sexual harassment seminar on a Saturday, much to everyone's displeasure. Given the comments and actions both Frasier and Bulldog have said and done throughout the series this incident seems almost the least offensive interaction to result in a sexual harassment meeting. Also, the consequences of his actions are seemingly dismissed as he does not seem to grasp why they are there; rather, he blames his misinterpreting her hostility for attraction and continues to accuse her, saying, "That's all there is to you. Ever since you arrived at this station we have reached out to you in friendship and all we've gotten in return is arrogance and unbridled rudeness."[52] Rather than Frasier learning from the situation, the scene ends with Julia promising she will not sue the station, allowing the staff to conclude their sexual harassment training without very much training.

Interestingly, the Frasier and Julia exchange also mirrors the *Cheers* moment in the Season 1 finale, in which Sam and Diane argue and Sam asks the same question: "Are you as turned on right now as I am?" Diane gives the opposite of Julia's response when she yells, "More!"[53] and the two share their first passionate kiss. Later in the *Frasier* episode during their sexual harassment course, when asked what Frasier did wrong, Bulldog comments, "People stopped saying 'turned on' twenty years ago."[54] The *Cheers* Season 1 finale was in March 1983; this episode of *Frasier* aired in February 2003. In 2017, the world is in a different place than when the *Cheers* episode aired. While the callback is remarkably clever, and the plot demonstrates that Frasier was in the wrong, his treatment of a female coworker deserved more repercussions then the staff just making sure nobody would get sued.

RACE

Frasier has a race problem. It actually has more than one race problem. The first is the almost complete absence of any characters of color on the show. The second is the almost universally stereotypical or antagonistic roles of any characters of color who do appear. Of course, anyone familiar with television history could almost assume such if told "*Frasier* was an NBC sitcom that aired in the 1990s." The series was part of a legendary era of NBC sitcoms, a golden age of the genre. But it was not a golden age of racial inclusivity.

At the same time *Frasier* was a hit for the network, *Seinfeld* and *Friends*, two of the most popular shows in the history of television, were airing. Both sitcoms were set in New York City, one of the most diverse cities in America, and both featured all-white casts. It should also be acknowledged that *Frasier* was also a spin-off of *Cheers*, a show where every single recurring character during its run was white.

Many noted the lack of racial representation on sitcoms in the 1990s. In the 2010 book *American Culture in the 1990s*, Colin Harrison looks back at the decade in hindsight and identifies the "glaring imbalance of racial representation in sitcoms."[55] But the issue was so blatant that no hindsight was needed to spot it. The lack of representation for people of color, particularly on network sitcoms, was being acknowledged and criticized even as it was happening. A 1996 article by Jonathan Storm examines race in sitcoms and reveals that "less than one-fifth of the season's network sitcoms have had racially mixed casts. More than half the dramas, however, have put black and white people together."[56] The same article quotes Sasha Torres, a professor of modern culture and media, arguing that many of the sitcoms of the time "figuratively and narratively [tried] to make urban spaces safe for white people."[57]

A *New York Times* article by James Sterngold from 1998 highlights not only the lack of diversity on NBC's most popular shows but also the resultant divide in the viewing habits of households. Sterngold notes that the 1997–1998 season of *Seinfeld*, the most watched show in white households, was only the fiftieth most watched show in black households, while *Between Brothers* was the most watched show in black households but the 112th most watched show in white households. A similar divide was appearing in the 1998–1999 season when *Friends* was the number one show in white households but the ninety-first among black households while *The Steve Harvey Show* was the most popular show in black households but the 118th most watched show in white households.[58]

According to Sterngold, in the 1990s shows became increasingly segregated, with most prime-time slots on major networks going to shows with entirely white casts. Shows with primarily black talent behind the scenes and in front of the camera were often asked to "broaden their appeal," which was taken as coded language for making the show more white. Network executives defended themselves by pointing out that their dramas such as *ER* or *Homicide: Life on the Street* were much more integrated than their comedy lineups. They also noted that they were simply meeting audience demand. Sterngold states that executives "are business people, not social reformers, and they maintained that there was generally little resistance from audiences to the trend of racial polarization, and thus little incentive to fight it."[59]

Consider the sitcoms that populated NBC's "Must See TV" lineup of the 1990s. This Thursday night lineup of shows was a ratings juggernaut for NBC and was primarily anchored by *Friends* at 8:00 p.m., *Seinfeld* at 9:00 p.m., and the drama *ER* at 10:00 p.m. (EST). In the 8:30 and 9:30 slots were a constantly rotating group of sitcoms that were put into time slots where they were almost guaranteed huge ratings and then moved to other time slots where it was hoped audiences would follow them. Among the shows launched in the in-between time slots were *Wings* (1990), *Frasier* (1993), *Caroline in the City* (1995), *Suddenly Susan* (1996), *Veronica's Closet* (1997), and *Just Shoot Me* (1997). There were also many other shows that only lasted one or two seasons that premiered in those time slots. What is universal about these sitcoms is that they feature primarily white casts, with many of them being exclusively white.

On *Frasier*, the first recurring character of color is Marta, Niles's maid. Hailing from Guatemala, Marta not only inhabits a stereotypical role for Latinos, hired help for a wealthy white family, her defining trait is speaking broken English. Her inability to speak English fluently is mined for laughs and used to drive plotlines when miscommunication is necessary,[60] though, in at least one instance, it is Frasier who mistranslates something into Spanish to escalate the humor.

In the early seasons, most of the characters of color who are seen are the waitresses at Café Nervosa who serve Frasier and Niles their coffee. There are a few other examples, such as Bulldog's producer for *The Gonzo Sports Show*. Later seasons see two recurring antagonists for Frasier, both of whom are African American. Mary is a loud, streetwise woman who takes over Frasier's radio show when he asks her to fill in for Roz for one week. Frasier found Mary "at a program called 'Second Start.' They offer career training for people who are stuck in tedious, low-paying jobs."[61] This storyline is loaded with stereotypes about lower-class African Americans, sassy African American women, and white guilt/political correctness creating more problems than it solves. Mary appears in one more episode, and derails one of Frasier's lifelong dreams with her overbearing personality.[62]

The other recurring African American character, Cam Winston, at least breaks away from the "lower-class" and "street-speak" stereotypes present in the Mary episodes. Cam is decidedly a problematic presence in Frasier's life, but he lives in and above Frasier's social standing and elite economic spheres. Perhaps the most progressive moment in terms of race representation in the series comes unexpectedly from Martin, who is often portrayed as being from a less enlightened generation when it comes to social issues. As a joke Martin and Cam Winston's mother pretend to be dating, but it becomes more serious. Other than one episode in which Frasier pursues an Asian woman and one in which Daphne flirts with an African American man, this is the only interracial relationship seen in the entire series.

Frasier's overwhelmingly white cast and worldview were indicative of most American network sitcoms in the 1990s. The context of the time period when it was created is important for understanding these issues, but if *Frasier* earns praise for never making homosexuality into a punch line, it also warrants some criticism for demonstrating very little effort to embrace racial diversity.

CONCLUSION

"Goodnight, Seattle!"

High-quality writing. A brilliant ensemble. Excellent directing. And, of course, catching lightning in a bottle that allows all the talent in front of and behind the camera to come together and make something even better than the sum of its parts. Television history is littered with failed series that had the first three ingredients but missed the fourth. *Frasier* luckily had all of the above.

There is still something more to *Frasier* that makes it endure. Some of it is a timelessness to the stories, as very few of the episodes are rooted in a specific moment in time. Some of it is the style of humor, which isn't observational to a specific cultural moment, but rather rooted in specific characters and more universal issues of family and human interactions. But perhaps what makes *Frasier* great is that underneath the smart writing and behind the transcendent acting there is an eleven-year-long theme that still resonates. The theme may not be revolutionary—it can be found in many, many other narratives—but that is because it is so significant a theme. *Frasier* is about the importance of warm, caring relationships and how those, more than the food you love or the entertainment you enjoy or the wealth you accumulate, add joy to your life.

Saying goodnight. Standing: David Hyde Pierce, Kelsey Grammer, and John Mahoney; seated: Jane Leeves and Peri Gilpin. © *NBC; Photographer: Greg Gorman; NBC/Photofest*

When the show begins, every character is in a worse off place than where they end, and primarily what is lacking for each is a happy relationship. Not a romantic relationship, but a warm, loving relationship of any kind. There is a famous study performed at Harvard called the Grant Study, which has been going for seventy-five years, collecting data on a group of men as they age to determine what factors lead to a healthy life. George Vaillant, who has directed the study for several decades, insists that there is a "powerful correlation between the warmth of your relationships and your health and happiness in old age."[1] To summarize the results of this massive, decades-long study, Vaillant says, "Happiness is love. Full stop."[2] That can also summarize the lessons presented in eleven seasons of *Frasier*.

In the pilot, Frasier is recently divorced and has moved across the country from his son and all his friends from *Cheers*. Niles is in a loveless marriage that seems to offer him little in the way of physical or emotional intimacy and seems to rarely even provide companionship. Besides literally never being seen together, there are frequent jokes to Maris sleeping in a separate room and taking long trips without Niles. Martin is a widower who does hang out at the bar and has his faithful Eddie, but lives alone and has no strong filial relationships. Roz has many romantic partners, but from the first season on makes comments about hoping to find a long-term relationship rather than her frequent short-lived flings. And Daphne has left her home country, and from what the audience learns through her hilariously absurd monologues and then through meeting them in later seasons, she has a strained relationship with her parents and siblings.

When these lonely characters begin engaging with each other in the first season, little seems to improve. Niles and Frasier barely see each other even though they live in the same city. Frasier and Martin literally cannot have a conversation. Frasier can't stand Daphne. Frasier and Roz have a cold professional relationship only. Roz and Niles only bicker (when Niles remembers who she is).

Contrast that with the finale eleven years later and their emotional good-byes, and it's clear that every character is happier, each one is a better person, and each one has healthier relationships because they value family and friendship despite their differences in taste and lifestyle. Family matters, warm relationships make life better, and strengthening filial bonds is worth the effort. These are not revolutionary concepts, but to be presented in a humorous manner without being saccharine and in the face of more cynical shows that had become common is a feat worth recognizing.

THE EPISODES

An Opinionated Compendium

The following is our subjective opinion about all 264 episodes of *Frasier* on a 4-star scale. Undoubtedly different viewers have their own reactions and may think we're giving too much credit to some episodes and are being unfair to others. In total, we gave fifty-five episodes 4-star ratings, a full 20.8 percent of the series. Conversely, we gave twenty-nine episodes, 10.9 percent of the series, a 1-star rating.

An example of the flaw that may result in a 1-star episode is seen in the Season 11 episode "A Man, a Plan and a Gal: Julia." Frasier is dating an immensely unlikable woman named Julia and during a game of Pictionary she clearly begins to choke on a peanut, but Martin, Niles, and Daphne all pretend not to notice. These three characters are willing to watch a woman die because she is unpleasant. This is problematic not only because they have, to this point, been generally moral and likable human beings, but it is literally a police officer, a health care worker, and a doctor who are ignoring a threat to life in the very room where they are sitting. This behavior was simultaneously so unlikable and out of character that it resulted in one of the very worst episodes of the series.

A 4-star episode provides genuine laughs but also has thematic unity and substance. For example, "The Innkeepers" sees Frasier and Niles buy a restaurant and seamlessly maintains a thematic focus while ensuring each scene is legitimately funny. The writers found organic ways to align seemingly random bits of comedy around a theme, specifically the question "What do we do with old things?" This theme gets kicked off with Gil Chesterton describing why the restaurant is closing: "Well, the owner's getting old, he wants to sell. And just between us, I'm afraid Orsini's a bit like wine that's stayed too long in the cellar. It retains only memories of its former glory."

The theme carries through when Niles visits the station. Writers had to give a "bit of business" to Niles as a reason for him to stop by the radio station—he had a message from Martin, he was dropping off tickets for the opera, he was paying back a loan, and so forth. But in this episode Niles actually contributes to the thematic spine of the episode. He has an antique book that introduces the idea of how we treat old things in our culture. Niles notes that it's a shame more people haven't read the book, but when Roz asks to see it he insists it not be opened because the smallest crease in the spine devalues the book. Niles of course misses the hypocrisy of his lament and subsequent action, but this highlights one way old things are treated: preserved without any function.

In the next scene, Frasier, Niles, Martin, and Daphne go to Orsini's for dinner, and addressing the run-down nature of the restaurant Niles offers another reaction to old things: pity. "It's like running into a movie star you worshipped as a child, only time has left her hair brittle, her eyes sunken and dull, her skin waxy and sallow. . . ." Daphne offers perhaps the most direct statement about a theme for the episode when she asks, "Why are Americans always in such an almighty rush to tear things down? At home, we treasure our antiquities but you people just can't wait to bring in the bulldozers." Of course, a third option is explored in the plot, to try and update and continue using the restaurant. After the purchase is complete the restaurant is completely remodeled with new furnishings and a bright, modern design. Otto, the octogenarian waiter, is a third old object presented to the audience. Unable to perform his duties, he is allowed to carry on in a new role due to nostalgia, but proves particularly unfit as a valet attendant.

What then, is the argument implicit in this episode about what to do with old things? Preserving them without functionality is immediately shown to be pointless. Pitying equally so. Tearing them down to make way for something new is "tragic," as Daphne puts it. And trying to either update it to keep it going or shift an old thing that is no longer working to a new purpose are both disasters.

The key, as is often the case in *Frasier*, lies with Martin. The final "old thing" in the episode. Martin raises a voice of warning based on his past experiences that would have prevented the chaos Frasier and Niles endure. First, he discourages them in his typically blunt fashion: "Wait a minute! Don't tell me you two are seriously considering doing a dumb-ass, idiotic thing like buying this place?" Then, he offers insight into his two sons that he has gained from knowing them their entire lives: "You see, that's what always gets you guys in trouble. You don't think about the hard work or the long hours. No, to you, owning a restaurant is just wearing fancy clothes, hobnobbing with your friends and turning your enemies away at the door." And finally, he offers pointed and specific advice about the very situation they are considering: "Look, when I was a cop walking the beat, there was this one restaurant on the corner. In ten years, it must have changed hands twenty times. First it was Ling Fun's Lichi Palace, then it was Tony's Meatball Hutch, then it was A Little Taste of Yorkshire—English food. Huh, big surprise, that lasted about five minutes." Of course, Frasier and Niles manage to simultaneously miss his point and completely ignore him:

Niles: You know, Frasier, Dad has a point. A lot of people have lost a lot of money in this business for one reason: they picked the wrong name.

Frasier: True, Niles, but I've got something very special. I was thinking about this while Dad was talking. [1]

This then, is the unlearned lesson that is the theme of the episode: we should learn from old things. We should build on the foundation of the past and not pointlessly preserve it, pity it, revive it, or repurpose it.

"The Innkeepers" is indicative of the quality we were looking for in a 4-star episode. Using a rating system not only allows us to rate each episode, it also allows us to see trends for entire seasons. This resulted in some surprises that depart from conventional wisdom regarding the series. Typically the first five seasons, which all won Emmys for Best Comedy Series, are praised as the best of the series, with an acknowledged decrease in quality from there. By averaging out our episodes' rankings across a season, we can see each season's average on a scale of from 1 to 4. Using this method, we had Season 3 as one of the weaker seasons, something we did not expect based on both reputations and awards.

Additionally, many critics point to Season 6 as a beginning of a decline for the series in terms of quality and that after five consistently high-quality seasons it suffered a slow lessening from there. But both Season 6 and 7 rank very high in our scale, higher than several seasons that did win Emmys. Of course, the lessening in quality did occur, just later than is typically described. Season 9 is our lowest-rated, and Season 10 ties with Season 3 as the next lowest.

Episode 1.1: "The Good Son" (September 16, 1993) ****

Frasier moves back to Seattle. His father, Martin, moves in with him with his dog, Eddie. They hire Daphne, a home health care worker. *Why 4 stars:* One of the best pilots in television history, it reveals enough about each character and their relationships while still being simultaneously funny and touching.

Frasier, Daphne, Niles, and Martin. *NBC/Photofest;* © *NBC*

Episode 1.2: "Space Quest" (September 23, 1993) ***

Frasier wants to get Martin and Daphne their own apartment but Martin tells him he's not going anywhere, their relationship will take time to get better.

Episode 1.3: "Dinner at Eight" (September 30, 1993) ****

Niles meets Daphne. Niles and Frasier are horrified at their dad's middle-class taste. *Why 4 stars:* This episode truly sets up the two defining relationships of the series: Niles meets Daphne and is instantly smitten, and Frasier's and Niles's snootiness is called out by Martin.

Episode 1.4: "I Hate Frasier Crane" (October 7, 1993) **

Frasier is challenged to a fight by a newspaper critic.

Episode 1.5: "Here's Looking at You" (October 14, 1993) *

Frasier buys Martin a telescope and Martin begins writing messages to a woman from another building who also has a telescope. *Why 1 star:* This episode just doesn't work. Frasier's voyeurism doesn't fit his strict moral code nor Martin's and the woman from the other building is never mentioned again.

Episode 1.6: "The Crucible" (October 21, 1993) ***

Frasier discovers a painting he purchased is a forgery.

Episode 1.7: "Call Me Irresponsible" (October 28, 1993) **

Frasier advises a caller to end his relationship and then begins dating the caller's ex-girlfriend.

Episode 1.8: "Beloved Infidel" (November 4, 1993) ****

Frasier and Niles begin to believe Martin had an affair decades ago and Martin admits he did. Later, Frasier learns it was his mother who had an affair. *Why 4 stars:* A crucial episode to the relationship between Martin and Frasier, and one of the best balances of humor and real, raw emotion yet in the series.

Episode 1.9: "Selling Out" (November 11, 1993) ***

Frasier's new agent, Bebe, wants him to do a TV commercial for a product he hates.

Episode 1.10: "Oops" (November 18, 1993) **

After overhearing Frasier gossip that Bulldog is about to be fired, Bulldog quits.

Episode 1.11: "Death Becomes Him" (December 2, 1993) ***

Frasier becomes obsessed with death.

Episode 1.12: "Miracle on Third or Fourth Street" (December 16, 1993) **

Frasier works his radio show on Christmas Day and is depressed.

Episode 1.13: "Guess Who's Coming to Breakfast" (January 6, 1994) *

During his radio show, Frasier mentions his father spent the night with a woman named Elaine from his building. *Why 1 star:* It is very out of character for Frasier, a man whose career depends on confidentiality, to blab such personal details.

Episode 1.14: "Can't Buy Me Love" (January 20, 1994) ***

At a date auction Frasier is "bought" by a model named Kristina. As Frasier's date arrives, she is pulled away by a sudden job and asks him to babysit her twelve-year-old daughter, Renetta.

Episode 1.15: "You Can't Tell a Crook by His Cover" (January 27, 1994) **

Martin has three friends over for a poker game and makes a bet that Frasier can't tell which one is the convicted felon. Daphne agrees to go on a date with the felon.

Episode 1.16: "The Show Where Lilith Comes Back" (February 3, 1994) ***

Lilith returns after finding a note from Frasier asking for her back, but the note was actually written a year ago.

Episode 1.17: "A Midwinter Night's Dream" (February 10, 1994) ****

Niles convinces Daphne to cook a meal for Maris. That night a storm knocks the power out and Daphne and Niles are left alone together. *Why 4 stars:* The first episode to focus on the Niles-Daphne relationship as the A-storyline and it delivers.

Episode 1.18: "And the Whimper Is . . ." (February 17, 1994) **

Frasier and Roz are nominated for a Seattle Broadcasting Award.

Episode 1.19: "Give Him the Chair!" (March 17, 1994) ***

Frasier buys Martin a new recliner. Martin wants his old chair back, but it has been thrown out.

Episode 1.20: "Fortysomething" (March 31, 1994) **

Frasier begins to feel his age and panics.

Episode 1.21: "Travels with Martin" (April 14, 1994) ***

Frasier decides to take Martin on a vacation and ends up in a Winnebago along with Daphne and Niles.

Episode 1.22: "Author, Author" (May 5, 1994) ****

Niles convinces Frasier to write a book with him on sibling relationships. *Why 4 stars:* This episode truly shows how dynamic and comedic it can be to have two similar characters interacting with each other. The finale in the hotel room is a perfect blend of physical comedy and line delivery.

Episode 1.23: "Frasier Crane's Day Off" (May 12, 1994) ***

Sick with the flu, Frasier is forced to take off work and sends Niles to cover his radio show.

Episode 1.24: "My Coffee with Niles" (May 19, 1994) ****

The entire episode takes place in "real time," so approximately twenty-two consecutive minutes of Frasier's day is shown, all at the coffee shop. *Why 4 stars:* The episode shows the growth of the brothers' relationship.

Episode 2.1: "Slow Tango in South Seattle" (September 20, 1994) *

The popular book *Slow Tango* turns out to be written about Frasier and his first romantic encounter with his piano teacher. *Why 1 star:* There are so many issues with this episode from a thematic point of view, but perhaps most galling is that it tries to make the audience feel as though the older member of a teacher-student sexual relationship is the victim.

Episode 2.2: "The Unkindest Cut of All" (September 27, 1994) **

Frasier takes Eddie to get neutered and Martin is very upset.

Episode 2.3: "The Matchmaker" (October 4, 1994) ****

Frasier sets Daphne up with the new station manager, Tom, by inviting him over for dinner. Unknown to Frasier, Tom is gay and thinks that Frasier has asked him out. *Why 4 stars:* The first farce episode of *Frasier*. On its own, this is a great episode, but this is also a key episode in setting a tone for the series.

Episode 2.4: "Flour Child" (October 11, 1994) ***

Niles, trying to decide if he wants a child, carries around a sack of flour.

Episode 2.5: "Duke's, We Hardly Knew Ye" (October 18, 1994) ***

Frasier and Niles are thrilled to be invited by Martin to join him for a drink at his favorite bar, Duke's, but realize they're part of an investment group tearing the bar down.

Episode 2.6: "The Botched Language of Cranes" (November 1, 1994) ****

Frasier offends all of Seattle, but when emceeing a hospital charity event in order to improve his reputation he unwittingly makes inappropriate jokes. *Why 4 stars:* A classic example of comedy rising from miscommunication, this represents one of the staple sources of comedy for the series.

Episode 2.7: "The Candidate" (November 8, 1994) ***

Frasier films an ad supporting a politician but discovers the candidate thinks he was abducted by aliens.

Episode 2.8: "Adventures in Paradise (1)" (November 15, 1994) ***

Frasier and his new girlfriend, Madeline, take a trip to Bora Bora and unexpectedly run into Lilith there.

Episode 2.9: "Adventures in Paradise (2)" (November 22, 1994) ***

The idea of one-upping Lilith takes over Frasier, ruining his romantic trip.

Episode 2.10: "Burying a Grudge" (November 29, 1994) **

Frasier sees one of Martin's old partners, Artie, and manipulates Martin into apologizing to Artie.

Episode 2.11: "Seat of Power" (December 13, 1994) ***

Frasier's plumbers turn out to be his and Niles's old school bullies.

Episode 2.12: "Roz in the Doghouse" (January 3, 1995) **

Bulldog asks Roz to be his new producer but is just trying to sleep with her.

Episode 2.13: "Retirement Is Murder" (January 10, 1995) ***

Martin has spent twenty years trying to solve a murder and Frasier concludes a monkey did it.

Episode 2.14: "Fool Me Once, Shame on You, Fool Me Twice . . ." (February 7, 1995) *

Despite Martin's cynical warnings, Frasier is repeatedly conned by the same criminal. *Why 1 star:* This episode works in the abstract, but something about the specific execution doesn't come together very well.

Episode 2.15: "You Scratch My Book . . ." (February 14, 1995) **

Frasier falls for Honey Snow, a self-help author whose work he does not respect.

Episode 2.16: "The Show Where Sam Shows Up" (February 21, 1995) **

Sam Malone from *Cheers* visits and when Frasier meets Sam's girlfriend he realizes that he slept with that woman three months ago.

Episode 2.17: "Daphne's Room" (February 28, 1995) ***

Frasier keeps ending up in Daphne's room and she is upset at the invasion of privacy.

Episode 2.18: "The Club" (March 21, 1995) ***

Niles and Frasier, wanting to get into a prestigious club, begin to sabotage each other's chances.

Episode 2.19: "Someone to Watch Over Me" (March 28, 1995) **

Frasier thinks he has a stalker.

Episode 2.20: "Breaking the Ice" (April 18, 1995) ***

Frasier joins Martin and Niles on an ice fishing weekend hoping to hear Martin say "I love you."

Episode 2.21: "An Affair to Forget" (May 2, 1995) ****

A caller tells Frasier that she thinks her husband is having an affair with a fencing student. Frasier puts it together that Maris is the student and then accidentally tells Niles. *Why 4 stars:* The buildup has great moments but the finale is some of the best comedy the show produced.

Episode 2.22: "Agents in America, Part III" (May 9, 1995) ***

Under Bebe's advice, Frasier holds out for a raise from the radio station.

Episode 2.23: "The Innkeepers" (May 16, 1995) ****

Frasier and Niles decide to buy a restaurant. *Why 4 stars:* The timing and pacing of this episode is impeccable. There is the perfect slow build to a manic finale.

Episode 2.24: "Dark Victory" (May 23, 1995) **

It's Martin's birthday but everyone is in a bad mood.

Episode 3.1: "She's the Boss" (September 19, 1995) **

Frasier has a power struggle with the new station manager, Kate Costas.

Episode 3.2: "Shrink Rap" (September 26, 1995) **

Frasier and Niles each tell their side of the story of the disastrous experience they had trying to go into practice together.

Episode 3.3: "Martin Does It His Way" (October 10, 1995) *

While going through boxes, Daphne finds a song Martin had started writing years ago. Frasier and Niles's mean aunt dies. *Why 1 star:* This episode feels like several different possible plots were tossed into one episode with no thematic coherence.

Episode 3.4: "Leapin' Lizards" (October 31, 1995) **

Frasier tries to play a joke on Bulldog but a lizard bites the station manager instead.

Episode 3.5: "Kisses Sweeter Than Wine" (November 7, 1995) ***

Frasier hires a contractor named Joe to whom Daphne is attracted.

Episode 3.6: "Sleeping with the Enemy" (November 14, 1995) **

The studio takes away the annual raises for the "nontalent" staff. Frasier negotiates on their behalf with Kate, and the two no longer fight their physical attraction.

Episode 3.7: "The Adventures of Bad Boy and Dirty Girl" (November 21, 1995) **

Frasier and Kate accidentally have sex in range of the radio station's on-air mic.

Episode 3.8: "The Last Time I Saw Maris" (November 28, 1995) ***

Niles and Maris have a massive fight, and she threatens him with divorce and kicks him out.

Episode 3.9: "Frasier Grinch" (December 19, 1995) **

Frederick comes for Christmas and Frasier searches for the perfect brainy and scientific toys.

Episode 3.10: "It's Hard to Say Goodbye If You Won't Leave" (January 9, 1996) *

Frasier confesses his feelings for Kate, then finds out she's leaving to take a job in Chicago. *Why 1 star:* Kate's turn from hard nosed to cutesy doesn't work at all.

Episode 3.11: "The Friend" (January 16, 1996) *

Frasier realizes that he has no friends other than Niles and tries to make friends with a man named Bob. *Why 1 star:* Building an episode around a guest who is supposed to be annoying is a delicate act, and too often it ends up just being annoying for the viewer, too.

Episode 3.12: "Come Lie with Me" (January 30, 1996) **

Frasier and Martin realize how much they need Daphne after she goes away with Joe for a weekend.

Episode 3.13: "Moon Dance" (February 6, 1996) ****

Niles takes Daphne dancing. *Why 4 stars:* This episode marks a turn toward the Niles-Daphne relationship (or lack thereof), and the show is better for it.

Episode 3.14: "The Show Where Diane Comes Back" (February 13, 1996) ***

Diane Chambers returns to Frasier's life when she's in Seattle for the opening of her play.

Episode 3.15: "A Word to the Wiseguy" (February 20, 1996) *

Maris contacts Niles for help and he turns to a man named Jerome Belasco, who has all the stereotypes of a member of the Mafia. *Why 1 star:* The end of the episode has Niles hiring Jerome's dim-witted fiancée as his new secretary, something that should have long-term ramifications but is never mentioned again.

Episode 3.16: "Look before You Leap" (February 27, 1996) ***

On Leap Day, Frasier challenges everyone to take a leap outside their comfort zone.

Episode 3.17: "High Crane Drifter" (March 12, 1996) ***

Frasier is overly annoyed by the lack of courtesy of people around him.

Episode 3.18: "Chess Pains" (March 26, 1996) ***

Martin beats Frasier in chess over and over again.

Episode 3.19: "Crane vs. Crane" (April 9, 1996) **

Frasier and Niles go head-to-head in the courtroom as expert witnesses.

Episode 3.20: "Police Story" (April 23, 1996) **

Frasier wants to ask out an attractive police officer and convinces Martin to come with him to the local bar, but the woman asks Martin out.

Episode 3.21: "Where There's Smoke There's Fired" (April 30, 1996) ****

The station is sold to Big Willy Boone who asks Frasier to get his fiancée, Frasier's agent Bebe, to quit smoking in three days. *Why 4 stars:* Harriet Harris's Bebe often gives a spark to the show in her guest appearances, but this is one of her best turns.

Episode 3.22: "Frasier Loves Roz" (May 7, 1996) **

Roz begins to believe Frasier is in love with her.

Episode 3.23: "The Focus Group" (May 14, 1996) **

Eleven out of twelve members of a focus group love *The Frasier Crane Show*, but Frasier fixates on the one negative voice.

Episode 3.24: "You Can Go Home Again" (May 21, 1996) ****

Frasier thinks about a time when Niles and Frasier were not very close and Martin and Frasier never talked. *Why 4 stars:* Perfectly and humorously provides the contrast of three years' time, which could easily be missed because the evolution in relationships has been handled naturally.

Episode 4.1: "The Two Mrs. Cranes" (September 17, 1996) ****

Daphne's ex-fiancé, Clive, calls to visit. Worried that he wants to rekindle their romance, she pretends Niles is her husband. Soon Clive thinks Frasier is married to Maris, Martin was an astronaut, and that Roz is Maris. *Why 4 stars:* The trick for this type of episode is presenting motivations for each character to be lying and acting the way they do. To set it all up, have it make clear sense, and be hilarious in only twenty-two minutes is a marvel.

Episode 4.2: "Love Bites Dog" (September 24, 1996) **

Bulldog falls in love with a woman who dumps him, crushing him.

Episode 4.3: "The Impossible Dream" (October 15, 1996) *

Frasier keeps having the same recurring dream—waking up in a motel room with Gil Chesterton. *Why 1 star:* There's very little that works in this episode, and the dream sequences, awkward conversations, and strained analysis are all more dull than entertaining.

Episode 4.4: "A Crane's Critique" (October 22, 1996) **

Frasier and Niles follow T. H. Houghton, a reclusive author who only wrote one book.

Episode 4.5: "Head Game" (November 12, 1996) ***

A basketball player thinks Niles is his good luck charm.

Episode 4.6: "Mixed Doubles" (November 19, 1996) ****

Daphne starts dating a new guy who is just like Niles. *Why 4 stars:* David Hyde Pierce. Really, that's about all that needs to be said; this episode is a master class in mining comedy from genuine emotion.

Episode 4.7: "A Lilith Thanksgiving" (November 26, 1996) **

The Cranes fly out to Boston for Thanksgiving when Freddie has a chance to enroll in a prestigious school.

Episode 4.8: "Our Father Whose Art Ain't Heaven" (December 9, 1996) ***

Frasier hates a painting that Martin bought for him but can't tell him.

Episode 4.9: "Dad Loves Sherry, the Boys Just Whine" (January 7, 1997) ***

The Crane men argue about how none of them date/marry anyone that the others like very much.

Episode 4.10: "Liar! Liar!" (January 14, 1997) **

Frasier feels guilty for a transgression from his youth.

Episode 4.11: "Three Days of the Condo" (January 21, 1997) ***

Frasier decides to run for the condo board, but a misunderstanding causes his speech to the condo board to go horribly awry.

Episode 4.12: "Death and the Dog" (February 11, 1997) **

Eddie is depressed and Martin hires a dog psychiatrist to figure it out.

Episode 4.13: "Four for the Seesaw" (February 18, 2001) ***

Frasier and Niles decide to take two women they've recently started seeing to a romantic outing at a cabin.

Episode 4.14: "To Kill a Talking Bird" (February 25, 1997) ****

Niles throws a dinner party that ends disastrously when his new bird begins repeating everything Niles and Frasier have been saying about the guests. *Why 4 stars:* Can we just say David Hyde Pierce again?

Episode 4.15: "Roz's Krantz & Gouldenstein Are Dead" (March 11, 1997) **

Roz has to do community service visiting a retirement home, and those she visits begin to die.

Episode 4.16: "The Unnatural" (April 1, 1997) **

Frederick comes to visit and wants to see his dad play in a softball game with his coworkers.

Episode 4.17: "Roz's Turn" (April 15, 1997) ***

An opening comes up at the radio station, and Roz auditions for it.

Episode 4.18: "Ham Radio" (April 22, 1997) ****

Frasier wants to put on a "classic" radio drama reading at the station. *Why 4 stars:* Somehow they manage to execute a farce in a closed room, and there are particularly strong performances from Peri Gilpin and David Hyde Pierce.

Episode 4.19: "Three Dates and a Breakup (1)" (April 29, 1997) ***

After a party Frasier ends up with three dates over a holiday weekend.

Episode 4.20: "Three Dates and a Breakup (2)" (April 29, 1997) ***

Frasier has three different dates three nights in a row and each time Sherry embarrasses Frasier.

Episode 4.21: "Daphne Hates Sherry" (May 6, 1997) ****

Upset with Sherry, Daphne runs to Niles's apartment to stay the night. *Why 4 stars:* The chemistry shared by Jane Leeves and David Hyde Pierce shines.

Episode 4.22: "Are You Being Served?" (May 13, 1997) ****

Niles thinks he and Maris are beginning to work it out when he gets served with divorce papers. *Why 4 stars:* We get to see growth in Niles's character as he finally stands up to Maris. Also, this episode features one of the greatest visual gags in the series when Niles walks out of a bathroom covered in foam.

Episode 4.23: "Ask Me No Questions" (May 21, 1997) *

Niles asks Frasier if he thinks Maris and he are meant to be together. *Why 1 star:* Montages are not a strong stylistic choice on *Frasier*.

Episode 4.24: "Odd Man Out" (May 21, 1997) *

Hoping for a love connection, Frasier goes to the airport to see a woman who has been leaving messages trying to reach someone else, but she's married. *Why 1 star:* Frasier often does cringeworthy things when it comes to women, but the desperation of meeting a stranger at the airport is upped by the creepiness of him following a second woman on her vacation.

Episode 5.1: "Frasier's Imaginary Friend" (September 23, 1997) ****

Frasier returns from Acapulco with a model/zoologist who has asked him to keep their relationship a secret. *Why 4 stars:* A frankly silly premise that still works, creating a hilarious setup and conclusion.

Episode 5.2: "The Gift Horse" (September 30, 1997) ****

Frasier and Niles compete with one another to give Martin the best birthday present. *Why 4 stars:* The episode portrays sibling rivalry at its best, but also highlights the importance of family relationships.

Episode 5.3: "Halloween" (October 28, 1997) ****

Roz tells Frasier she thinks she might be pregnant. At a costume party characters have significant miscommunications about who is pregnant by whom. *Why 4 stars:* One of the best-structured episodes, and truly incredible given the complicated storyline yet how easy it is to follow.

Episode 5.4: "The Kid" (November 4, 1997) **

Roz decides that she is going to keep the baby and raise it on her own.

Episode 5.5: "The 1000th Show" (November 11, 1997) *

It's the one thousandth episode for *The Frasier Crane Show* and the mayor names it "Frasier Crane Day." *Why 1 star:* While it is interesting to see them on location in Seattle, the energy feels off.

Episode 5.6: "Voyage of the Damned" (November 18, 1997) ****

Everyone goes on a cruise; unknown to them, Maris is on the cruise. *Why 4 stars:* An episode centered around a character who is never shown can be tricky, but when done right the comedic reward is priceless.

Episode 5.7: "My Fair Frasier" (November 25, 1997) ****

Frasier begins a relationship with a high-powered attorney but they argue over their gender role reversal in the relationship. *Why 4 stars:* Very funny, but with thematic heft as this episode expertly explores gender roles within our society.

Episode 5.8: "Desperately Seeking Closure" (December 9, 1997) ***

Frasier realizes he was after his girlfriend's lifestyle more than the woman herself.

Episode 5.9: "Perspectives on Christmas" (December 16, 1997) ****

Everyone retells their version of a rough Christmas Eve to a masseur. *Why 4 stars:* Generally, episodes that experiment with nonlinear structures are a miss on *Frasier*, but this is the exception to that rule.

Episode 5.10: "Where Every Bloke Knows Your Name" (January 6, 1998) **

Frasier goes with Daphne to her local bar and begins frequenting it.

Episode 5.11: "Ain't Nobody's Business If I Do" (January 13, 1998) **

Martin wants to propose to Sherry, but Frasier and Niles are concerned when they find out how many times she has previously been married.

Episode 5.12: "The Zoo Story" (January 20, 1998) ***

Renegotiations are up at the radio station again. Frasier hires another agent for cutthroat negotiations, Ben, a Mormon scoutmaster.

Episode 5.13: "The Maris Counselor" (February 3, 1998) ****

Niles discovers Maris and their marriage counselor are having an affair. *Why 4 stars:* The episode is simultaneously hilarious and very emotional with the Crane men's vulnerable moment together at the finale.

Episode 5.14: "The Ski Lodge" (February 24, 1998) ****

Frasier takes everyone on a weekend at a ski lodge. A hilarious mix-up of who is interested in whom occurs. *Why 4 stars:* This episode is perfect, one of the best in television history. Expertly written, performed, and executed.

Episode 5.15: "Room Service" (March 3, 1998) *

Lilith comes to Seattle, upset that her husband has left her for a man; and, feeling vulnerable, Lilith sleeps with Niles. *Why 1 star:* Our greatest debate as coauthors. While the setup is hilarious, it feels too out of character to have Niles ever sleep with Lilith.

Episode 5.16: "Beware of Greeks" (March 17, 1998) *

Frasier's cousin Nikos is getting married. *Why 1 star:* It is too ridiculous to be funny and it doesn't work to bring in local family members such as Martin's brother, who is introduced but never referenced again.

Episode 5.17: "The Perfect Guy" (March 24, 1998) **

An extremely good-looking new guy is hired at the station, making Frasier jealous.

Episode 5.18: "Bad Dog" (April 7, 1998) ***

Bulldog is falsely praised as being a hero and Frasier tries to guilt Bulldog into confessing the truth.

Episode 5.19: "Frasier Gotta Have It" (April 21, 1998) *

Frasier meets a new woman, but Niles thinks the attraction is purely physical. *Why 1 star:* It's a hollow episode built on a shallow premise that is never elevated to anything more.

Episode 5.20: "First Date" (April 28, 1998) ****

Niles decides he's finally going to ask Daphne out on a date but is unable to do so. *Why 4 stars:* Yet another strong episode exploring the growth of Daphne and Niles's relationship.

Episode 5.21: "Roz and Schnoz" (May 5, 1998) ****

Roz learns that the father of her baby comes from a family of large noses. *Why 4 stars:* A successful shift in gear toward broad comedy built on big noses and puns.

Episode 5.22: "The Life of the Party" (May 12, 1998) ***

Frasier and Niles are struggling to find dates and they decide to hold a singles party.

Episode 5.23: "Party, Party" (May 19, 1998) **

Frasier meets a new woman, but keeps missing their date due to various issues.

Episode 5.24: "Sweet Dreams" (May 19, 1998) **

Frasier manages to get everyone at KACL fired.

Episode 6.1: "Good Grief" (September 24, 1998) **

Having just lost his job, Frasier goes through the various stages of grief.

Episode 6.2: "Frasier's Curse" (October 1, 1998) **

Frasier has his high school reunion but does not want to attend because he has no job.

Episode 6.3: "Dial M for Martin" (October 8, 1998) ****

Martin and Frasier begin to get on each other's nerves and Martin decides to go live with Niles. *Why 4 stars:* Niles's and Frasier's parallel frustrations build perfectly, and Pierce and Grammer rise to the occasion.

Episode 6.4: "Hot Ticket" (October 15, 1998) **

A new play comes to Seattle, but Frasier and Niles are unable to get tickets.

Episode 6.5: "First, Do No Harm" (October 29, 1998) **

Frasier realizes he likes his new girlfriend so much because he enjoys analyzing her.

Episode 6.6: "Secret Admirer" (November 5, 1998) ***

Frasier believes he has a secret admirer but the gifts are all actually for Niles from Maris.

Episode 6.7: "How to Bury a Millionaire" (November 12, 1998) ****

Having lost access to Maris's money, Niles has to adjust his lifestyle to match his income, and Frasier helps and they find a place within his budget, the Shangri-La. It is everything Niles is not. *Why 4 stars:* Niles at the Shangri-La: the contrast is perfection.

Episode 6.8: "The Seal Who Came to Dinner" (November 19, 1998) ****

Niles has to get rid of a dead seal on the beach before his dinner party begins. *Why 4 stars:* Absurd premise, great physical comedy, and a theme that unites all the scenes (efforts to make ourselves look good often make us look more foolish).

Episode 6.9: "Roz, a Loan" (December 10, 1998) **

Frasier lends Roz some money but becomes concerned with how she spends it. Everyone gets their jobs back at KACL.

Episode 6.10: "Merry Christmas, Mrs. Moskowitz" (December 17, 1998) ****

Frasier pretends to be Jewish while his new girlfriend's mother is visiting on Christmas Eve. *Why 4 stars:* Niles dressed up as Jesus standing next to a Christmas tree while Frasier is pretending to be Jewish. Not much more needs to be said.

Episode 6.11: "Good Samaritan" (January 7, 1999) *

Frasier imagines the worst things that could happen from doing good service. *Why 1 star:* The reveal that this was all in Frasier's imagination makes the whole episode meaningless.

Episode 6.12: "Our Parents, Ourselves" (January 21, 1999) ***

Roz and Frasier set up their parents together.

Episode 6.13: "The Show Where Woody Shows Up" (February 4, 1999) ***

Frasier's old friend from Boston, Woody, shows up.

Episode 6.14: "Three Valentines" (February 11, 1999) ****

Niles is in Frasier's apartment preparing for a Valentine's date, while Frasier can't figure out if he is on a date or a business meeting, and Daphne and Martin are out together and start bickering. *Why 4 stars:* David. Hyde. Pierce. While there is not a weak link in the three stories, Niles's is the strongest.

Episode 6.15: "To Tell the Truth" (February 18, 1999) ***

Niles's divorce lawyer Donny digs up where Maris's family really came from, and she settles.

Episode 6.16: "Decoys" (February 25, 1999) ****

Donny and Daphne's new relationship devastates Niles, and his attempts to foil it lead to farce. *Why 4 stars:* These episodes shouldn't be done too often, but *Frasier* can safely dip into the farce well once a season for a classic episode.

Episode 6.17: "Dinner Party" (March 11, 1999) **

Frasier and Niles attempt to plan another dinner party.

Episode 6.18: "Taps at the Montana" (March 25, 1999) ****

Niles throws a dinner party for his neighbors and they play a murder mystery game; however, one of the guests actually dies of natural causes. *Why 4 stars:* The absurd efforts to secretly remove a dead body are great comedy, as is Roz's reaction to being near the corpse.

Episode 6.19: "IQ" (April 8, 1999) ****

At a charity event, Frasier and Niles competitively bid on a lunch with three geniuses. *Why 4 stars:* Again an excellent blend of true filial issues, the brothers' rivalry, and laugh-out-loud performances from Grammer and Pierce.

Episode 6.20: "Dr. Nora" (April 29, 1999) ***

Frasier selects a new psychiatrist for the radio station, Dr. Nora.

Episode 6.21: "When a Man Loves Two Women" (May 6, 1999) **

Frasier begins to date both Cassandra and Faye and can't choose between the two.

Episode 6.22: "Visions of Daphne" (May 13, 1999) ***

Donny proposes to Daphne and Daphne says yes.

Episode 6.23: "Shutout in Seattle (1)" (May 20, 1999) ***

Frasier gets worried Niles has gone back to Maris, but he has just started to date a new woman, a young waitress from Café Nervosa.

Episode 6.24: "Shutout in Seattle (2)" (May 20, 1999) ***

The three Crane men are all single again.

Episode 7.1: "Momma Mia" (September 23, 1998) ****

Frasier does not realize his new girlfriend looks exactly like his mother. *Why 4 stars:* A fantastic blend of silly reactions and heartfelt emotions.

Episode 7.2: "Father of the Bride" (October 1, 1998) ***

A misunderstanding leads to Daphne thinking Frasier has offered to pay for her wedding.

Episode 7.3: "Radio Wars" (October 7, 1999) ***

New radio hosts at KACL keep playing practical jokes on Frasier.

Episode 7.4: "Everyone's a Critic" (October 14, 1999) **

Niles is the new art critic for a highbrow newspaper. Frasier is jealous.

Episode 7.5: "The Dog That Rocks the Cradle" (October 21, 1999) **

Roz hires Bulldog to be her babysitter and he wants a real relationship with Roz.

Episode 7.6: "Rivals" (November 4, 1999) ****

Frasier and Niles think they're pursuing the same woman, but they're not. *Why 4 stars:* Another great misunderstanding episode that is easy to follow.

Episode 7.7: "A Tsar Is Born" (November 11, 1999) ****

The three Crane men bond over *Antiques Roadshow* and an antique bear clock. *Why 4 stars:* This episode expertly highlights just how ridiculous Frasier's and Niles's snobbery can be.

Episode 7.8: "The Late Dr. Crane" (November 18, 1999) **

The mistaken news that Frasier Crane is dead is read over the air.

Episode 7.9: "The Apparent Trap" (November 25, 1999) ***

Freddie manipulates both Frasier and Lilith into thinking that each wants to get back together with the other.

Episode 7.10: "Back Talk (1)" (March 10, 2000) ****

Frasier throws out his back while blowing out a candle on a cupcake for his birthday. Under pain medication he tells Daphne that Niles loves her. *Why 4 stars:* The moment audiences have been waiting for—Daphne finding out about Niles.

Episode 7.11: "The Fight before Christmas" (December 16, 1999) ***

Niles brings his new girlfriend, Mel, to the KACL holiday party and Daphne is conflicted seeing Niles in a new relationship.

Episode 7.12: "RDWRER" (January 6, 2000) **

Frasier, Niles, and Martin take a road trip to a wine event for New Year's Eve.

Episode 7.13: "They're Playing Our Song" (January 13, 2000) **

The station manager asks Frasier to write a song for his show.

Episode 7.14: "Big Crane on Campus" (February 3, 2000) ***

Frasier has a date with his high school crush but the next morning he sees a different side of her.

Episode 7.15: "Out with Dad" (February 10, 2000) ****

Frasier is interested in a woman and after a mix-up she sets Martin up with her gay uncle. *Why 4 stars:* A hilarious episode with an ending that highlights just how much Martin loves his son.

Episode 7.16: "Something about Dr. Mary" (February 17, 2000) **

Frasier hires Mary, an African American woman from a local college, to fill in for Roz.

Episode 7.17: "Whine Club" (February 24, 2000) **

Frasier and Niles both want to be named the next "Cork Master" for their wine club.

Episode 7.18: "Hot Pursuit" (March 23, 2000) **

Roz and Frasier have to share a room at a conference and become more interested in each other as the night goes on.

Episode 7.19: "Morning Becomes Entertainment" (April 6, 2000) ***

Frasier's show gets put on hold and Frasier and Bebe host a Seattle morning show.

Episode 7.20: "To Thine Own Self Be True" (April 27, 2000) ***

Frasier attempts to plan a bachelor party for Donny.

Episode 7.21: "Three Faces of Frasier" (May 4, 2000) *

A local restaurant puts a caricature picture of Frasier on their walls. *Why 1 star:* His actions are ridiculous and the timeline throughout the episode does not work.

Episode 7.22: "Dark Side of the Moon" (May 11, 2000) ****

Daphne thinks Niles is going to confess how he feels to her, but instead he is planning a surprise bridal shower. *Why 4 stars:* Such a crucial episode in the Niles-Daphne saga.

Episode 7.23: "Something Borrowed, Someone Blue (1)" (May 18, 2000) ***

Daphne begins to realize she has feelings for Niles and wants to tell him. But Niles tells everyone he and Mel got married, crushing Daphne.

Episode 7.24: "Something Borrowed, Someone Blue (2)" (May 18, 2000) ****

The night before Daphne and Donny's wedding Frasier sees that Daphne and Niles love each other. Niles confronts Daphne and begs her to end it with Donny and be with him. *Why 4 stars:* FINALLY.

Episode 8.1: "And the Dish Ran Away with the Spoon (1)" (October 24, 2000) ***

Donny is suing Daphne. Mel tells Niles she'll give him a divorce, but she wants them to keep up appearances and remain a couple until she breaks up with him.

Episode 8.2: "And the Dish Ran Away with the Spoon (2)" (October 24, 2000) ***

Because Mel and Niles pretend to still be a couple, Daphne and Niles get into a huge fight.

Episode 8.3: "The Bad Son" (October 31, 2000) ***

Frasier sees an attractive woman and takes Martin to the retirement home where she works, pretending that Martin is interested in living there.

Episode 8.4: "The Great Crane Robbery" (November 14, 2000) **

There is another new station owner, a computer tech millionaire who knows nothing about culture or style, who ends up stealing Frasier's style and decor.

Episode 8.5: "Taking Liberties" (November 21, 2000) ****

Frasier hires a butler (Victor Garber), and delights in having him around. *Why 4 stars:* Victor Garber is so underrated.

Episode 8.6: "Legal Tender Love and Care" (November 28, 2000) ***

Frasier asks out his lawyer from his lawsuit with Donny.

Episode 8.7: "The New Friend" (December 5, 2000) ***

Frasier meets Roz's new boyfriend, Luke, and the two become quick friends.

Episode 8.8: "Mary Christmas" (December 12, 2000) *

Frasier and his former coworker Mary are asked to cohost the Christmas parade. Frasier doesn't like how Mary doesn't follow the script for the show, but everyone loves her. *Why 1 star:* Nothing in this episode really works.

Episode 8.9: "Frasier's Edge" (January 9, 2001) **

Frasier receives the Lifetime Achievement Award at the SeaBees, sending him spiraling down in self-exploration.

Episode 8.10: "Cranes Unplugged" (January 16, 2001) **

Frasier brings Freddie out to Seattle for the weekend and takes him camping with Martin.

Episode 8.11: "Motor Skills" (January 30, 2001) ***

Frasier and Niles sign up for a night class about car mechanics.

Episode 8.12: "The Show Must Go Off" (February 6, 2001) **

Frasier sees one of his favorite Shakespearean actors at a sci-fi convention, and Frasier and Niles realize they can create their own production for the stage and hire the actor for it.

Episode 8.13: "Sliding Frasiers" (February 13, 2001) **

The episode shows two different realities, where Frasier makes one small decision that changes the outcome.

Episode 8.14: "Hungry Heart" (February 20, 2001) ***

Through a mix-up, Frasier has a date with Kenny's wife. Daphne gains weight.

Episode 8.15: "Hooping Cranes" (February 27, 2001) ***

Niles ends up making a halftime half-court shot at an NBA game.

Episode 8.16: "Docu.Drama" (March 6, 2001) **

Roz gets to produce a space documentary. She hires Frasier to narrate but neither can handle the role reversal very well.

Episode 8.17: "It Takes Two to Tangle" (March 27, 2001) **

Martin tries to date two women at once and it does not go well.

Episode 8.18: "Forgotten but Not Gone" (April 17, 2001) *

Frasier and Niles fight at their wine club, and Martin goes down there to yell at both of them. *Why 1 star:* As if Martin would go down to the Wine Club just to yell at his kids.

Episode 8.19: "Daphne Returns" (May 1, 2001) ****

Niles picks up Daphne from her "spa retreat" where she lost the weight she had been gaining. Daphne and Niles face serious issues in their relationship. *Why 4 stars:* Another crucial exploration in the Daphne-Niles dynamic.

Episode 8.20: "The Wizard and Roz" (May 8, 2001) **

Roz and Frasier's old mentor begin dating. Frasier sees him in one of Roz's robes when he is at Roz's house and can't get that image out of his head and has to analyze why.

Episode 8.21: "Semi-decent Proposal" (May 15, 2001) **

Frasier meets an interesting woman, Claire, and tries to use their mutual friend to secure a date with her.

Episode 8.22: "A Passing Fancy" (May 15, 2001) *

Frasier is tutoring Lana's son, Kirby, and Frasier strikes a deal with Kirby to help motivate him to get a better grade by getting Roz to attend prom with Kirby. *Why 1 star:* Roz on a prom date should never have been allowed to happen.

Episode 8.23: "A Day in May" (May 22, 2001) *

Frasier goes with Lana as she tries to sell a house. Niles gets jealous of another dog owner and his friendship with Daphne. Martin is at a parole hearing for the guy who shot him. *Why 1 star:* No thematic coherence and none of the plots work particularly well individually.

Episode 8.24: "Cranes Go Caribbean" (May 22, 2001) ***

Everyone takes a trip to Belize. Despite being with Claire, Frasier has a dream about Lana.

Episode 9.1: "Don Juan in Hell (1)" (September 25, 2001) **

Still in Belize, Frasier begins to doubt his relationship with Claire even more.

Episode 9.2: "Don Juan in Hell (2)" (September 25, 2001) **

Frasier has visions of Lilith, Diane, and his first wife as representations of his unconscious.

Episode 9.3: "The First Temptation of Daphne" (October 2, 2001) **

Daphne sees one of Niles's patients' files revealing that the woman is in love with Niles.

Episode 9.4: "The Return of Martin Crane" (October 9, 2001) **

Martin begins a new job as a security guard.

Episode 9.5: "Love Stinks" (October 16, 2001) **

Roz begins dating Roger, a garbageman. She adores him but is embarrassed by his career.

Episode 9.6: "Room Full of Heroes" (October 30, 2001) **

Frasier hosts a heroes party where everyone dresses up as their hero.

Episode 9.7: "Bla-Z-Boy" (November 6, 2001) ****

Frasier accidentally destroys Martin's beloved chair as he knocks it off the balcony. *Why 4 stars:* Expertly displays the growth of Martin and Frasier's relationship.

Episode 9.8: "The Two Hundredth" (November 13, 2001) *

Frasier celebrates his two thousandth episode of *The Frasier Crane Show* and meets an obsessed fan. *Why 1 star:* Too bizarre and uncomfortable to work well.

Episode 9.9: "Sharing Kirby" (November, 20, 2001) **

Frasier and Niles compete to win over Kirby, who can get one guest into a wine collector's cellar.

Episode 9.10: "Junior Agent" (November 27, 2001) **

Frasier's agent has passed him on to a junior agent.

Episode 9.11: "Bully for Martin" (December 11, 2001) **

Frasier sees Martin's boss at work bullying him.

Episode 9.12: "Mother Overload (1)" (January 8, 2002) **

Daphne and Niles decide to move in together.

Episode 9.13: "Mother Overload (2)" (January 15, 2002) **

Daphne tells her mother she is moving in with Niles, but Daphne's mother moves in, too.

Episode 9.14: "Juvenilia" (January 22, 2002) ***

Frasier agrees to appear on *Teen Scene*, a show hosted by high schoolers; however, they quickly turn on him and reveal some embarrassing events from his past.

Episode 9.15: "The Proposal" (February 4, 2002) ***

Niles is ready to propose to Daphne and plans an over-the-top celebration.

Episode 9.16: "Wheels of Fortune" (February 26, 2002) **

Lilith's con-man brother Blaine Sternin (Michael Keaton) comes to visit.

Episode 9.17: "Three Blind Dates" (March 5, 2002) **

Roz, Daphne, and Niles try to set Frasier up with people, but all the setups fail.

Episode 9.18: "War of the Words" (March 12, 2002) *

Freddie wins the National Spelling Bee in Seattle, but is accused of cheating. *Why 1 star:* The stakes are weirdly too big and too small at the same time.

Episode 9.19: "Deathtrap" (April 2, 2002) ***

Frasier and Niles visit their childhood home and find a skull.

Episode 9.20: "The Love You Fake" (April 9, 2002) ***

Frasier and his neighbor Cam Winston are fighting again. Martin and Cam's mother decide to play a joke on Cam and Frasier and pretend they're dating.

Episode 9.21: "Cheerful Goodbyes" (April 30, 2002) **

Frasier is speaking at a conference in Boston and everyone comes along. While in the airport Frasier runs into his friend Cliff, and everyone attends his retirement party.

Episode 9.22: "Frasier Has Spokane" (May 7, 2002) **

The Frasier Crane Show gets picked up to be aired in Spokane.

Episode 9.23: "The Guilt Trippers" (May 14, 2002) *

Roz is upset over breaking up with Roger and ends up sleeping with Frasier. *Why 1 star:* Roz and Frasier together is a storyline that just does not work.

Episode 9.24: "Moons over Seattle" (May 21, 2002) **

Daphne tells Niles she wants to marry him.

Episode 10.1: "The Ring Cycle" (September 24, 2002) ***

Daphne and Niles elope to Reno and get married but have to pretend to not be married when everyone wants to attend the ceremony.

Episode 10.2: "Enemy at the Gate" (September 18, 2002) *

Frasier refuses to pay the $2 to exit a parking garage. *Why 1 star:* Frasier being annoying just becomes annoying for the viewer.

Episode 10.3: "Proxy Prexy" (October 8, 2002) **

Frasier decides to have Martin run for condo board president with Frasier trying to put in his policies through Martin.

Episode 10.4: "Kissing Cousin" (October 15, 2002) ***

Roz's younger cousin (Zooey Deschanel) comes to visit and makes everyone feel uncool. Roz goes out every night with her but eventually can't keep up with it anymore.

Episode 10.5: "Tales from the Crypt" (October 29, 2002) ***

After Bulldog pranks him, Frasier is determined to get Bulldog back with a prank of his own.

Episode 10.6: "Star Mitzvah" (November 5, 2002) ***

Freddie is having his Bar Mitzvah, and Frasier wants to deliver his speech in Hebrew. Noel teaches Frasier the speech in Klingon.

Episode 10.7: "Bristle While You Work" (November 12, 2002) **

Frasier is trying to hire a new housecleaner, but can't find the right one.

Episode 10.8: "Rooms with a View" (November 19, 2002) ***

Niles is at the hospital for heart surgery. Everyone is there as he gets taken to the operating room. Flashbacks are shown of various times when they were at the hospital.

Episode 10.9: "Don't Go Breaking My Heart" (November 26, 2002) ***

Niles is fine after his operation and determined to live life to the fullest. However, he's actually scared to really live.

Episode 10.10: "We Two Kings" (December 10, 2002) **

Niles and Daphne want to host Christmas at their place this year. Frasier is upset because he wants to host it and doesn't like that everything is changing.

Episode 10.11: "Door Jam" (January 7, 2003) ***

Frasier receives some of Cam Winston's mail and sees an invitation to an exclusive club that turns out to be a spa.

Episode 10.12: "The Harassed" (January 14, 2003) **

At first Frasier argues with a new employee, Julia, but then makes advances that land all the employees in a sexual harassment course.

Episode 10.13: "Lilith Needs a Favor" (February 4, 2003) **

Lilith flies to Seattle to ask Frasier a favor—she wants another child and wants Frasier's sperm.

Episode 10.14: "Daphne Does Dinner" (February 11, 2003) ****

Niles wants to throw a dinner party for a piece of art he's donating to a museum. Daphne decides to throw the party, assuming this will stop their bad luck at dinner parties. She is wrong. *Why 4 stars:* The opening scene alone is worth 4 stars.

Episode 10.15: "Trophy Girlfriend" (February 18, 2003) **

Frasier begins dating a PE teacher, which brings back unfortunate memories.

Episode 10.16: "Fraternal Schwinns" (February 25, 2003) *

KACL hosts a bike-a-thon. Frasier and Niles confess that they don't know how to ride a bike. *Why 1 star:* Another failed montage . . .

Episode 10.17: "Kenny on the Couch" (March 4, 2003) **

Kenny's divorce is finalized and he begins to see Frasier as a therapist to help him.

Episode 10.18: "Roe to Perdition" (March 18, 2003) ***

Niles and Frasier begin to sell caviar to their friends in exchange for invitations to social events.

Episode 10.19: "Some Assembly Required" (April 1, 2003) **

KACL helps build a house for a family.

Episode 10.20: "Farewell, Nervosa" (April 22, 2003) **

Frasier has issues with his coworker Julia and the affair she is having with his college friend Avery.

Episode 10.21: "The Devil and Dr. Phil" (April 29, 2003) **

Frasier runs into Bebe, who tries to seduce Frasier while also getting him back as a client.

Episode 10.22: "Father and Sons" (May 6, 2003) ****

Hester Crane's old lab partner, Leland, comes to visit. Martin begins to wonder if he really is Frasier and Niles's biological father. *Why 4 stars:* Despite how far they have come, this is one of the first times we see Martin trying to strengthen his relationship with his sons.

Episode 10.23: "Analyzed Kiss" (May 13, 2003) **

Julia is upset when her affair is over with Avery but then agrees to go out with Frasier.

Episode 10.24: "A New Position for Roz" (May 20, 2003) *

Roz is upset about Frasier's relationship with Julia and quits KACL. *Why 1 star:* Roz's ultimatum feels forced to try to cause a dramatic finale and is out of character.

Episode 11.1: "No Sex Please, We're Skittish" (September 23, 2003) **

Frasier thinks Roz quit because she is in love with him.

Episode 11.2: "A Man, a Plan and a Gal: Julia" (September 23, 2003) *

The rest of the family can't stand Julia and want Frasier to break up with her. *Why 1 star:* The scene where Julia is choking in front of a cop, a health care professional, and a doctor who all look the other way is one of the stupidest and most out of character in all eleven years of the show.

Episode 11.3: "The Doctor Is Out" (September 30, 2003) ****

Patrick Stewart guest-stars as Alistair, the director of the Seattle Opera. Frasier believes the two are great friends, when really Alistair is dating him. *Why 4 stars:* A farce with Patrick Stewart playing an opera director named Alistair. That's a 4-star episode.

Episode 11.4: "The Babysitter" (October 7, 2003) **

Niles and Frasier run into their old babysitter, Ronee. Frasier and Martin compete over Ronee, but she is interested in Martin.

Episode 11.5: "The Placeholder" (October 14, 2003) ***

Roz tries to set up Frasier with one of her friends, Ann.

Episode 11.6: "I'm Listening" (October 28, 2003) ***

Frasier accidentally eavesdrops on Ronee making plans with another man.

Episode 11.7: "Maris Returns" (November 4, 2003) ****

Maris asks Niles to meet her for lunch. We later learn that Maris has been arrested for the murder of her boyfriend. *Why 4 stars:* Welcome back, Maris.

Episode 11.8: "Murder Most Maris" (November 11, 2003) ****

News of Maris's act of murder spreads; Niles handles it all very calmly and well until he finally snaps at Café Nervosa. *Why 4 stars:* Niles's breakdown is fantastic comedy.

Episode 11.9: "Guns 'N Neuroses" (November 18, 2003) ***

Lilith is coming to town and her friend unknowingly sets up Lilith and Frasier.

Episode 11.10: "SeaBee Jeebies" (December 2, 2003) **

Frasier begins to feel jealous about Niles's celebrity from Maris's murder trial.

Episode 11.11: "High Holidays" (December 9, 2003) ****

Freddie is coming for the holidays, and everyone is shocked to see his new goth look. Niles realizes that he never had a rebellious phase and gets a pot brownie; however, Martin accidentally eats the brownie. *Why 4 stars:* Freddie appearing as a goth is one of the best shocking moments on the show. And Niles's fake high is hilarious, while Martin's real high is even better.

Episode 11.12: "Frasier-Lite" (January 6, 2004) **

KACL is doing a weight-loss competition against another radio station.

Episode 11.13: "The Ann Who Came to Dinner" (January 13, 2004) **

While Ann is at Frasier's apartment she slips in the kitchen and breaks her leg. Afraid of being sued, Frasier invites her to stay.

Episode 11.14: "Freudian Sleep" (February 3, 2004) *

Everyone goes to Ronee's boss's cabin in the mountains. They all have dreams about what they are stressed about in their life. *Why 1 star:* The worst deviation from the established storytelling style on this series.

Episode 11.15: "Caught in the Act" (February 24, 2004) **

Roz is trying to get tickets to a child performer, Nanny G. Turns out she is Frasier's ex-wife.

Episode 11.16: "Boo! (a.k.a. I'm with Her)" (March 2, 2004) ***

Frasier tries to scare Martin by dressing up as a clown and gives him a heart attack.

Episode 11.17: "Coots and Ladders" (March 16, 2004) ***

Frasier tells Niles he has stolen a trinket from his neighbor.

Episode 11.18: "Match Game" (March 30, 2004) **

Frasier meets a woman who is a matchmaker. Frasier begins to realize he is interested in the matchmaker, Charlotte; unfortunately, she has a boyfriend.

Episode 11.19: "Miss Right Now" (April 6, 2004) **

Frasier can't get Charlotte out of his head. Frasier tries to go out with other women, but Charlotte comes to his apartment after a fight with her boyfriend.

Episode 11.20: "And Frasier Makes Three" (April 20, 2004) ***

Frasier begins spending time with both Charlotte and her boyfriend Frank (Aaron Eckhart) but bonds with her boyfriend. Charlotte breaks up with Frank and decides to move back to Chicago.

Episode 11.21: "Detour" (April 27, 2004) **

Frasier offers to drive Charlotte to the train station, but his car breaks down in the middle of nowhere and they have to go to a random house to get help.

Episode 11.22: "Crock Tales" (May 4, 2004) **

Frasier remembers his time in the apartment with his family and Roz.

Episode 11.23: "Goodnight, Seattle (Part 1)" (May 13, 2004)
****

At Martin and Ronee's wedding Daphne goes into labor. *Why 4 stars:* Niles holding a baby monkey after Daphne gives birth surprisingly works.

Episode 11.24: "Goodnight, Seattle (Part 2)" (May 13, 2004)
****

Frasier decides to take a job in San Francisco when he realizes everyone else is moving on to a new chapter in their lives. But there is one final twist before the show concludes. *Why 4 stars:* The farewells the characters say are genuinely moving after spending eleven years together.

NOTES

INTRODUCTION

1. Tom Hubbell, "Re: Frasier Archives Inquiry," personal e-mail, July 12, 2016.
2. Mandi Bierly, "The All-Timers: An Oral History of the Classic 'Ski Lodge' Episode of 'Frasier,'" Yahoo.com, March 1, 2016, https://www.yahoo.com/tv/frasier-ski-lodge-oral-history-164309203.html.

1. FRASIER BEFORE *FRASIER*

1. Dennis A. Bjorklund, *Toasting* Cheers: *An Episode Guide to the 1982–1993 Comedy Series with Cast Biographies and Character Profiles* (Jefferson, NC: McFarland, 1997), 35.
2. David Bianculli, "*Cheers* and Farewell to One of the Best Crafted Sitcoms," *New York Daily News*, May 16, 1993.
3. Ken Tucker, "A Farewell Tribute to *Cheers*," *Entertainment Weekly*, May 14, 1993.
4. "A Repeat of *Cheers* Finale," *New York Times*, May 22, 1993.
5. "One for the Road." *Cheers*. S11E25. Written by Glen Charles and Les Charles. NBC, May 1993.
6. "Give Me a Ring Sometime." *Cheers*. S1E1. Written by Glen Charles and Les Charles. NBC, September 1982.
7. "One for the Road." *Cheers*. S11E25.
8. Dave Nemetz, "How *Cheers* Replaced Coach: James Burrows Looks Back 30 Years Later," Yahoo.com, December 15, 2015, accessed June 20, 2016,

https://www.yahoo.com/tv/bp/cheers-james-burrows-coach-woody-010936771.
html.

9. Elana Levine, "Sex as a Weapon: Programming Sexuality in the 1970s,"
in *NBC: America's Network*, ed. Michele Hilmes (Berkeley: University of California Press, 2007), 228.

10. Warren Littlefield, *Top of the Rock: Inside the Rise and Fall of Must See
TV*, with T. R. Pearson (New York: Doubleday, 2012), 20.

11. Paul L. Klein, "Why You Watch What You Watch When You Watch,"
TV Guide, July 24, 1971, 7.

12. Seth Shiesel, "Paul L. Klein, 69, a Developer of TV Pay-Per-View Channels," *New York Times*, July 13, 1998.

13. Vince Waldron, *Classic Sitcoms: A Celebration of the Best Prime-Time
Comedy* (New York: Collier Books, 1987), 471.

14. Ken Levine, "It's James Burrows Night on NBC," . . . *by Ken Levine: The
World as Seen by a TV Comedy Writer* (blog), February 21, 2016, http://
kenlevine.blogspot.com/2016/02/its-james-burrows-night-on-nbc.html.

15. Brian Raftery, "The Best TV Show That's Ever Been," *GQ*, September
27, 2012, http://www.gq.com/story/cheers-oral-history-extended.

16. Waldron, *Classic Sitcoms*, 471.

17. Waldron, *Classic Sitcoms*, 471.

18. "Reviews of New Television Shows." *Variety* (Los Angeles), October 6,
1982.

19. Bill Carter, "Why *Cheers* Proved So Intoxicating," *New York Times*, May
9, 1993, http://www.nytimes.com/1993/05/09/arts/television-why-cheers-
proved-so-intoxicating.html?pagewanted=all.

20. Mark Harris, "*Cheers* Celebrates Its 200th Episode," *Entertainment
Weekly*, October 26, 1990, http://www.ew.com/article/1990/10/26/cheers-
celebrates-its-200th-episode.

21. Susan King, "The Creative Brew: Glen and Les Charles, James Burrows," *Los Angeles Times*, May 16, 1993.

22. Littlefield, *Top of the Rock*, 31.

23. Martin Gitlin, *The Greatest Sitcoms of All Time* (Lanham, MD: Scarecrow Press, 2014), 43.

24. Gitlin, *Greatest Sitcoms*, 45.

25. Bjorklund, *Toasting* Cheers, 107.

26. Bjorklund, *Toasting* Cheers, 107.

27. Bjorklund, *Toasting* Cheers, 107.

28. Harris, "*Cheers* Celebrates Its 200th Episode."

29. Gary Hoppenstand, "Re: Chapter of Frasier Book," personal e-mail, August 22, 2016.

30. Hoppenstand, personal e-mail, August 22, 2016.

31. Bjorklund, *Toasting* Cheers, 58.

32. Bjorklund, *Toasting* Cheers, 58.

33. Bjorklund, *Toasting* Cheers, 58.

34. Bjorklund, *Toasting* Cheers, 58.

35. "I Do, Adieu." *Cheers*. S5E26. Directed by James Burrows. Written by Glen Charles and Les Charles. NBC, May 1987.

36. "Mixed Reaction to the Post-Seinfeld Era," Pew Research Center, May 10, 1998, accessed July 26, 2016, http://www.people-press.org/1998/05/10/mixed-reaction-to-post-seinfeld-era/.

37. Kelsey Grammer, *So Far . . .* (New York: Dutton, 1995), 5.

38. Bjorklund, *Toasting* Cheers, 57.

39. Grammer, *So Far . . .* , 99.

40. Grammer, *So Far . . .* , 116.

41. Grammer, *So Far . . .* , 116–17.

42. Littlefield, *Top of the Rock*, 32.

43. Littlefield, *Top of the Rock*, 32.

44. Grammer, *So Far . . .* , 7–8.

45. Grammer, *So Far . . .* , 9.

46. Raftery, "Best TV Show."

47. "The Matchmaker." *Frasier*. S2E3. Written by Joe Keenan. NBC, October 1994.

2. FRASIER ON HIS OWN

1. John Corry, "NBC Presents *The Tortellis*, a *Cheers* Spinoff," *New York Times*, January 22, 1987.

2. John J. O'Connor, "Review/Television: A *Cheers* Spinoff, Set in Seattle," *New York Times*, October 21, 1993, http://www.nytimes.com/1993/10/21/arts/review-television-a-cheers-spinoff-set-in-seattle.html.

3. Warren Littlefield, *Top of the Rock: Inside the Rise and Fall of Must See TV*, with T. R. Pearson (New York: Doubleday, 2012), 131.

4. Littlefield, *Top of the Rock*, 131.

5. Littlefield, *Top of the Rock*, 41.

6. Littlefield, *Top of the Rock*, 131.

7. Martin Gitlin, *The Greatest Sitcoms of All Time* (Lanham, MD: Scarecrow Press, 2014), 59.

8. Gitlin, *Greatest Sitcoms*, 135.

9. Kelsey Grammer, *So Far . . .* (New York, Dutton, 1995), 212.

10. Littlefield, *Top of the Rock*, 137.

11. Littlefield, *Top of the Rock*, 136.

12. Grammer, *So Far . . .* , 213.

13. Ken Tucker, "Frasier," *Entertainment Weekly*, October 22, 1993, http://www.ew.com/article/1993/10/22/tv-show-review-frasier.

14. Grammer, *So Far . . .* , 213.

15. "The Good Son." *Frasier*. S1E1. Directed by James Burrows. Written by David Angell, Peter Casey, and David Lee. NBC, September 1993.

16. Peter Casey and David Lee. "Commentary." Disc 1. *Frasier: Season 1*, DVD, Hollywood, CA: CBS DVD.

17. Jeff Richman, "Observations, Analyses, and Goodbyes." Disc 4. *Frasier: The Final Season*, DVD, Hollywood: CA, CBS DVD.

18. Ken Levine, "*Frasier* Starring Lisa Kudrow??" *. . . by Ken Levine: The World as Seen by a TV Comedy Writer* (blog), December 8, 2006, http://kenlevine.blogspot.com/2006/12/frasier-starring-lisa-kudrow.html.

19. Casey and Lee. "Commentary."

20. Levine, "*Frasier* Starring Lisa Kudrow??"

21. "Two Girls for Every Boyd." *Cheers*. S8E9. Directed by James Burrows. Written by Dan O'Shannon and Tom Anderson. NBC, November 1989. "Woody Gets an Election." *Cheers*. S11E21. Directed by James Burrows. Written by Dan O'Shannon, Tom Anderson, Dan Staley, and Rob Long. NBC, April 1993.

22. Littlefield, *Top of the Rock*, 133.

23. Littlefield, *Top of the Rock*, 141.

24. Levine, "*Frasier* Starring Lisa Kudrow??"

25. Levine, "*Frasier* Starring Lisa Kudrow??"

26. Littlefield, *Top of the Rock*, 142.

27. "The Pilot." *Friends*. S1E1. Directed by James Burrows. Written by David Crane and Marta Kauffman. NBC, September 1994.

28. Littlefield, *Top of the Rock*, 142.

29. Levine, "*Frasier* Starring Lisa Kudrow??"

30. Grammer, *So Far . . .* , 216.

31. Littlefield, *Top of the Rock*, 139.

32. Littlefield, *Top of the Rock*, 140.

33. Grammer, *So Far . . .* , 214.

34. Ken Levine, "How *Frasier* Came to Be," *. . . by Ken Levine: The World as Seen by a TV Comedy Writer* (blog), December 15, 2010, http://kenlevine.blogspot.com/2010/12/how-frasier-came-to-be.html.

35. Alan Carter, "David Hyde Pierce: Frasier's Junger Brother," *Entertainment Weekly*, November 12, 1993, http://www.ew.com/article/1993/11/12/david-hyde-pierce-frasiers-junger-brother.

36. Grammer, *So Far . . .* , 214.

37. Jefferson Graham, *Frasier* (New York: Pocket Books, 1996), 86.

38. "The Show Where Sam Shows Up." *Frasier.* S2E16. Directed by James Burrows. Written by Ken Levine and David Isaacs. NBC, February 1995.

39. "Are You Being Served?" *Frasier.* S4E22. Directed by Gordon Hunt. Written by William Lucas Walker. NBC, May 1997.

40. Scott D. Pierce, "*Frasier* Rated a Rave Review," *Deseret News* (Salt Lake City, UT), May 13, 2004.

41. Casey and Lee. "Commentary."

42. Ken Levine, "Questions about *Frasier*," . . . *by Ken Levine: The World as Seen by a TV Comedy Writer* (blog), September 18, 2008, http://kenlevine. blogspot.com/2008/09/questions-about-frasier.html.

43. Littlefield, *Top of the Rock*, 143.

44. Graham, *Frasier*, 17.

45. Littlefield, *Top of the Rock*, 138.

46. Graham, *Frasier*, 18.

47. Graham, *Frasier*, 18.

48. Littlefield, *Top of the Rock*, 138.

49. Graham, *Frasier*, 18.

50. "Do Not Forsake Me, O' My Postman." *Cheers.* S11E5. Directed by James Burrows. Written by Ken Levine and David Isaacs. NBC, October 1992.

51. Ken Levine, "More on *Frasier* You Didn't Know," . . . *by Ken Levine: The World as Seen by a TV Comedy Writer* (blog), December 12, 2006, http:// kenlevine.blogspot.com/2006/12/more-on-frasier-you-didnt.html.

52. Littlefield, *Top of the Rock*, 139.

53. "'Primal Fear' Gives Mahoney New Role," *Orlando (FL) Sentinel*, April 9, 1996.

54. Graham, *Frasier*, 163.

55. Graham, *Frasier*, 163.

56. Levine, "How *Frasier* Came to Be."

57. Levine, "How *Frasier* Came to Be."

58. David Isaacs, "Sitcom Master Class: Creating Comedy through Character," in *Inside the Room: Writing Television with the Pros at UCLA Extension Writers' Program*, ed. Linda Venis (New York: Gotham Books, 2013), 189.

59. Levine, "How *Frasier* Came to Be."

60. Casey and Lee. "Commentary."

61. "The Virgin." *Seinfeld.* S4E10. Directed by Tom Cherones. Written by Peter Mehlman. NBC, November 1992.

62. Casey and Lee. "Commentary."

63. Casey and Lee. "Commentary."

64. Grammer, *So Far . . .* , 215.

65. Grammer, *So Far . . .* , 216.

66. Graham, *Frasier*, 19.

67. Harry Castleman and Walter J. Podrazik, *Watching Six Decades of American Television* (Syracuse, NY: Syracuse University Press, 2010)..

68. Gitlin, *Greatest Sitcoms*, 59.

69. Gitlin, *Greatest Sitcoms*, 137.

70. Scott D. Pierce, "Sam Visits *Frasier* but the Reunion Is Sort of a Letdown," *Deseret News* (Salt Lake City, UT), February 21, 1995.

71. William Keck, "Three NBC Hits Are Coming Back to the Future," *Entertainment Weekly*, March 22, 2002.

72. Scott D. Pierce, "Everything Old Is New Again on TV During May Sweeps," *Deseret News* (Salt Lake City, UT), April 26, 2002.

73. Pierce, "Everything Old Is New Again."

74. Pierce, "Everything Old Is New Again."

75. Lynn Elber, "*Frasier* Hears Last Call," *Cincinnati Enquirer*, May 11, 2004.

76. Graham, *Frasier*, 59.

77. Graham, *Frasier*, 59.

78. Caryn Mandabach, "The Art of the Sitcom," in *Writing Long-Running Television Series*, ed. Julian Friedmann (Luton, UK: University of Luton Press, 1996).

79. Ken Tucker, "What'd You Think of the Finale? Here's Our Take," *Entertainment Weekly*, May 13, 2004.

80. Stephen Coles, "Cheers Logo and Opening Titles," Fonts in Use, October 29, 2013, http://fontsinuse.com/uses/5067/cheers-logo-and-opening-titles.

81. Littlefield, *Top of the Rock*, 23.

82. Littlefield, *Top of the Rock*, 144.

83. Littlefield, *Top of the Rock*, 138.

84. Casey and Lee. "Commentary."

85. Casey and Lee. "Commentary."

86. "Brother from Another Series." *Simpsons*. S8E16. Directed by Pete Michels. Written by Ken Keeler. FOX, February 1997.

87. Ken Levine, "The Story behind 'Tossed Salad and Scrambled Eggs,'" . . . *by Ken Levine: The World as Seen by a TV Comedy Writer* (blog), April 9, 2012, http://kenlevine.blogspot.com/2012/04/story-behind-tossed-salad-and-scrambled.html.

88. *Must-See TV: A Tribute to James Burrows*. Directed by Ryan Polito. NBC, February 21, 2016.

89. Lanford Beard, "*Frasier* Theme Decoded," *Entertainment Weekly*, April 10, 2012, http://www.ew.com/article/2012/04/10/frasier-theme-song-explained.

90. Levine, "Story behind 'Tossed Salad.'"

91. Levine, "Story behind 'Tossed Salad.'"

92. Levine, "Story behind 'Tossed Salad.'"

93. Levine, "Story behind 'Tossed Salad.'"

94. Levine, "Story behind 'Tossed Salad.'"

95. Brian Raftery, "The Best TV Show That's Ever Been," *GQ*, September 27, 2012, http://www.gq.com/story/cheers-oral-history-extended.

96. "The Show Where Sam Shows Up." *Frasier*. S2E16. Directed by James Burrows. Written by Ken Levine and David Isaacs. NBC, February 1995.

97. "Death Takes a Holiday on Ice." *Cheers*. S8E7. Directed by James Burrows. Written by Ken Levine and David Isaacs. NBC, November 1989.

98. "Diane Meets Mom." *Cheers*. S3E8. Directed by James Burrows. Written by David Lloyd. NBC, November 1984.

99. Graham, *Frasier*, 21.

100. "The Show Where Sam Shows Up." *Frasier*. S2E16.

101. Graham, *Frasier*, 26.

102. "The Perfect Guy." *Frasier*. S5E17. Directed by Jeff Melman. Written by Rob Greenburg. NBC, March 1998.

103. "The Ski Lodge." *Frasier*. S5E14. Directed by David Lee. Written by Joe Keenan. NBC, February 1998.

104. "Our Founders," Angell Foundation, http://www.angellfoundation.org/content.php?pgID=240.

3. THREE CRANES AND A DOG

1. David Isaacs, "Sitcom Master Class: Creating Comedy through Character," in *Inside the Room: Writing Television with the Pros at UCLA Extension Writers' Program*, ed. Linda Venis (New York: Gotham Books, 2013), 176.

2. Susan King, "The Creative Brew: Glen and Les Charles, James Burrows," *Los Angeles Times*, May 16, 1993.

3. David Lee, "Observations, Analyses, and Goodbyes." Disc 4. *Frasier: The Final Season*, DVD, Hollywood: CA, CBS DVD.

4. Jefferson Graham, *Frasier* (New York: Pocket Books, 1996), 26.

5. Ken Tucker, "Mad about *Frasier*," *Entertainment Weekly*, November 29, 1996, http://www.ew.com/article/1996/11/29/mad-about-frasier.

6. Jon E. Lewis and Penny Stempel, *Cult TV : The Comedies* (London: Pavilion Books, 1998).

7. Martin Gitlin, *The Greatest Sitcoms of All Time* (Lanham, MD: Scarecrow Press, 2014).

8. Andy Greenwald, "Summer TV Mailbag!" Grantland.com, July 24, 2014, http://grantland.com/features/summer-tv-mailbag-homeland-better-call-saul-game-of-thrones-scott-bakula/.

9. David Bailey and Warren Martyn. *Goodnight Seattle: The Unauthorised Guide to the World of Frasier* (London: Virgin Books, 1996).

10. "Observations, Analyses, and Good-byes," *Frasier: The Final Season*, DVD special feature, Disc 4 (Paramount, 2004).

11. Anita Gates, "Yes, America Has a Class System. See *Frasier*," *New York Times*, April 19, 1998, http://www.nytimes.com/1998/04/19/arts/television-yes-america-has-a-class-system-see-frasier.html?pagewanted=all.

12. Isaacs, "Sitcom Master Class," 187.

13. Graham, *Frasier*, 59.

14. Brian Raftery, "The Best TV Show That's Ever Been," *GQ*, September 27, 2012, http://www.gq.com/story/cheers-oral-history-extended.

15. Michael Joseph Gross, "Goodbye, *Frasier*; Hello, Kelsey Grammer?" *New York Times*, April 25, 2004, http://www.nytimes.com/2004/04/25/arts/television-goodbye-frasier-hello-kelsey-grammer.html?_r=0.

16. Gross, "Goodbye, *Frasier*."

17. Gross, "Goodbye, *Frasier*."

18. "Don Juan In Hell Part 2." *Frasier*. S9E2. Directed by Kelsey Grammer. Written by Lori Kirkland. NBC, September 2001.

19. Scott D. Pierce, "*Frasier* Proves NBC Wrong," *Deseret News* (Salt Lake City, UT), May 14, 2001, http://beta.deseretnews.com/article/842668/Frasier-proves-NBC-wrong.html?pg=allro.

20. "Actor-Director David Hyde Pierce." PBS, August 12, 2016, http://www.pbs.org/wnet/tavissmiley/interviews/david-hyde-pierce/.

21. Tom Shales, "Pierce Doesn't Even Like Niles Crane," *Los Angeles Times*, April 6, 1996.

22. Graham, *Frasier*, 85.

23. Graham, *Frasier*, 74.

24. Graham, *Frasier*, 8.

25. Lynette Rice, "*Frasier*—1993/2004," *Entertainment Weekly*, October 18, 2013, http://www.ew.com/article/2013/10/18/frasier-19932004.

26. Graham, *Frasier*, 8.

27. Graham, *Frasier*, 8.

28. Lucy Magnan, "The *Cheers* Spinoff Is a Delight from Start to Finish—as Long as You Ignore Daphne's Accent," *Guardian*, August 10, 2010, https://www.theguardian.com/tv-and-radio/2010/aug/10/cable-girl-frasier.

29. Graham, *Frasier*, 83.

30. Alan Carter, "David Hyde Pierce: Frasier's Junger Brother," *Entertainment Weekly*, November 12, 1993, http://www.ew.com/article/1993/11/12/david-hyde-pierce-frasiers-junger-brother.

31. "The Ski Lodge." *Frasier*. S5E14. Directed by David Lee. Written by Joe Keenan. NBC, February 1998.

32. Mandi Bierly, "The All-Timers: An Oral History of the Classic 'Ski Lodge' Episode of *Frasier*," Yahoo.com, March 1, 2016, https://www.yahoo.com/tv/frasier-ski-lodge-oral-history-164309203.html.

33. "You Can Go Home Again." *Frasier*. S3E24. Directed by David Lee. Written by Linda Morris and Vic Rauseo. NBC, May 1996.

34. *EW* Staff. "Beyond Therapy." *Entertainment Weekly*, November 3, 1995, http://www.ew.com/article/1995/11/03/beyond-therapy/2.

35. *EW* Staff, "Beyond Therapy."

36. "When a Man Loves Two Women." *Frasier*. S6E21. Directed by David Lee. Written by Alex Gregory. NBC, May 1999.

37. "Daphne Returns." *Frasier*. S8E19. Directed by Lory Fryman. Written by Dan O'Shannon and Bob Daily. NBC, May 2001.

38. "Dinner at Eight." *Frasier*. S1E3. Directed by James Burrows. Written by Anne Fleet and Chuck Ranberg. NBC, September 1993.

39. "Miss Right Now." *Frasier*. S11E19. Directed by Scott Ellis. Written by Ken Levine and David Isaacs. NBC, April 2004.

40. "My Fair Frasier." *Frasier*. S5E7. Directed by Jeff Melman. Directed by Jay Kogen. NBC, November 1997.

41. "High Crane Drifter." *Frasier*. S3E17. Directed by Philip Charles MacKenzie. Written by Jack Burditt. NBC, March 1996.

42. "Come Lie with Me." *Frasier*. S3E12. Directed by Philip Charles MacKenzie. Written by Steven Levitan. NBC, June 2000.

43. "Our Father Whose Art Ain't Heaven." *Frasier*. S4E8. Directed by Jeff Melman. Written by Michael Kaplan. NBC, December 1996.

44. "The Show Where Lilith Comes Back." *Frasier*. S1E16. Directed by James Burrows. Written by Christopher Lloyd. NBC, February 1994.

45. "Sorry, Sir. That's the Last Straw," *Protagonist Podcast*, no. 64, March 14, 2016.

46. "Flour Child." *Frasier*. S2E4. Directed by James Burrows. Written by Christopher Lloyd. NBC, October 1994.

47. "Murder Most Maris." *Frasier*. S11E8. Directed by Scott Ellis. Written by Sam Johnson. NBC, November 2003.

48. "Goodnight, Seattle." *Frasier*. S11E24. Directed by David Lee. Written by Christopher Lloyd and Joe Keenan. NBC, May 2004.

49. "A Word to the Wiseguy." *Frasier*. S3E15. Directed by Philip Charles MacKenzie. Written by Joe Keenan. NBC, February 1996.

50. "Dad Loves Sherry, the Boys Just Whine." *Frasier*. S4E9. Directed by James Burrows. Written by Joe Keenan. NBC, January 1997.

51. "Odd Man Out." *Frasier*. S4E24. Directed by Jeff Melman. Written by Suzanne Martin. NBC, May 1997.

52. "Beloved Infidel." *Frasier*. S1E8. Directed by Andy Ackerman. Written by Leslie Eberhard. NBC, November 1993.

53. "The Two Mrs. Cranes." *Frasier*. S4E1. Directed by David Lee. Written by Joe Keenan. NBC, September 1996.

54. Graham, *Frasier*, 72.

55. "Signing Off: A *Dateline* Special," YouTube video, 7:53, uploaded May 28, 2008, https://www.youtube.com/watch?v=CI47WsBCMDQ.

56. "The Good Son." *Frasier*. S1E1. Directed by James Burrows. Written by David Angell, Peter Casey, and David Lee. NBC, September 1993.

57. "Space Quest." *Frasier*. S1E2. Directed by James Burrows. Written by Sy Dukane and Denise Moss. NBC, September 1993.

58. "I Hate Frasier Crane." *Frasier*. S1E4. Directed by David Lee. Written by Christopher Lloyd. NBC, October 1993.

59. "You Can Go Home Again." *Frasier*. S3E24.

60. "Mixed Doubles." *Frasier*. S4E6. Directed by David Lee. Written by Christopher Lloyd. NBC, November 1996.

61. "Fathers and Sons." *Frasier*. S10E22. Directed by Kelsey Grammer. Written by Jon Sherman. NBC, May 2003.

62. *My Dog Skip*, directed by Jay Russell (Warner Bros., 2000).

63. Alan Carter, "Eddie Unleashed," *Entertainment Weekly*, December 3, 1993.

64. Graham, *Frasier*, 123.

65. "Gary Gero's Birds & Animals Unlimited," BirdsandAnimals.com, accessed August 25, 2016. http://www.birdsandanimals.com/about-us/.

66. Graham, *Frasier*, 123.

67. Graham, *Frasier*, 123.

68. Graham, *Frasier*, 128.

69. Graham, *Frasier*, 124.

70. Graham, *Frasier*, 125.

71. "Shut Out in Seattle (1)." *Frasier*. S6E23. Directed by Pamela Fryman. Written by David Isaacs. NBC, May 1999.

72. Carter, "Eddie Unleashed."

73. "Frasier's Dog Eddie Dies, Aged 16," BBC News, June 28, 2006, http://news.bbc.co.uk/2/hi/entertainment/5124104.stm.

74. Cover, *Entertainment Weekly*, December 1993.

75. Brian Hargrove, *My Life as a Dog* (New York: HarperCollins, 2000).

76. "Beyond Blunderdome." *The Simpsons*. S11E1. Directed by Steven Dean Moore. Written by Mike Scully. FOX, September 1999.

77. Graham, *Frasier*, 73.

78. "And Then There Was Eddie," *Frasier: The Complete Second Season*, DVD special feature, Disc 4 (Paramount, 2004).

79. Graham, *Frasier*, 128.

80. Graham, *Frasier*, 129.

81. Graham, *Frasier*, 73–74.

82. Tom Shales, "Frasier, off the Couch," *Washington Post*, October 16, 1994, https://www.washingtonpost.com/archive/lifestyle/style/1994/10/16/frasier-off-the-couch/5386d6bc-e37a-446b-ba08-e9bf4dbae363/.

83. Kelsey Grammer, *So Far . . .* (New York: Dutton, 1995), 217.

84. Graham, *Frasier*, 61.

85. Judy Faber, "*Frasier* Pooch Dies in L.A.," CBS News, June 28, 2006, http://www.cbsnews.com/news/frasier-pooch-dies-in-la-28-06-2006/.

4. DAPHNE AND ROZ

1. "You Can't Tell a Crook by His Cover." *Frasier*. S1E15. Directed by Andy Ackerman. Written by David Lloyd. NBC, January 1994.

2. "Selling Out." *Frasier*. S1E9. Directed by Andy Ackerman. Written by Lloyd Garver. NBC, November 1993.

3. "Daphne Returns." *Frasier*. S8E19. Directed by Lory Fryman. Written by Dan O'Shannon and Bob Daily. NBC, May 2001.

4. Betty Goodwin, "Frasier, a Well-Dressed Man," *Los Angeles Times*, February 18, 1994, http://articles.latimes.com/1994-02-18/news/vw-24293_1_frasier-crane.

5. "The Wizard and Roz." *Frasier*. S8E20. Directed by Sheldon Epps. Written by Saladin K. Patterson. NBC, May 2001.

6. "Visions of Daphne." *Frasier*. S6E22. Directed by Robert H. Egan. Written by Janis Hirsch and Lori Kirkland. NBC, May 1999.

7. Jefferson Graham, *Frasier* (New York: Pocket Books, 1996), 98.

8. Lina Das, "How Benny Hill Babe Jane Leeves Became the Queen of U.S. TV," *Daily Mail*, July 30, 2010, http://www.dailymail.co.uk/tvshowbiz/article-1298828/How-Benny-Hill-babe-Jane-Leeves-queen-U-S-TV.html#ixzz4IS49BSF4.

9. Kara Kovalchik, "18 Things You Might Not Know about *Frasier*," *Mental Floss*, April 5, 2016, http://mentalfloss.com/article/60555/18-things-you-might-not-know-about-frasier.

10. Susan King, "Also Starring: Daffy, with a Touch of Class: Jane Leeves Makes Daphne on *Frasier* a Crane Necessity," *Los Angeles Times*, July 2, 1995, http://articles.latimes.com/1995-07-02/news/tv-19314_1_jane-leeves.

11. "Selling Out." *Frasier*. S1E9.

12. Graham, *Frasier*, 9.

13. Graham, *Frasier*, 109.

14. "The Maris Counselor." *Frasier*. S5E13. Directed by Jeff Melman. Written by David Lloyd. NBC, February 1998.

15. "The Maris Counselor." *Frasier*. S5E13.

16. "Roz, a Loan." *Frasier*. S6E9. Directed by Pamela Fryman. Written by Janis Hirsch. NBC, December 1998.

17. Graham, *Frasier*, 109.

18. "Dark Victory." *Frasier*. S2E24. Directed by James Burrows. Written by Christopher Lloyd, Linda Morris, and Vic Rauseo. NBC, May 1995.

19. "Dark Victory." *Frasier*. S2E24.

20. "Death Becomes Him." *Frasier*. S1E11. Directed by Andy Ackerman. Written by Leslie Eberhard. NBC, December 1993.

21. Graham, *Frasier*, 109.

22. "The Unkindest Cut of All." *Frasier*. S2E2. Directed by Rick Beren. Written by Dave Hackel. NBC, September 1994.

23. Graham, *Frasier*, 110.

24. "How to Bury a Millionaire." *Frasier*. S6E7. Directed by Pamela Fryman. Written by Lori Kirkland. NBC, November 1998.

25. "Agents in America, Part Three." *Frasier*. S2E22. Directed by David Lee. Written by Joe Keenan. NBC, May 1995.

26. "The Kid." *Frasier*. S5E4. Directed by Jeff Melman. Written by Jeffrey Richman and Suzanne Martin. NBC, November 1997.

27. Scott D. Pierce, "A Drop in Quality? No Way, Insists Emmy-Winning Team." *Deseret News* (Salt Lake City, UT), May 2, 1999, http://beta. deseretnews.com/article/694473/A-drop-in-quality-No-way-insists-Emmy-winning-team.html?pg=all.

28. "Hot Pursuit." *Frasier*. S7E18. Directed by Sheldon Epps. Written by Charlie Hauck. NBC, April 2000.

29. "Goodnight, Seattle (Part 2)." *Frasier*. S11E24. Directed by David Lee. Written by Christopher Lloyd and Joe Keenan. NBC, May 2004.

30. "The Crucible." *Frasier*. S1E6. Directed by James Burrows. Written by Sy Dukane and Denise Moss. NBC, October 1993.

5. THE EVOLUTIONS ARE TELEVISED

1. David Isaacs, "Sitcom Master Class: Creating Comedy through Character," in *Inside the Room: Writing Television with the Pros at UCLA Extension Writers' Program*, ed. Linda Venis (New York: Gotham Books, 2013), 189.

2. John J. O'Connor, "Review/Television: A *Cheers* Spinoff, Set in Seattle," *New York Times*, October 21, 1993, http://www.nytimes.com/1993/10/21/arts/review-television-a-cheers-spinoff-set-in-seattle.html.

3. "Space Quest." *Frasier* S2E2. Directed by James Burrows. Written by Sy Dukane and Denise Moss. NBC, September 1993.

4. "Breaking the Ice." *Frasier.* S2E20. Directed by Phillip Charles MacKenzie. Written by Steven Levitan. NBC, April 1995.

5. Quoted in Victoria O'Donnell, *Television Criticism* (Thousand Oaks, CA: Sage, 2007), 104.

6. O'Donnell, *Television Criticism*, 90.

7. Diana Friedman, *Sitcom Style: Inside America's Favorite TV Homes* (New York: Random House, 2005), 111.

8. "The Good Son." Frasier. S1E1. Directed by James Burrows. Written by David Angell, Peter Casey, and David Lee. NBC, September 1993.

9. "The Good Son." Frasier. S1E1.

10. "Four for the Seesaw." *Frasier.* S4E13. Directed by Jeff Melman. Written by David Lloyd. NBC, February 1997.

11. "Give Him the Chair!" *Frasier.* S1E19. Directed by James Burrows. Written by Chuck Ranberg and Anne Flett-Giordano. NBC, March 1994.

12. "Bla-Z-Boy." *Frasier.* S9E7. Directed by Robert H. Egan. Written by Jon Sherman. NBC, November 2001.

13. "The Good Son." *Frasier.* S1E1.

14. "Goodnight, Seattle (Part 2)." *Frasier.* S11E24. Directed by David Lee. Written by Christopher Lloyd and Joe Keenan. NBC, May 2004.

15. *Must-See TV: A Tribute to James Burrows.* Directed by Ryan Polito. NBC, February 21, 2016.

16. Ken Tucker, "Frasier," *Entertainment Weekly*, October 22, 1993, http://www.ew.com/article/1993/10/22/tv-show-review-frasier.

17. Warren Littlefield, *Top of the Rock: Inside the Rise and Fall of Must See TV*, with T. R. Pearson (New York: Doubleday, 2012), 140.

18. "Observations, Analyses, and Goodbyes," *Frasier: The Final Season*, DVD special feature, Disc 4 (Paramount, 2004).

19. "Marching onto Season Two," *Frasier: The Complete Second Season*, DVD special feature, Disc 4 (Paramount, 2004).

20. "The Friend." *Frasier.* S3E11. Directed by Philip Charles MacKenzie. Written by Jack Burditt. NBC, January 1996.

21. "The Friend." *Frasier.* S3E11.

22. "Something Borrowed, Someone Blue (1)." *Frasier.* S7E23. Directed by Pamela Fryman. Written by Christopher Lloyd and Joe Keenan. NBC, May 2000.

23. "You Can Go Home Again." *Frasier.* S3E24. Directed by David Lee. Written by Linda Morris and Vic Rauseo. NBC, May 1996.

24. "Goodnight, Seattle (Part 2)." *Frasier.* S11E24.

25. Alan Carter, "David Hyde Pierce: Frasier's Junger Brother," *Entertainment Weekly*, November 12, 1993. http://www.ew.com/article/1993/11/12/david-hyde-pierce-frasiers-junger-brother.

26. "Fortysomething." *Frasier.* S1E20. Directed by Rick Beren. Written by Sy Dukane and Denise Moss. NBC, March 1994.

27. "Dinner Party." *Frasier.* S6E17. Directed by David Lee. Written by Jeffrey Richman. NBC, March 1999.

28. "The Show Where Woody Shows Up." *Frasier.* S6E13. Directed by Pamela Fryman. Written by Rob Greenberg. NBC, February 1999.

29. "The Friend." *Frasier.* S3E11. Directed by Philip Charles MacKenzie. Written by Jack Burditt. NBC, January 1996.

30. "The Club." *Frasier.* S2E18. Directed by David Lee. Written by Elias Davis and David Pollock. NBC, March 1995.

31. "IQ." *Frasier.* S6E19. Directed by David Lee. Written by Rob Hanning and Jay Kogen. NBC, April 1999.

32. "Author, Author." *Frasier.* S1E22. Directed by James Burrows. Written by Don Seigel and Jerry Perzigian. NBC, May 1994.

33. "IQ." *Frasier.* S6E19.

34. "Forgotten but Not Gone." *Frasier.* S8E18. Directed by Pamela Fryman. Written by David Lloyd. NBC, April 2001.

35. "IQ." *Frasier.* S6E19.

36. "Everyone's a Critic." *Frasier.* S7E4. Directed by Pamela Fryman. Written by Joe Keenan. NBC, October 1999.

37. "The Good Son." *Frasier.* S1E1.

38. "And the Whimper Is . . ." *Frasier.* S1E18. Directed by James Burrows. Written by Sy Dukane and Denise Moss. NBC, February 1994.

39. "Bad Dog." *Frasier.* S5E18. Directed by Pamela Fryman. Written by Suzanne Martin. NBC, April 1998.

40. "The Gift Horse." *Frasier.* S5E2. Directed by Pamela Fryman. Written by Ron Darian. NBC, September 1997.

41. Littlefield. *Top of the Rock*, 140.

42. "The Innkeepers." *Frasier.* S2E23. Directed by James Burrows. Written by David Lloyd. NBC, May 1995.

43. "Shrink Rap." *Frasier.* S3E2. Directed by David Lee. Written by Christopher Lloyd. NBC, September 1995.

44. "The Good Son." *Frasier.* S1E1.

45. Wendy Lesser, "Television/Radio: Couples Who Aren't (or Who Shouldn't Be)," *New York Times*, November 26, 2000, http://www.nytimes.com/2000/11/26/arts/television-radio-couples-who-aren-t-or-who-shouldn-t-be.html.

46. "Signing Off: A *Dateline* Special," YouTube video, 7:53, uploaded May 28, 2008, https://www.youtube.com/watch?v=CI47WsBCMDQ.

47. "My Coffee with Niles." *Frasier.* S1E24. Directed by James Burrows. Written by David Angell and Peter Casey. NBC, May 1994.

48. Jefferson Graham, *Frasier* (New York: Pocket Books, 1996), 85.

49. Graham, *Frasier*, 85.

50. Graham, *Frasier*, 98.

51. Bruce Fretts, "Leeves of Autumn," *Entertainment Weekly*, November 18, 1994, http://www.ew.com/article/1994/11/18/leeves-autumn.

52. "Back Talk." *Frasier.* S7E10. Directed by Pamela Fryman. Written by Lori Kirkland. NBC, December 1999.

53. "Something Borrowed, Someone Blue (2)." *Frasier.* S7E24. Directed by Pamela Fryman. Written by Christopher Lloyd and Joe Keenan. NBC, May 2000.

54. Lesser, "Couples Who Aren't."

55. Ken Tucker, "Why Switching *Frasier* to Tuesdays is a Shrewd Move," *Entertainment Weekly*, May 16, 2000, http://www.ew.com/article/2000/05/16/why-switching-frasier-tuesdays-shrewd-move.

56. Lesser. "Couples Who Aren't."

57. "I Am Curious . . . Maddie." *Moonlighting.* S3E14. Directed by Alan Arkush. Written by Glenn Gordon Caron. CBS, March 1987.

58. Bill Carter, "2 Disappointments for ABC, Low Ratings and an Ending," *New York Times*, May 9, 1989, http://www.nytimes.com/1989/05/09/arts/2-disappointments-for-abc-low-ratings-and-an-ending.html.

59. Lesser, "Couples Who Aren't."

60. Lesser, "Couples Who Aren't."

61. "Daphne Returns." *Frasier.* S8E19. Directed by Lory Fryman. Written by Dan O'Shannon and Bob Daily. NBC, May 2001.

62. "Daphne Returns." *Frasier.* S8E19.

63. "Hungry Heart." *Frasier.* S8E14. Directed by Kelsey Grammer. Written by Gayle Abrams. NBC, February 2001.

6. SET DESIGN

1. Diana Friedman, *Sitcom Style: Inside America's Favorite TV Homes* (New York: Random House, 2005).

2. Michelle Manetti, "7 Lessons from *Frasier* on Home Decor, Living and the Finer Things in Life," *Huffington Post*, September 26, 2013, http://www.huffingtonpost.com/2013/09/25/lessons-from-frasier-home-_n_3989071.html.

3. "TV and Movie Houses—Dr. Frasier Crane's Apartment," *Southgate* (blog), March 12, 2011, http://southgateresidential.blogspot.com/2011/03/tv-and-movie-houses-dr-frasier-cranes.html.

4. Joe McGauley, "Inside Frasier Crane's Plush Seattle Digs," *Thrillist*, October 21, 2014,https://www.thrillist.com/home/photo-tour-of-frasier-crane-s-seattle-apartment.

5. Dan Snierson, "Frasier: Sleekness in Seattle," *Entertainment Weekly*, December 8, 1995, http://www.ew.com/article/1995/12/08/frasier-sleekness-seattle.

6. Edward Rothstein, "A Place Comfortable with Boeing, Anarchists and *Frasier*," *New York Times*, December 28, 2012, http://www.nytimes.com/2012/12/29/arts/design/museum-of-history-industry-reopens-in-seattle.html?_r=0.

7. "Give Him the Chair!" *Frasier.* S1E19. Directed by James Burrows. Written by Chuck Ranberg and Anne Flett-Giordano. NBC, March 1994.

8. Roy Christopher, "Frasier Crane's Apartment," *Frasier: The Complete First Season*, DVD special feature, Disc 4 (Paramount, 2003).

9. Friedman, *Sitcom Style*, 114.

10. Friedman, *Sitcom Style*, 111.

11. Jefferson Graham, *Frasier* (New York: Pocket Books, 1996), 23.

12. Graham, *Frasier*.

13. Christopher, interview, part 5 of 7, Archive of American Television, accessed August 12, 2016, http://www.emmytvlegends.org/interviews/people/roy-christopher.

14. Ken Levine, "The *Frasier* Living Room" . . . *by Ken Levine: The World as Seen by a TV Comedy Writer* (blog), September 3, 2009, http://kenlevine.blogspot.com/2009/09/frasier-living-room.html.

15. Graham, *Frasier*, 23.

16. Christopher, "Frasier Crane's Apartment."

17. "Daphne's Room." *Frasier.* S2E17. Directed by David Lee. Written by Linda Morris and Vic Rauseo. NBC, February 1995.

18. Ken Levine, "*Frasier* Starring Lisa Kudrow??" . . . *by Ken Levine: The World as Seen by a TV Comedy Writer* (blog), December 8, 2006, http://kenlevinc.blogspot.com/2009/09/frasier-living-room.html.

19. Levine, "The *Frasier* Living Room."

20. Levine, "The *Frasier* Living Room."

21. Levine, "The *Frasier* Living Room."

22. Levine, "The *Frasier* Living Room."

23. Mary Daniels, "No Props for Frasier," *Orlando (FL) Sentinel*, July 21, 1994, http://articles.orlandosentinel.com/1994-07-21/lifestyle/9407190658_1_frasier-crane-kelsey-grammer-viljoen.

24. Mary Daniels, "Room with a View into *Frasier*'s Psyche," *Chicago Tribune*, July 3, 1994, http://articles.chicagotribune.com/1994-07-03/entertainment/9407030126_1_real-interior-designer-sharon-viljoen-dr-frasier-crane.

25. "The Good Son." *Frasier*. S1E1. Directed by James Burrows. Written by David Angell, Peter Casey, and David Lee. NBC, September 1993.

26. Christopher, "Frasier Crane's Apartment."

27. Christopher, "Frasier Crane's Apartment."

28. Christopher Wilk, *Modernism : Designing a New World, 1914–1939* (London: V&A Publications, 2006), chapter 6.

29. "Three Dates and a Breakup (1)." *Frasier*. S4E19. Directed by Jeff Melman. Written by Rob Greenberg. NBC, April 1997.

30. Sandy Isenstadt, *The Modern American House* (Cambridge: Cambridge University Press, 2006), 4.

31. Isenstadt, *The Modern American House.*

32. Isenstadt, *The Modern American House.*

33. "Daphne's Room." *Frasier.* S2E17. "The Unnatural." *Frasier.* S4E16. Directed by Pamela Fryman. Written by Michael Kaplan. NBC, April 1997.

34. "Flour Child." *Frasier*. S2E4. Directed by James Burrows. Written by Christopher Lloyd. NBC, October 1994.

35. "The Candidate." *Frasier*. S2E7. Directed by James Burrows. Written by Chuck Ranberg and Anne Flett-Giordano. NBC, November 1994.

36. "The Show Where Lilith Comes Back." *Frasier*. S1E16. Directed by James Burrows. Written by Christopher Lloyd. NBC, February 1994.

37. "The Fight before Christmas." *Frasier*. S7E11. Directed by Pamela Fryman. Written by Jon Sherman. NBC, December 1999.

38. "The Maris Counselor." *Frasier*. S5E13. Directed by Jeff Melman. Written by David Lloyd. NBC, February 1998.

39. Edward Gardiner, "Why Frasier Deserves More Recognition," FlickeringMyth.com, February 26, 2016, http://www.flickeringmyth.com/2016/02/why-frasier-deserves-more-recognition/.

40. Christopher, interview, part 5 of 7.

41. "How to Bury a Millionaire." *Frasier*. S6E7. Directed by Pamela Fryman. Written by Lori Kirkland. NBC, November 1998.

42. "A Crane's Critique." *Frasier*. S4E4. Directed by Jeff Melman. Written by Dan Cohen and F. J. Pratt. NBC, October 1996.

43. Roy Christopher, "Frasier Crane's Apartment, " *Frasier: The Complete First Season*, DVD special feature, Disc 4 (Paramount, 2003).

44. "How to Bury a Millionaire." *Frasier*. S6E7.

45. "How to Bury a Millionaire." *Frasier*. S6E7.

46. Wilk, *Modernism*, chapter 6.

47. Clare Cooper Marcus, *House as a Mirror of Self : Exploring the Deeper Meaning of Home* (Berwick, ME: Nicolas-Hays, 2006), 4.

48. "Taps at the Montana." *Frasier*. S6E18. Directed by David Lee. Written by David Lloyd. NBC, March 1999.

49. Chuck Taylor, "*Frasier* Meets the Real Seattle—Belltown Is Transformed and a Bit Bemused as Sitcom Finally Comes Home," *Seattle Times*, September 9, 1997, http://community.seattletimes.nwsource.com/archive/?date=19970909&slug=2559279

50. Taylor, "*Frasier* Meets the Real Seattle."

51. Ken Levine, "How *Frasier* Came to Be," . . . *by Ken Levine: The World as Seen by a TV Comedy Writer* (blog), December 15, 2010, http://kenlevine.blogspot.com/2010/12/how-frasier-came-to-be.html.

52. Melanie McFarland, "More Seattle Hits Than Misses for 'Frasier,'" *Seattle PI*, May 12, 2004, http://www.seattlepi.com/ae/tv/article/More-Seattle-hits-than-misses-for-Frasier-1144568.php.

53. "The Botched Language of Cranes." *Frasier*. S2E6. Directed by David Lee. Written by Joe Keenan. NBC, November 1994.

54. "Farewell, Nervosa." *Frasier*. S10E20. Directed by Kelsey Grammer. Written by Eric Zicklin. NBC, April 2003.

55. *EW* Staff, "TV's Gotta Whole Latte Love," *Entertainment Weekly*, October 21, 1994, http://www.ew.com/article/1994/10/21/tvs-gotta-whole-latte-love.

56. Christopher, interview, part 5 of 7.

57. Roy Christopher, "A Conversation with Roy Christopher," *Frasier: The Complete Third Season*, DVD special feature (Paramount, 2004).

58. "Frasier Says Farewell," *Frasier: The Complete Final Season*, DVD special feature, Disc 4 (Paramount, 2004).

7. CURATING THE SPACES

1. Beverly Gordon, "Material Culture in a Popular Vein," in *Symbiosis: Popular Culture and Other Fields*, ed. Ray B. Browne and Marshall W. Fishwick (Bowling Green, OH: Bowling Green State University Popular Press, 1988), 175.

2. "The Good Son." *Frasier*. S1E1. Directed by James Burrow. Written by David Angell, Peter Casey, and David Lee. NBC, September 1993. "The Great Crane Robbery." *Frasier*. S8E4. Directed by Katy Garretson. Written by Gayle Abrams. NBC, November 2000. "Father and Sons." *Frasier*. S10E22. Directed by Kelsey Grammer. Written by Jon Sherman. NBC, May 2003.

3. Diana Friedman, *Sitcom Style : Inside America's Favorite TV Homes* (New York: Random House, 2005), 110.

4. Mary Daniels, "No Props for Frasier," *Orlando (FL) Sentinel*, July 21, 1994, http://articles.orlandosentinel.com/1994-07-21/lifestyle/9407190658_1_frasier-crane-kelsey-grammer-viljoen.

5. Daniels, "No Props for Frasier."

6.   Sharon Overton, "Sitcom Décor—Popular TV Programs Offer Clues about the Way We Live in the '90s," *Seattle Times*, November 3, 1996, http://community.seattletimes.nwsource.com/archive/?date=19961103&slug=2357628.

7.   Stevenson Swanson, "50 Years Later, Eames Chair Sits Well with Design Lovers," *Chicago Tribune*, July 9, 2006, http://www.sandiegouniontribune.com/uniontrib/20060709/news_1hs09eamesch.html.

8.   "The Good Son." *Frasier.* S1E1.

9.   Roy Christopher, "Frasier Crane's Apartment," *Frasier: The Complete First Season*, DVD special feature, Disc 4 (Paramount, 2003).

10.   Mary Daniels, "Room with a View into *Frasier*'s Psyche," *Chicago Tribune*, July 3, 1994, http://articles.chicagotribune.com/1994-07-03/entertainment/9407030126_1_real-interior-designer-sharon-viljoen-dr-frasier-crane.

11.   Christopher, "Frasier Crane's Apartment."

12.   Friedman, *Sitcom Style*, 111.

13.   Friedman, *Sitcom Style*, 111.

14.   "The Good Son." *Frasier.* S1E1.

15.   "Robert Adam: Neo-Classical Architect and Designer," Victoria and Albert Museum, vam.ac.uk, 2015, accessed July 1, 2015.

16.   "The Anne Who Came to Dinner." *Frasier.* S11E13. Directed by Scott Ellis. Written by Sam Johnson and Chris Marcil. NBC, January 2004.

17.   LeGene Quesenberry and Bruce W. Sykes, "Leveraging the Internet to Promote Fine Art: Perspectives of Art Patrons," *Journal of Arts Management, Law, and Society* 38, no 2, (2008): 121.

18.   Sarah Pugh, "The Absolute Definitive Guide to *Frasier* Christmas Episodes," *Sarah TV* (blog), December 14, 2015, https://sarahtv3.com/tag/frasier-christmas-episodes/.

19.   "The Great Crane Robbery." *Frasier.* S8E4. Directed by Katy Garretson. Written by Gayle Abrams. NBC, November 2000.

20.   Clare Cooper Marcus, *House as a Mirror of Self: Exploring the Deeper Meaning of Home* (Berwick, ME: Nicolas-Hays, 2006), xv.

21.   Daniels, "Room with a View."

22.   Friedman, *Sitcom Style*, 10.

23.   Mayer Rus, "Television's Smart Set," *Interior Design* 65, no. 8 (August 1, 1994). ISSN: 0020-5508.

24.   Daniels, "Room with a View."

25.   "The Good Son." *Frasier.* S1E1.

26.   "The Focus Group." *Frasier.* S3E23. Directed by Philip Charles MacKenzie. Written by Rob Greenberg. NBC, May 1996.

27. "Death Becomes Him." *Frasier.* S1E11. Directed by Andy Ackerman. Written by Leslie Eberhard. NBC, December 1993.

28. Emma Reynolds, "Roy Lichtenstein Painting Sells for Record $43 Million at Christie's Auction in New York," *Daily Mail*, November 9, 2011, http://www.dailymail.co.uk/news/article-2059314/Roy-Lichtenstein-painting-sells-record-27m-Christies-auction.html.

29. "The Focus Group." *Frasier.* S3E23.

30. Roy Christopher, interview, part 5 of 7, Archive of American Television, http://www.emmytvlegends.org/interviews/people/roy-christopher.

31. Christopher, interview, part 5 of 7.

32. Christopher, interview, part 5 of 7.

33. Christopher, interview, part 5 of 7.

34. Casey, Peter, and David Lee. "Commentary." Disc 1. *Frasier: Season 1*, DVD, Hollywood, CA: CBS DVD.

35. Christopher, "Frasier Crane's Apartment."

36. Christopher, "Frasier Crane's Apartment."

37. Friedman, *Sitcom Style*, 114.

38. Christopher, "Frasier Crane's Apartment."

39. Mike Hughes, "Little-Known Tidbits about *Frasier*," *Honolulu Advertiser*, May 13, 2004, http://the.honoluluadvertiser.com/article/2004/May/13/il/il06a.html.

40. Chuck Taylor, "*Frasier* Meets the Real Seattle—Belltown Is Transformed and a Bit Bemused as Sitcom Finally Comes Home," *Seattle Times*, September 9, 1997, http://community.seattletimes.nwsource.com/archive/?date=19970909&slug=2559279.

41. Christopher, interview, part 5 of 7.

42. Hughes, "Little-Known Tidbits about *Frasier*."

43. Quesenberry and Sykes, "Leveraging the Internet," 121.

44. Christopher, interview, part 5 of 7.

45. Christopher, "Frasier Crane's Apartment."

46. Christopher, "Frasier Crane's Apartment."

47. Michael Buckley, "Stage to Screens: Carla Gugino, David Hyde Pierce, and *In Treatment* Writer Leight," *Playbill*, May 3, 2009, http://www.playbill.com/article/stage-to-screens-carla-gugino-david-hyde-pierce-and-in-treatment-writer-leight-com-160506.

48. "Actor-Director David Hyde Pierce," PBS, accessed August 12, 2016, http://www.pbs.org/wnet/tavissmiley/interviews/david-hyde-pierce/.

49. *EW* Staff, "Beyond Therapy," *Entertainment Weekly*, November 3, 1995, http://www.ew.com/article/1995/11/03/beyond-therapy/3.

50. "Signing Off: A *Dateline* Special," YouTube video, 7:53, uploaded May 28, 2008, https://www.youtube.com/watch?v=CI47WsBCMDQ.

51. Tom Gliatto, "Exist Laughing," *People* 61, no. 19 (May 17, 2004), http://www.people.com/people/archive/article/0,,20150110,00.html.

52. Design Museum, *Fifty Chairs That Changed the World* (London: Conran, 2010), 6.

53. Design Museum, *Fifty Chairs*, 6.

54. Judy Hevrdejs, "How Will *Frasier* Recliner Kick Back?" *Chicago Tribune*, January 26, 2003, http://articles.chicagotribune.com/2003-01-26/features/0301260345_1_martin-crane-recliner-easy-chair.

55. Christopher, "Frasier Crane's Apartment."

56. Grace Lees-Maffei, *Iconic Designs: 50 Stories about 50 Things* (London: Bloomsbury Visual Arts, 2014), 169.

57. Christopher Wilk, *Modernism: Designing a New World, 1914–1939* (London: V&A Publications, 2006), chapter 6.

58. Wilk, *Modernism*, chapter 6.

59. "The Good Son." *Frasier*. S1E1.

60. "Kisses Sweeter Than Wine." *Frasier*. S3E5. Directed by Philip Charles MacKenzie. Written by Anne Flett-Giordano. NBC, November 1995.

61. "Wassily Chair," Knoll.com, accessed August 18, 2016, http://www.knoll.com/product/wassily-chair.

62. "Wassily Chair."

63. Design Museum, *Fifty Chairs*, 20.

64. "Wassily Chair."

65. Lees-Maffei, *Iconic Designs*, 170.

66. Wilk, *Modernism*, chapter 6.

67. Lees-Maffei, *Iconic Designs*, 169.

68. Christopher Wilk, *Marcel Breuer, Furniture and Interiors* (New York: Museum of Modern Art, 1981).

69. Lees-Maffei, *Iconic Designs*, 171.

70. Lees-Maffei, *Iconic Designs*, 171.

71. "They're Playing Our Song." *Frasier*. S7E13. Directed by David Lee. Written by David Lloyd. NBC, January 2000.

72. "The Botched Language of Cranes." *Frasier*. S2E6. Directed by David Lee. Written by Joe Keenan. NBC, November 1994.

73. "The Good Son." *Frasier*. S1E1.

74. "Eames Chair and Ottoman," HermanMiller.com, accessed August 18, 2016, http://www.hermanmiller.com/products/seating/lounge-seating/eames-lounge-chair-and-ottoman.

75. Colin Marshall, "Charles and Ray Eames' Iconic Lounge Chair Debuts on American TV," *Open Culture*, August 18, 2014, http://www.openculture.com/2014/08/debut-of-charles-and-ray-eames-iconic-lounge-chair.html.

76. "Eames Chair and Ottoman."

77.   Roberta Smith, "Eames Lounge Chair Exhibition at the Museum of Arts and Design," *New York Times*, May 26, 2006, http://www.nytimes.com/2006/05/26/arts/design/26eame.html?_r=1.

78.   Design Museum, *Fifty Chairs*, 56.

79.   Smith, "Eames Lounge Chair Exhibition."

80.   "Eames Chair and Ottoman."

81.   "Eames Chair and Ottoman."

82.   "Goodnight, Seattle (Part 2)." *Frasier*. S11E24. Directed by David Lee. Written by Christopher Lloyd and Joe Keenan. NBC, May 2004.

83.   "Back Talk." *Frasier*. S7E10. Directed by Pamela Fryman. Written by Lori Kirkland. NBC, December 1999.

84.   Smith, "Eames Lounge Chair Exhibition."

85.   "Eames Chair and Ottoman."

86.   Smith, "Eames Lounge Chair Exhibition."

87.   Smith, "Eames Lounge Chair Exhibition."

88.   Overton, "Sitcom Décor."

89.   Overton, "Sitcom Décor."

90.   Christopher, "Frasier Crane's Apartment."

91.   Christopher, "Frasier Crane's Apartment."

92.   Casey and Lee. "Commentary."

93.   Quesenberry and Sykes, "Leveraging the Internet," 121.

94.   "Merry Christmas, Mrs. Moskowitz." *Frasier*. S6E10. Directed by Kelsey Grammer. Written by Jay Kogen. NBC, December 1998.

95.   "The Good Son." *Frasier*. S1E1.

96.   "To Kill a Talking Bird." *Frasier*. S4E14. Directed by David Lee. Written by Jeffrey Richman. NBC, February 1997.

97.   *EW* Staff, "The Art of Saying Goodbye," *Entertainment Weekly*, April 10, 2014, http://www.ew.com/article/2014/04/10/art-saying-goodbye/4.

98.   "Goodnight, Seattle (Part 2)." *Frasier*. S11E24.

99.   Gordon, "Material Culture," 171.

100.   "Give Him the Chair!" *Frasier*. S1E19. Directed by James Burrows. Written by Chuck Ranberg and Anne Flett-Giordano. NBC, March 1994.

101.   "The Crucible." *Frasier*. S1E6. Directed by James Burrows. Written by Sy Dukane and Denise Moss. NBC, October 1993.

102.   "A Tsar Is Born." *Frasier*. S7E7. Directed by Pamela Fryman. Written by Charlie Hauck. NBC, November 1999.

103.   "Crock Tales." *Frasier*. S11E22. Directed by Sheldon Epps. Written by John Sherman and Bob Daily. NBC, May 2004.

8. GENDER . . . AND RACE?

1. Dustin Gann, "'I'm Listening': Analyzing the Masculine Example of Frasier Crane," in *Screening Images of American Masculinity in the Age of Postfeminism*, ed. Elizabeth Abele and John A. Gronbeck-Tedesco (Lanham, MD: Lexington Books, 2016), 103.

2. "The Innkeepers." *Frasier*. S2E23. Directed by James Burrows. Written by David Lloyd. NBC, May 1995.

3. "Motor Skills." *Frasier*. S8E11. Directed by Pamela Fryman. Written by Sam Johnson and Chris Marcil. NBC, January 2001.

4. Gann, "I'm Listening," 107.

5. "My Fair Frasier." *Frasier*. S5E7. Directed by Jeff Melman. Written by Jay Kogen. NBC, November 1997.

6. Lee Wright, "The Suit: A Common Bond or Defeated Purpose?," in *The Gendered Object*, ed. Pat Kirkham (Manchester, UK: Manchester University Press, 1996), 153.

7. "Watches," Cartier, accessed July 28, 2016, http://www.cartier.com/en-us/collections/watches.html.

8. "My Fair Frasier." *Frasier*. S5E7.

9. "The Doctor Is Out." *Frasier*. S11E3. Directed by David Lee. Written by Joe Keenan. NBC, September 2003.

10. "Desperately Seeking Closure." *Frasier*. S5E8. Directed by Pamela Fryman. Written by Rob Hanning. NBC, December 1997.

11. "Desperately Seeking Closure." *Frasier*. S5E8.

12. Gann, "I'm Listening," 115.

13. Curtis M. Wong, "David Hyde Pierce Looks Back on *Frasier* and Its Then-Progressive Takes on Gay Issues," *Huffington Post*, May 26, 2015, updated February 2, 2016, http://www.huffingtonpost.com/2015/05/26/david-hyde-pierce-frasier-gay-stereotypes-_n_7444176.html.

14. Gann, "I'm Listening," 116.

15. "Liar! Liar!" *Frasier*. S4E10. Directed by James Burrows. Written by Anne Flett-Giordano and Chuck Ranberg. NBC, January 1997. "Father and Sons." *Frasier*. S10E22. Directed by Kelsey Grammer. Written by Jon Sherman. NBC, May 2003.

16. Wong, "David Hyde Pierce Looks Back."

17. "The Impossible Dream." *Frasier*. S4E3. Directed by David Lee. Written by Rob Greenberg. NBC, October 1996.

18. "The Matchmaker." *Frasier*. S2E3. Directed by David Lee. Written by Joe Keenan. NBC, October 1994.

19. Louis Peitzman, "Classic Gay TV: Frasier, 'The Matchmaker,'" *New-NowNext*, November 2, 2012, http://www.newnownext.com/classic-gay-tv-frasier-the-matchmaker/11/2012/.

20. "The Matchmaker." *Frasier*. S2E3.

21. Peitzman, "Classic Gay TV."

22. "The Matchmaker." *Frasier*. S2E3.

23. Peitzman, "Classic Gay TV."

24. Wong, "David Hyde Pierce Looks Back."

25. Wong, "David Hyde Pierce Looks Back."

26. Brian Stelter, "Gay on TV: It's All in the Family," *New York Times*, May 8, 2012, http://www.nytimes.com/2012/05/09/business/media/gay-on-tv-its-all-in-the-family.html?_r=0.

27. Gann, "I'm Listening," 103.

28. Lynn Spigel, *Make Room for TV: Television and the Family Ideal in Postwar America* (Chicago: University of Chicago Press, 1992).

29. Stelter, "Gay on TV."

30. Stelter, "Gay on TV."

31. Stelter, "Gay on TV."

32. Alonso Duralde, "Pretty Witty—and Gay." Advocate.com, January 17, 2006, http://www.advocate.com/politics/commentary/2006/01/17/pretty-witty%E2%80%94and-gay.

33. "Ski Lodge." *Frasier*. S5E14. Directed by David Lee. Written by Joe Keenan. NBC, February 1998.

34. "Out with Dad." *Frasier*. S7E15. Directed by David Lee. Written by Joe Keenan. NBC, February 2000.

35. "The Doctor Is Out." *Frasier*. S11E3. Directed by David Lee. Written by Joe Keenan. NBC, September 2003.

36. Andy Greenwald, "Summer TV Mailbag!" Grantland.com, July 24, 2014, http://grantland.com/features/summer-tv-mailbag-homeland-better-call-saul-game-of-thrones-scott-bakula/.

37. Ray Richmond, *TV Moms: An Illustrated Guide* (New York: TV Books, 2000), 150.

38. Bonnie J. Dow, *Prime-Time Feminism: Television, Media Culture, and the Women's Movement since 1970* (Philadelphia: University of Pennsylvania Press, 1996), 153.

39. Dow, *Prime-Time Feminism*, 153.

40. "The Kid." *Frasier*. S5E4. Directed by Jeff Melman. Written by Jeffrey Richman and Suzanne Martin. NBC, November 1997.

41. "Docu.Drama." *Frasier*. S8E16. Directed by David Lee. Written by Sam Johnson and Chris Marcil. NBC, March 2001.

42. "Dark Victory." *Frasier*. S2E24. Directed by James Burrows. Written by Christopher Lloyd, Linda Morris, and Vic Rauseo. NBC, May 1995.

43. "The Seal Who Came to Dinner." *Frasier*. S6E8. Directed by David Lee. Written by Joe Keenan. NBC, November 1998.

44. Gann, "I'm Listening," 114.

45. "She's the Boss." *Frasier*. S3E1. Directed by Philip Charles MacKenzie. Written by Chuck Ranberg and Anne Flett-Giordano. NBC, September 1995.

46. "Frasier-Lite." *Frasier*. S11E12. Directed by Sheldon Epps. Written by Sam Johnson, Chris Marcil, Jeffrey Richman, Jon Sherman, Bob Daily, and Patricia Breen. NBC, January 2004.

47. "To Kill a Talking Bird." *Frasier*. S4E14. Directed by David Lee. Written by Jeffrey Richman. NBC, February 1997.

48. "Dr. Nora." *Frasier*. S6E20. Directed by Katy Garretson. Written by Joe Keenan. NBC, April 1999.

49. "Frasier-Lite." *Frasier*. S11E12.

50. "The Harassed." *Frasier*. S10E12. Directed by Kelsey Grammer. Written by Chris Marcil. NBC, January 2003.

51. "Sleeping with the Enemy." *Frasier*. S3E6. Directed by Jeff Melman. Written by Linda Morris and Vic Rauseo. NBC, November 1995.

52. "The Harassed." *Frasier*. S10E12.

53. "Show Down: Part 2." *Cheers*. S1E22. Directed by James Burrows. Written by Glen Charles and Les Charles. NBC, March 1983.

54. "The Harassed." *Frasier*. S10E12.

55. Colin Harrison, *American Culture in the 1990s* (Edinburgh: Edinburgh University Press, 2010).

56. Jonathan Storm, "Segregated Situation on Television Comedies: Sitcoms Are Either Black or White—With *Friends* Like That, *Living Single* Has Appeal," *Philadelphia Inquirer*, April 14, 1996.

57. Storm, "Segregated Situation on Television Comedies."

58. James Sterngold, "A Racial Divide Widens on Network TV," *New York Times*, December 29, 1998.

59. Sterngold, "Racial Divide."

60. See "An Affair to Forget," Season 2, Episode 21, as a prime example.

61. "Something about Dr. Mary." *Frasier*. S7E16. Directed by Wil Shriner. Written by Jay Kogen. NBC, February 2000.

62. "Mary Christmas." *Frasier*. S8E8. Directed by Pamela Fryman. Written by Eric Zicklin. NBC, December 2000.

CONCLUSION

1. Scott Stossel, "What Makes Us Happy, Revisited," *Atlantic*, May 2013.
2. Stossel, "What Makes Us Happy."

THE EPISODES

1. "The Innkeepers." *Frasier.* S2E23. Directed by James Burrows. Written by David Lloyd. NBC, May 1995.

BIBLIOGRAPHY

"Actor-Director David Hyde Pierce." PBS. Accessed August 12, 2016. http://www.pbs.org/wnet/tavissmiley/interviews/david-hyde-pierce/.

"And Then There Was Eddie." *Frasier: The Complete Second Season.* DVD special feature, Disc 4. Paramount, 2004.

Angell, David, Peter Casey, and David Lee. *The Frasier Scripts.* New York: Newmarket, 1999.

The A.V. Club. *Inventory: 16 Films Featuring Manic Pixie Dream Girls, 10 Great Songs Nearly Ruined by Saxophone, and 100 More Obsessively Specific Pop-Culture Lists.* New York: Scribner, 2009.

Bailey, David, and Warren Martyn. *Goodnight Seattle: The Unauthorised Guide to the World of Frasier.* London: Virgin Books, 1996.

Baker, Kathryn. "*Cheers* Starts 6th Season with New Co-star." *Fort Scott (KS) Tribune,* August 17, 1987.

Bawden, Jim. "Critic Nibbles on Tidbits with TV Stars." *Toronto Star,* June 24, 1986.

Beard, Lanford. "*Frasier* Theme Decoded." *Entertainment Weekly,* April 10, 2012. http://www.ew.com/article/2012/04/10/frasier-theme-song-explained.

Bianculli, David. "*Cheers* and Farewell to One of the Best Crafted Sitcoms." *New York Daily News,* May 16, 1993.

Bierly, Mandi. "The All-Timers: An Oral History of the Classic 'Ski Lodge' Episode of *Frasier.*" Yahoo.com. March 1, 2016. https://www.yahoo.com/tv/frasier-ski-lodge-oral-history-164309203.html.

Bjorklund, Dennis A. *Toasting* Cheers*: An Episode Guide to the 1982–1993 Comedy Series with Cast Biographies and Character Profiles.* Jefferson, NC: McFarland, 1997.

Bly, Robert W. *What's Your Frasier IQ: 501 Questions and Answers for Fans.* New York: Citadel, 1996.

Brant, Marley. *Happier Days: Paramount Television's Classic Sitcoms 1974–1984.* New York: Billboard Books, 2006.

Buck, Jerry. "Rhea Perlman Mixes Real Life with Her Series." *Oxnard (CA) Press-Courier,* April 24, 1983.

Buckley, Michael. "Stage to Screens: Carla Gugino, David Hyde Pierce, and *In Treatment* Writer Leight." *Playbill,* May 3, 2009. http://www.playbill.com/article/stage-to-screens-carla-gugino-david-hyde-pierce-and-in-treatment-writer-leight-com-160506.

Carter, Alan. "David Hyde Pierce: Frasier's Junger Brother." *Entertainment Weekly,* November 12, 1993. http://www.ew.com/article/1993/11/12/david-hyde-pierce-frasiers-junger-brother.

———. "Eddie Unleashed." *Entertainment Weekly,* December 3, 1993.

Carter, Bill. "2 Disappointments for ABC, Low Ratings and an Ending." *New York Times*, May 9, 1989. http://www.nytimes.com/1989/05/09/arts/2-disappointments-for-abc-low-ratings-and-an-ending.html.

———. "Why *Cheers* Proved So Intoxicating." *New York Times*, May 9, 1993. http://www.nytimes.com/1993/05/09/arts/television-why-cheers-proved-so-intoxicating.html?pagewanted=all.

Casey, Peter, and David Lee. "Commentary." Disc 1. *Frasier: Season 1*, DVD, Hollywood, CA: CBS DVD.

Castleman, Harry, and Walter J. Podrazik. *Watching Six Decades of American Television*. Syracuse, NY: Syracuse University Press, 2010.

Channel 4 Books. *The Very Best of Frasier*. London: Channel 4 Books, 2002.

Christopher, Roy. Interview. Archive of American Television. Accessed August 12, 2016. http://www.emmytvlegends.org/interviews/people/roy-christopher.

———. "A Conversation with Roy Christopher." *Frasier: The Complete Third Season*. DVD special feature. Paramount, 2004.

———. "Frasier Crane's Apartment." *Frasier: The Complete First Season*. DVD special feature, Disc 4. Paramount, 2003.

Cover. *Entertainment Weekly*, December 1993.

Cronin, Brian. "TV Legends Revealed: Why You Don't Mess with Carla on *Cheers*." Comic Book Resources. January 10, 2013. http://spinoff.comicbookresources.com/2013/01/10/tv-legends-revealed-why-you-dont-mess-with-carla-on-cheers/.

Daniels, Mary. "No Props for Frasier." *Orlando (FL) Sentinel*, July 21, 1994. http://articles.orlandosentinel.com/1994-07-21/lifestyle/9407190658_1_frasier-crane-kelsey-grammer-viljoen.

———. "Room with a View into *Frasier*'s Psyche." *Chicago Tribune*, July 3, 1994. http://articles.chicagotribune.com/1994-07-03/entertainment/9407030126_1_real-interior-designer-sharon-viljoen-dr-frasier-crane.

Das, Lina. "How Benny Hill Babe Jane Leeves Became the Queen of U.S. TV." *Daily Mail*, July 30, 2010. http://www.dailymail.co.uk/tvshowbiz/article-1298828/How-Benny-Hill-babe-Jane-Leeves-queen-U-S-TV.html#ixzz4IS49BSF4.

Design Museum. *Fifty Chairs That Changed the World*. London: Conran, 2010.

Dow, Bonnie J. *Prime-Time Feminism: Television, Media Culture, and the Women's Movement since 1970*. Philadelphia: University of Pennsylvania Press, 1996.

Duralde, Alonso. "Pretty Witty—and Gay." Advocate.com. January 17, 2006. http://www.advocate.com/politics/commentary/2006/01/17/prettywitty%E2%80%94and-gay.

"Eames Chair and Ottoman." HermanMiller.com. Accessed August 18, 2016. http://www.hermanmiller.com/products/seating/lounge-seating/eames-lounge-chair-and-ottoman.

Elber, Lynn. "*Frasier* Hears Last Call." *Cincinnati Enquirer*, May 11, 2004.

EW Staff. "The Art of Saying Goodbye." *Entertainment Weekly*, April 10, 2014. http://www.ew.com/article/2014/04/10/art-saying-goodbye/4.

———. "Beyond Therapy." *Entertainment Weekly*, November 3, 1995. http://www.ew.com/article/1995/11/03/beyond-therapy/.

———. "TV's Gotta Whole Latte Love." *Entertainment Weekly*, October 21, 1994. http://www.ew.com/article/1994/10/21/tvs-gotta-whole-latte-love.

———. "The Year That Was." *Entertainment Weekly*, December 24, 1993. http://www.ew.com/article/1993/12/24/year-was.

Faber, Judy. "*Frasier* Pooch Dies in L.A." CBS News, June 28, 2006. http://www.cbsnews.com/news/frasier-pooch-dies-in-la-28-06-2006/.

Fisher, Julie. *Café Nervosa: The Connoisseur's Cookbook*. Tampa, FL: Oxmoor House, 1996.

"Frasier Says Farewell." *Frasier: The Complete Final Season*. DVD special feature, Disc 4. Paramount, 2004.

"Frasier's Dog Eddie Dies, Aged 16." BBC News. June 28, 2006. http://news.bbc.co.uk/2/hi/entertainment/5124104.stm.

Fretts, Bruce. "Leeves of Autumn." *Entertainment Weekly*, November 18, 1994. http://www.ew.com/article/1994/11/18/leeves-autumn.

Friedman, Diana. *Sitcom Style: Inside America's Favorite TV Homes.* New York: Random House, 2005.

Gann, Dustin. "'I'm Listening': Analyzing the Masculine Example of Frasier Crane." In *Screening Images of American Masculinity in the Age of Postfeminism*, edited by Elizabeth Abele and John A. Gronbeck-Tedesco, 103–19. Lanham, MD: Lexington Books, 2016.

Gardiner, Edward. "Why Frasier Deserves More Recognition." FlickeringMyth.com. February 26, 2016. http://www.flickeringmyth.com/2016/02/why-frasier-deserves-more-recognition/.

Garratt, Sheryl. "Dale Chihuly's Glass Menagerie." *Telegraph*, January 25, 2014. http://www.telegraph.co.uk/luxury/design/22959/dale-chihulys-glass-menagerie.html.

"Gary Gero's Birds & Animals Unlimited." BirdsandAnimals.com. Accessed August 25, 2016. http://www.birdsandanimals.com/about-us/.

Gates, Anita. "Yes, America Has a Class System. See *Frasier*." *New York Times*, April 19, 1998. http://www.nytimes.com/1998/04/19/arts/television-yes-america-has-a-class-system-see-frasier.html?pagewanted=all.

Gitlin, Martin. *The Greatest Sitcoms of All Time.* Lanham, MD: Scarecrow Press, 2014.

Gliatto, Tom. "Exist Laughing." *People* 61, no. 19 (May 17, 2004). http://www.people.com/people/archive/article/0,,20150110,00.html.

Goodwin, Betty. "Frasier, a Well-Dressed Man." *Los Angeles Times*, February 18, 1994. http://articles.latimes.com/1994-02-18/news/vw-24293_1_frasier-crane.

Gordon, Beverly. "Material Culture in a Popular Vein." In *Symbiosis: Popular Culture and Other Fields*, edited by Ray B. Browne and Marshall W. Fishwick, 170–76. Bowling Green, OH: Bowling Green State University Popular Press, 1988.

Graham, Jefferson. *Frasier.* New York: Pocket Books, 1996.

Grammer, Kelsey. *So Far . . .* New York: Dutton, 1995.

Greenwald, Andy. "Summer TV Mailbag!" Grantland.com. July 24, 2014. http://grantland.com/features/summer-tv-mailbag-homeland-better-call-saul-game-of-thrones-scott-bakula/.

Gross, Michael Joseph. "Goodbye, 'Frasier'; Hello, Kelsey Grammer?" *New York Times*, April 25, 2004. http://www.nytimes.com/2004/04/25/arts/television-goodbye-frasier-hello-kelsey-grammer.html?_r=0.

Hargrove, Brian. *My Life as a Dog.* New York: HarperCollins, 2000.

Harris, Mark. "*Cheers* Celebrates Its 200th Episode." *Entertainment Weekly*, October 26, 1990. http://www.ew.com/article/1990/10/26/cheers-celebrates-its-200th-episode.

Harrison, Colin. *American Culture in the 1990s.* Edinburgh: Edinburgh University Press, 2010.

Hevrdejs, Judy. "How Will *Frasier* Recliner Kick Back?" *Chicago Tribune*, January 26, 2003. http://articles.chicagotribune.com/2003-01-26/features/0301260345_1_martin-crane-recliner-easy-chair.

"History." Pilchuck Glass School. Accessed August 12, 2016. http://www.pilchuck.com/about_us/history.

Hoppenstand, Gary. "Re: Chapter of Frasier Book." Personal e-mail. August 22, 2016.

Hubbell, Tom. "Re: Frasier Archives Inquiry." Personal e-mail. July 12, 2016.

Hughes, Mike. "Little-Known Tidbits about *Frasier*." *Honolulu Advertiser*, May 13, 2004. http://the.honoluluadvertiser.com/article/2004/May/13/il/il06a.html.

Isaacs, David. "Sitcom Master Class: Creating Comedy through Character." In *Inside the Room: Writing Television with the Pros at UCLA Extension Writers' Program*, edited by Linda Venis, 174–91. New York: Gotham Books, 2013.

Isenstadt, Sandy. *The Modern American House.* Cambridge: Cambridge University Press, 2006.

Keck, William. "Three NBC Hits Are Coming Back to the Future." *Entertainment Weekly*, March 22, 2002.

King, Susan. "Also Starring: Daffy, with a Touch of Class: Jane Leeves Makes Daphne on *Frasier* a Crane Necessity." *Los Angeles Times*, July 2, 1995. http://articles.latimes.com/1995-07-02/news/tv-19314_1_jane-leeves.

———. "The Creative Brew: Glen and Les Charles, James Burrows." *Los Angeles Times*, May 16, 1993.

Klein, Paul L. "Why You Watch What You Watch When You Watch." *TV Guide*, July 24, 1971.

Kovalchik, Kara. "18 Things You Might Not Know about *Frasier*." *Mental Floss*. April 5, 2016. http://mentalfloss.com/article/60555/18-things-you-might-not-know-about-frasier.

Lee, David, "Observations, Analyses, and Goodbyes." Disc 4. *Frasier: The Final Season*, DVD, Hollywood: CA, CBS DVD.

Lees-Maffei, Grace. *Iconic Designs: 50 Stories about 50 Things.* London: Bloomsbury Visual Arts, 2014.

Lesser, Wendy. "Television/Radio: Couples Who Aren't (or Who Shouldn't Be)." *New York Times*, November 26, 2000. http://www.nytimes.com/2000/11/26/arts/television-radio-couples-who-aren-t-or-who-shouldn-t-be.html.

Lévi-Strauss, Claude. "The Structural Study of Myth." In *Literary Theory: An Anthology*, edited by Julie Rivkin and Michael Ryan, 101–18. Malden, MA: Blackwell, 2002.

Levine, Elana. "Sex as a Weapon: Programming Sexuality in the 1970s." In *NBC: America's Network*, edited by Michele Hilmes, 224–39. Berkeley: University of California Press, 2007.

Levine, Ken. "It's James Burrows Night on NBC." . . . *by Ken Levine: The World as Seen by a TV Comedy Writer* (blog). February 21, 2016. http://kenlevine.blogspot.com/2016/02/its-james-burrows-night-on-nbc.html.

———. "The Frasier Living Room." . . . *by Ken Levine: The World as Seen by a TV Comedy Writer* (blog). September 3, 2009. http://kenlevine.blogspot.com/2009/09/frasier-living-room.html.

———. "*Frasier* Starring Lisa Kudrow??" . . . *by Ken Levine: The World as Seen by a TV Comedy Writer* (blog). December 8, 2006. http://kenlevine.blogspot.com/2006/12/frasier-starring-lisa-kudrow.html.

———. "How *Frasier* Came to Be." . . . *by Ken Levine: The World as Seen by a TV Comedy Writer* (blog). December 15, 2010. http://kenlevine.blogspot.com/2010/12/how-frasier-came-to-be.html.

———. "The Kiss of Death for Eddie LeBec." . . . *by Ken Levine: The World as Seen by a TV Comedy Writer* (blog). July 21, 2006. http://kenlevine.blogspot.com/2006/07/kiss-of-death-for-eddie-lebec.html.

———. "More on *Frasier* You Didn't Know." . . . *by Ken Levine: The World as Seen by a TV Comedy Writer* (blog). December 12, 2006. http://kenlevine.blogspot.com/2006/12/more-on-frasier-you-didnt.html.

———. "One More Question . . ." . . . *by Ken Levine: The World as Seen by a TV Comedy Writer* (blog). June 6, 2008. http://kenlevine.blogspot.com/2008/06/one-more-question.html.

———. "Questions about *Frasier*." . . . *by Ken Levine: The World as Seen by a TV Comedy Writer* (blog). September 18, 2008. http://kenlevine.blogspot.com/2008/09/questions-about-frasier.html.

———. "The Story behind 'Tossed Salad and Scrambled Eggs.'" . . . *by Ken Levine: The World as Seen by a TV Comedy Writer* (blog). April 9, 2012. http://kenlevine.blogspot.com/2012/04/story-behind-tossed-salad-and-scrambled.html.

Lewis, Jon E., and Penny Stempel. *Cult TV: The Comedies.* London: Pavilion Books, 1998.

Littlefield, Warren. *Top of the Rock: Inside the Rise and Fall of Must See TV.* With T. R. Pearson. New York: Doubleday, 2012.

Magnan, Lucy. "The *Cheers* Spinoff Is a Delight from Start to Finish—as Long as You Ignore Daphne's Accent." *Guardian*, August 10, 2010. https://www.theguardian.com/tv-and-radio/2010/aug/10/cable-girl-frasier.

Mandabach, Caryn. "The Art of the Sitcom." In *Writing Long-Running Television Series*, edited by Julian Friedmann. Luton, UK: University of Luton Press, 1996.

Manetti, Michelle. "7 Lessons from *Frasier* on Home Decor, Living and the Finer Things in Life." *Huffington Post*, September 26, 2013. http://www.huffingtonpost.com/2013/09/25/lessons-from-frasier-home-_n_3989071.html.

"Marching onto Season Two." *Frasier: The Complete Second Season.* DVD special feature, Disc 4. Paramount, 2004.

Marcus, Clare Cooper. *House as a Mirror of Self: Exploring the Deeper Meaning of Home.* Berwick, ME: Nicolas-Hays, 2006.

Marshall, Colin. "Charles and Ray Eames' Iconic Lounge Chair Debuts on American TV." *Open Culture*, August 18, 2014. http://www.openculture.com/2014/08/debut-of-charles-and-ray-eames-iconic-lounge-chair.html.

McFarland, Melanie. "More Seattle Hits Than Misses for *Frasier*." *Seattle PI*, May 12, 2004. http://www.seattlepi.com/ae/tv/article/More-Seattle-hits-than-misses-for-Frasier-1144568.php.

McGauley, Joe. "Inside Frasier Crane's Plush Seattle Digs." Thrillist. October 21, 2014. https://www.thrillist.com/home/photo-tour-of-frasier-crane-s-seattle-apartment.

"Mixed Reaction to the Post-Seinfeld Era." Pew Research. May 10, 1998. Accessed July 26, 2016. http://www.people-press.org/1998/05/10/mixed-reaction-to-post-seinfeld-era/.

Must-See TV: A Tribute to James Burrows. Directed by Ryan Polito. NBC, February 21, 2016.

My Dog Skip. Directed by Jay Russell. Warner Bros., 2000.

Nemetz, Dave. "How *Cheers* Replaced Coach: James Burrows Looks Back 30 Years Later." Yahoo.com. December 15, 2015. Accessed June 20, 2016. https://www.yahoo.com/tv/bp/cheers-james-burrows-coach-woody-010936771.html.

"Observations, Analyses, and Goodbyes." *Frasier: The Final Season*. DVD special feature, Disc 4. Paramount, 2004.

O'Connor, John J. "Review/Television: A *Cheers* Spinoff, Set in Seattle." *New York Times*, October 21, 1993. http://www.nytimes.com/1993/10/21/arts/review-television-a-cheers-spinoff-set-in-seattle.html.

———. "Critic's Notebook: *Cheers* Is Dead, but There's Always the Wake. . . ." *New York Times*, May 21, 1993.

O'Donnell, Victoria. *Television Criticism*. Thousand Oaks, CA: Sage, 2007.

"Our Founders." Angell Foundation. http://www.angellfoundation.org/content.php?pgID=240.

Overton, Sharon. "Sitcom Décor—Popular TV Programs Offer Clues about the Way We Live in the '90s." *Seattle Times*, November 3, 1996. http://community.seattletimes.nwsource.com/archive/?date=19961103&slug=2357628.

Peitzman, Louis. "Classic Gay TV: Frasier, 'The Matchmaker.'" NewNowNext. November 2, 2012. http://www.newnownext.com/classic-gay-tv-frasier-the-matchmaker/11/2012/.

Pierce, David Hyde. Tony Acceptance Speech, 2007. https://www.youtube.com/watch?v=kw6yqCHyy-g.

Pierce, Scott D. "A Drop in Quality? No Way, Insists Emmy-Winning Team." *Deseret News* (Salt Lake City, UT), May 2, 1999. http://beta.deseretnews.com/article/694473/A-drop-in-quality-No-way-insists-Emmy-winning-team.html?pg=all.

———. "Everything Old Is New Again on TV During May Sweeps." *Deseret News* (Salt Lake City, UT), April 26, 2002.

———. "*Frasier* Proves NBC Wrong." *Deseret News* (Salt Lake City, UT), May 14, 2001. http://beta.deseretnews.com/article/842668/Frasier-proves-NBC-wrong.html?pg=allro.

———. "*Frasier* Rated a Rave Review." *Deseret News* (Salt Lake City, UT), May 13, 2004.

———. "Sam Visits *Frasier* but the Reunion Is Sort of a Letdown." *Deseret News* (Salt Lake City, UT), February 21, 1995.

"'Primal Fear' Gives Mahoney New Role." *Orlando (FL) Sentinel*, April 9, 1996.

Pugh, Sarah. "The Absolute Definitive Guide to *Frasier* Christmas Episodes." *Sarah TV* (blog). December 14, 2015. https://sarahtv3.com/tag/frasier-christmas-episodes/.

Quesenberry, LeGene, and Bruce W. Sykes. "Leveraging the Internet to Promote Fine Art: Perspectives of Art Patrons." *Journal of Arts Management, Law, and Society* 38, no. 2 (2008): 121.

Raftery, Brian. "The Best TV Show That's Ever Been." *GQ*, September 27, 2012. http://www.gq.com/story/cheers-oral-history-extended.

"A Repeat of *Cheers* Finale." *New York Times*, May 22, 1993.

Reuters. "Leno Calls Telecast on *Cheers* 'a Mistake': Drunken Cast Members Ruined *Tonight* Broadcast from Boston Bar, He Says." *Los Angeles Times*, May 28, 1993.

"Reviews of New Television Shows." *Variety* (Los Angeles), October 6, 1982.

Reynolds, Emma. "Roy Lichtenstein Painting Sells for Record $43 Million at Christie's Auction in New York." *Daily Mail*, November 9, 2011. http://www.dailymail.co.uk/news/article-2059314/Roy-Lichtenstein-painting-sells-record-27m-Christies-auction.html.

Rice, Lynette. "'Frasier'—1993/2004." *Entertainment Weekly*, October 18, 2013. http://www. ew.com/article/2013/10/18/frasier-19932004.

Richman, Jeff, "Observations, Analyses, and Goodbyes." Disc 4. *Frasier: The Final Season*, DVD, Hollywood: CA, CBS DVD.

Richmond, Ray. *TV Moms: An Illustrated Guide*. New York: TV Books, 2000.

"The Rise of Venetian Glassmaking." Corning Museum of Glass. Accessed August 12, 2016. http://www.cmog.org/collection/galleries/rise-of-venetian-glassmaking.

"Robert Adam: Neo-Classical Architect and Designer." Victoria and Albert Museum. vam.ac. uk. 2015. Accessed July 1, 2015.

Rothstein, Edward. "A Place Comfortable with Boeing, Anarchists and 'Frasier.'" *New York Times*, December 28, 2012. http://www.nytimes.com/2012/12/29/arts/design/museum-of-history-industry-reopens-in-seattle.html?_r=0.

Rus, Mayer. "Television's Smart Set." *Interior Design* 65, no. 8 (August 1, 1994). ISSN: 0020-5508.

Scigliano, Eric. "Heart of Glass." Slate. June 10, 1999. http://www.slate.com/articles/life/letter_from_washington/1999/06/heart_of_glass.html.

Shales, Tom. "Frasier, off the Couch." *Washington Post*, October 16, 1994. https://www. washingtonpost.com/archive/lifestyle/style/1994/10/16/frasier-off-the-couch/5386d6bc-e37a-446b-ba08-e9bf4dbae363/.

———. "Pierce Doesn't Even Like Niles Crane." *Los Angeles Times*, April 6, 1996.

Shiesel, Seth. "Paul L. Klein, 69, a Developer of TV Pay-Per-View Channels." *New York Times*, July 13, 1998.

"Signing Off: A *Dateline* Special." YouTube video, 7:53. Uploaded May 28, 2008. https:// www.youtube.com/watch?v=CI47WsBCMDQ.

Smith, Roberta. "Eames Lounge Chair Exhibition at the Museum of Arts and Design." *New York Times*, May 26, 2006. http://www.nytimes.com/2006/05/26/arts/design/26eame.html?_r=1.

Snierson, Dan. "Frasier: Sleekness in Seattle." *Entertainment Weekly*, December 8, 1995. http://www.ew.com/article/1995/12/08/frasier-sleekness-seattle.

"Sorry, Sir. That's the Last Straw." *Protagonist Podcast*, no. 64. March 14, 2016.

Spigel, Lynn. *Make Room for TV: Television and the Family Ideal in Postwar America*. Chicago: University of Chicago Press, 1992.

Stelter, Brian. "Gay on TV: It's All in the Family." *New York Times*, May 8, 2012. http://www. nytimes.com/2012/05/09/business/media/gay-on-tv-its-all-in-the-family.html?_r=0.

Sterngold, James. "A Racial Divide Widens on Network TV." *New York Times*, December 29, 1998.

Storm, Jonathan. "Segregated Situation on Television Comedies: Sitcoms Are Either Black or White—With *Friends* Like That, *Living Single* Has Appeal." *Philadelphia Inquirer*, April 14, 1996.

Stossel, Scott. "What Makes Us Happy, Revisited." *Atlantic*, May 2013.

Swanson, Stevenson. "50 Years Later, Eames Chair Sits Well with Design Lovers." *Chicago Tribune*, July 9, 2006. http://www.sandiegouniontribune.com/uniontrib/20060709/news_1hs09eamesch.html.

Taylor, Chuck. "*Frasier* Meets the Real Seattle—Belltown Is Transformed and a Bit Bemused as Sitcom Finally Comes Home." *Seattle Times*, September 9, 1997. http://community. seattletimes.nwsource.com/archive/?date=19970909&slug=2559279.

Tucker, Ken. "A Farewell Tribute to *Cheers*." *Entertainment Weekly*, May 14, 1993.

———. "Frasier." *Entertainment Weekly*, October 22, 1993. http://www.ew.com/article/1993/10/22/tv-show-review-frasier.

———. "Mad about *Frasier*." *Entertainment Weekly*, November 29, 1996. http://www.ew. com/article/1996/11/29/mad-about-frasier.

———. "What'd You Think of the Finale? Here's Our Take." *Entertainment Weekly*, May 13, 2004.

———. "Why Switching *Frasier* to Tuesdays Is a Shrewd Move." *Entertainment Weekly*, May 16, 2000.

"TV and Movie Houses—Dr. Frasier Crane's Apartment." *Southgate* (blog). March 12, 2011. http://southgateresidential.blogspot.com/2011/03/tv-and-movie-houses-dr-frasiercranes. html.

Various Artists. *Tossed Salad and Scrambled Eggs.* Lifetime B00004ZBDM, 2001. CD.

Waldron, Vince. *Classic Sitcoms: A Celebration of the Best Prime-Time Comedy.* New York: Collier Books, 1987.

"Wassily Chair." Knoll.com. Accessed August 18, 2016. http://www.knoll.com/product/ wassily-chair.

"Watches." Cartier. Accessed July 28, 2016. http://www.cartier.com/en-us/collections/watches. html.

Wilk, Christopher. *Marcel Breuer, Furniture and Interiors.* New York: Museum of Modern Art, 1981.

———. *Modernism: Designing a New World, 1914–1939.* London: V&A Publications, 2006.

Wong, Curtis M. "David Hyde Pierce Looks Back on *Frasier* and Its Then-Progressive Takes on Gay Issues." *Huffington Post,* May 26, 2015. Updated February 2, 2016. http://www. huffingtonpost.com/2015/05/26/david-hyde-pierce-frasier-gay-stereotypes-_n_7444176. html.

Wright, Lee. "The Suit: A Common Bond or Defeated Purpose?" In *The Gendered Object,* edited by Pat Kirkham, 153–61. Manchester, UK: Manchester University Press, 1996.

INDEX

ABOUT THE AUTHORS

Joseph J. Darowski has a PhD in American studies from Michigan State University and teaches English at Brigham Young University. He is the author of *X-Men and the Mutant Metaphor: Race and Gender in the Comic Books* (Rowman & Littlefield, 2014) and the editor of The Ages of Superheroes essay series, which has volumes on Superman, Wonder Woman, the X-Men, the Avengers, Iron Man, the Incredible Hulk, and the Justice League. He has published almost two dozen book chapters, journal articles, and encyclopedia entries on popular culture topics.

Kate Darowski has a master's degree from Parsons School of Design, where she studied the history of decorative arts and design, with an emphasis on twentieth-century modern design and pop culture in design. She attended Brigham Young University, Hawaii, where she majored in cultural studies. She has written about design for *Modern Magazine*.